THE FIRST VICTIM

Mark Kevin Ramsey searched the densely wooded area while Kosta Fotopoulos and Deidre Hunt went back to the car. Kosta opened the trunk and took out some rope, a Mag flashlight, an AK-47, his video camera and a .22 semi-automatic pistol.

Grinning while they tied him to the tree, Ramsey listened as Kosta assured him that they were only going to shoot bullets at his feet. It was all part of his initiation into "The Club." Ramsey nodded and said he was hungry.

Deidre took the .22 pistol and Kosta started the video.

"Is this okay," she asked Kosta.

"No, move this way . . . Okay."

Deidre aimed and fired three rapid shots into the young man's chest. He twisted in agony and began screaming. Deidre calmly walked over, grabbed a handful of Ramsey's hair, jerked back his head and fired point-blank into his left temple. Blood splattered onto her jeans and sneakers. The videotape took only fifty-seven seconds.

"Too bad he had to die hungry," Kosta said.

"Yeah," Deidre answered. "What a bummer."

SEX, MONEY AND MURDER IN DAYTONA BEACH

Lee Butcher

PINNACLE BOOKS
WINDSOR PUBLISHING CORP.

To my dear friend Julia Jordan Trinler,
with thanks for your many acts of kindness.

PINNACLE BOOKS

are published by

Windsor Publishing Corp.
475 Park Avenue South
New York, NY 10016

First printing: November, 1991

Printed in the United States of America

Acknowledgements

This book could not have been written without the generous cooperation of many busy people and official organizations. I would like to thank the personnel from the Daytona Beach Police Department, Ormond Beach Police Department, Volusia County Sheriff's Department, Florida Department of Law Enforcement, U.S. Secret Service, Daytona Beach Fire and Rescue Service, the *Orlando Sentinel* Library, the photography department of the *News-Journal* of Daytona Beach, and the Seventh District Court Clerk Office of Appeals. I am particularly grateful to Assistant State Attorney David Damore and State Attorney Investigator Joe Gallagher, who took time from their busy schedules to give me insights into this case. Many thanks also to the consistently courteous and helpful people from the Clerk of Court Office, particularly Reba Carter, assistant superintendent of appeals, Karen Blevins, and Diane Winfrey, appeals clerks.

My thanks also to Chief Paul Crow, William Adamy, John Powers and Greg Smith of the Daytona Beach Police Department.

Thanks also to my editor, Paul Dinas, and my agent, Peter Miller.

Author's Note

Sex, Money and Murder in Daytona Beach is not a so-called fictionalized account of the murders of Mark Kevin Ramsey, Bryan Chase, and the numerous attempted murders of Lisa Fotopoulos. This is a true story based on scores of interviews with personnel from the Volusia County Sheriff's Department, Daytona Beach Police Department, Ormond Beach Police Department, the U.S. Secret Service, State Attorney's Office, Florida Department of Law Enforcement, and private citizens who wish to remain anonymous.

All of the information in this book is authenticated by thousands of pages of police reports, additional thousands of pages of court records, recorded interviews, and good, hard journalistic legwork. The dialogue has been reconstructed from official police reports, sworn depositions, official police video and audiotaped interviews, and official court records.

Prologue

David Damore sipped a cup of coffee on Sunday morning. November 5, 1989, and read the story in the Daytona Beach *News-Journal*. The story was headlined in large type across the top of the front page. Just before dawn on November 3, the story reported, an intruder had broken into a luxurious home on the Halifax River that belonged to Mary Paspalakis, the widow of Augustine Paspalakis, who had been one of the wealthiest and most powerful men in Daytona Beach, Florida. The Paspalakis family, which included Mary, her son Dino, her daughter Lisa and her husband Kosta Fotopoulos was still rich and powerful.

All four of them lived in the house on the banks of the Halifax River, which was about a mile wide at that point, giving the family a great deal of privacy from the less affluent people in Daytona Beach who lived on the other side. The river that shielded them from other people and offered an exclusive waterfront view also gave potential intruders the privacy to go about their business of breaking and entering. Mary Paspalakis had taken that into consideration and had installed a sophisticated burglar alarm system and unbreakable plexiglass in the windows and doors that faced the waterfront.

According to the newspaper story, the intruder was a burglar. He had broken into a downstairs window in the basement that wasn't connected to the burglar alarm system. He had made his way through the basement, which served as a game room and a place where Kosta made bullets for his large collection of weapons, and walked up two flights of stairs to the top floor.

It was about four a.m. when the intruder walked down the hall on the third floor, bypassing the bedrooms of Mary and Dino, and entered the bedroom where Lisa and Kosta Fotopoulos slept. The room was dimly lit by the eerie lighting from a large aquarium.

According to the newspaper, the intruder had for some unknown reason stood over Lisa Fotopoulos and fired a bullet point blank into her head. Lisa's husband, Kosta, had awakened when the gun went off. He had reacted quickly. Kosta, the story said, reached under his bed, grabbed a 9-millimeter semiautomatic pistol, and fired several shots that struck the intruder in the chest before he could shoot Lisa again.

The intruder was hit several times and was knocked down by Kosta's hail of bullets, the story said, but still managed to stagger to his feet, gun in hand. Kosta fired another shot that struck the intruder in the head and killed him.

The story portrayed Kosta as a hero who had saved his wife and perhaps the whole family from certain death. Lisa had a bullet in her brain but was still alive. She was rushed to the Halifax Medical Center where a team in the trauma unit was standing by. The intruder was dead.

Damore read the story and alarm bells went off in his head. As a criminal lawyer in private practice and as an assistant state attorney, his experience told him that something was wrong. As a prosecutor, Damore never began an investigation with a preconceived notion of guilt or innocence. Instead, he kept an open mind and probed for facts, and looked upon a legal trial as a search for the truth. Damore was six feet tall, rapier thin, and even in repose he gave the impression of intense energy. His brown eyes reflected intelligence honed to a keen cutting edge. Everything about him, from his dark wavy hair to his neatly trimmed mustache and sharply pressed clothes, suggested that he was so finely tuned that he could step on a coin and tell you if it were heads or tails.

He was not about to be swayed by a newspaper story into forming a conclusion based on information that had not been corroborated by an official investigation. But his instincts went on red alert.

On Sunday mornings Damore gave his wife, Nona, a break and fixed breakfast for them and their two pre-teenage children, Ryan and Jacqueline. It was a special treat for the whole family when Damore whipped up pancakes and sausages or bacon and eggs. The children were still asleep when Damore read the newspaper.

He looked up at Nona, whom he relied on as a sounding board for his thoughts and for emotional support. Nona frequently had uncanny insights into the cases Damore worked on.

Damore said, "There'll be more to this story, you just watch and see. This is like something made for a TV movie. I'll be getting a phone call from the detectives at Homicide."

Nona nodded. "Probably so. Something's wrong here."

A lot of people thought that Nona looked like a model. She was five feet, eight inches tall, slender, and carried herself well. Nona had a trace of Blackfoot Indian in her blood, and it manifested itself in high, sculpted cheekbones and dark hair that she wore to her shoulders.

Damore was a 1973 honor graduate from the Florida State Law School in Tallahassee and started working as an assistant state attorney in Broward County, where he was soon named Chief of Trial Division, responsible for prosecuting all felony cases in the district. Later Damore stepped to the opposite end of the spectrum and became a criminal defense lawyer in private practice. Now Damore was an assistant state attorney for the Seventh Judicial Circuit and had his office in Daytona Beach. Damore had never lost a murder case, either as a prosecutor or as a defense attorney.

Damore was currently busy preparing to prosecute a man charged with murders in a nursing home and tried to put the burglary-killing out of his mind. He had more than enough work to do on his present case. Even so, he expected a telephone call that would get him involved in the incident on Halifax Drive. He had no idea that the newspaper only revealed the tip of the iceberg and that the greater part of it had not yet surfaced. The case would involve two cold-blooded murders, attempted murder, solicitation to commit murder, and would reveal a web of intrigue that touched the lives of both gutter-snipes and prominent political figures. It was destined to become one of the most bizarre criminal cases in the history of Florida jurisprudence.

1

The Greek community in Daytona Beach had rarely seen a wedding to rival that of Lisa Paspalakis when she married Konstantinos (Kosta) Fotopoulos. Even the weather cooperated by providing a clear sunny day that was pleasantly cool and not too humid, one of the golden days in Daytona Beach, Florida. It was January 4, 1986, and St. Demetrios Greek Orthodox Church spilled over with flowers and important guests. Both the men and women wore diamonds, gold, and other precious stones. Some of the most powerful people in Daytona Beach were there to see Lisa and Kosta tie the knot.

The bride was twenty-six years old, a slim brunette of medium height, with a quick smile, keen mind, and a sunny disposition. The groom, also twenty-six, was a graduate student at Embry-Riddle Aeronautical University, studying for his master's degree in aeronautical engineering.

Lisa was quite a catch. Not only was she smart and cheerful, she was rich. She was the daughter of Augustine and Mary Paspalakis, who were highly regarded and influential in Daytona Beach and Volusia County. Augustine contributed a great deal of money to political campaigns, and because the candidates he backed usually were elected, he had a great deal of power. Among the closely knit Greek community in Daytona Beach, which numbers about three hundred, the family was respected and admired. Augustine was an example of what a man could achieve through hard work.

Augustine was a Greek immigrant who had pulled himself up by his bootstraps. He moved to Daytona Beach from Cleveland before Lisa was born, looking for opportunities that would provide security for himself and his family. Daytona Beach was a quiet place when Augustine moved there, but it attracted tourists, and all of Florida was on the verge of explosive growth. Fortunes could be made by people who were in a position to take advantage of the expected growth and increasing tourism.

The major attractions of Florida are sand, sea, and sun. Like most other Florida cities, Daytona Beach capitalized on those assets and vigorously promoted them. Augustine turned his attention to the boardwalk along the Atlantic Ocean, similar to the one in Atlantic City, New Jersey. This, he believed, was the future for him.

Augustine created an entertainment center called Joyland Amusement Park on the Boardwalk to cater to the growing tourist trade. Daytona Beach became famous for stock-car races that drew tens of thousands of people to the city each year. This was followed by Biker Week and Spring Break, which brought additional thousands of dollars to spend. Florida's real estate boom increased the population. Money poured into Daytona Beach and Joyland.

Augustine started other businesses, but Joyland represented the heart of his fortune. It was a huge money cow that produced millions of dollars every year from the tourist trade, mostly in cash. Few local residents visited Joyland because the Boardwalk attracted a lot of sleazy and unsavory characters.

"It's the first place the riffraff go when they hit town," said Sergeant Gregg Anderson, a detective with the Daytona Beach Police Department.

Augustine had operated a business on the Boardwalk since 1960, but he never associated with the transients who prowled the area. He didn't like the tough element

14

the Boardwalk attracted and had been trying to do something about it. It was also something that was on Lisa's agenda.

Augustine Paspalakis wasn't squeaky clean. He ran a cash business, which made it difficult to keep records that satisfied the Internal Revenue Service. He had been convicted of income tax evasion and had served three months of an eighteen-month sentence in a federal prison. There were persistent rumors that Augustine got money from the Chicago mob to start Joyland and, because it was a cash business, it was whispered that he repaid his benefactors by laundering money.

The State Attorney's office and, later, the Organized Crime Strike Force investigated Augustine and Joyland and found nothing that warranted bringing charges. Augustine's prison sentence for income tax evasion wasn't considered a black mark on his record by those who knew him. They believed that Augustine had been railroaded. He enjoyed power, wealth, respect, and the admiration of hundreds of friends and acquaintances.

Lisa had earned her place in the sun, too. She was the daughter of a millionaire, but she had not been born rich and was far from being a pampered debutante. Possessed by the same spunk and drive as her father, Lisa started to learn about the family businesses as a youngster. She didn't acquire her knowledge by sitting on the sidelines; she pitched in with a great deal of elbow grease.

Lisa had graduated from the University of South Florida, where she earned a degree in accounting, then passed the examination to become a Certified Public Accountant. By that time, Lisa was already a seasoned businesswoman with years of hands-on experience in commerce. She was respected not only by the Greek business community but by colleagues in women's business associations. Once she completed her education, Lisa played an increasingly important role in family business affairs. The Paspalakis family was generous in the funds and leadership it provided in the Greek community affairs and in the church. The entire family was

15

well-liked.

"Lisa had it all," friends said. "She had everything but a husband."

The Greeks have a time-honored tradition of matchmaking. The matchmakers specialize in finding husbands for women and wives for men. Although they weren't encouraged to do so, Paspalakis family friends sometimes cast themselves in that role by trying to find a husband for Lisa. They kept an eye out for a young man who would make a suitable husband for a young woman they loved and respected.

People were suspicious that some young, ambitious man with good looks and a smooth way of talking might try to marry Lisa for her money or, more accurately, for the money she would inherit. Lisa needed no help finding boyfriends, and she was nobody's fool when it came to sizing people up, but friends knew that the heart often dominated the head.

Lisa had dates, but she was in no particular hurry to get married. All of that changed when she was introduced to Kosta. At first glance, Lisa and Kosta made an unlikely pair. Lisa was rich and would get richer when she received inheritances from her parents. Kosta, besides being a student, was a lowly waiter at Lenny's Barbecue, a beachside restaurant that specialized in barbecued ribs and chicken. Kosta had no money and few, if any, prospects for becoming wealthy.

But Kosta had other qualities that Lisa and her family found attractive. He came from a moderate-income family in Greece, and he showed initiative and ambition by working to help pay his way through college. Kosta had lived with various uncles in the Chicago area while he attended Lewis University in Lockport, Illinois, where he earned a bachelor's degree.

"The help from my uncles was not a gift," Kosta said. "I am expected to pay them back. I intend to pay them back."

When he received his bachelor's degree, Kosta moved to Daytona Beach. He was only six months away from

16

completing his studies in aeronautical science at Embry-Riddle when he met Lisa.

Kosta was born in Athens, Greece, the son of Charalampas and Despine Fotopoulos. Charalampas was an engineer for Olympia Airlines. He earned a good income and was able to send Kosta and his sister to private schools. When it was time for Kosta to attend college, Charalampas made arrangements for him to live with his brother in Illinois. Charalampas looked forward to the day his son would earn his degree in aeronautical science and join him as an engineer with Olympia Airlines.

This may have been Kosta's plan, too, but when he met Lisa, everything changed. He embarked on an intense campaign to win her hand and the approval of her friends and family. Kosta had little money to spend on Lisa, but he compensated by being thoughtful and considerate. He seemed to anticipate her every need and appeared to have a nurturing character. Lisa considered him exceptionally attentive, and her parents thought Kosta was a fine young man who would make a good husband for their daughter. Lisa's mother, Mary, loved him like a son, and all of the family's friends liked Kosta.

Lisa was attracted by Kosta's physical appearance. He was six feet, two inches tall, weighed a solid 220 pounds, had thick dark hair parted in the middle, brooding brown eyes, and a full, sensual mouth. He was strong and manly with a hint of mystery that was intriguing. Lisa believed she was more intelligent than Kosta, and she was somewhat concerned because he rarely showed any emotion. She also noted that she seemed to love Kosta much more than he loved her. Nevertheless, she was smitten and described him as being "wonderful."

Three weeks after they met, Lisa's parents announced that she and Kosta were engaged to be married in two months. Kosta abandoned all plans to return to Greece; he had struck it rich. Lisa's family friends approved of the match. Kosta had shown enterprise by nearly completing his studies to earn a master's degree in aeronautical science and was generally thought of as a thoughtful,

17

enterprising, intelligent young man.

The courtship had been a whirlwind affair, and Lisa was truly in love with Kosta. Yet there were those who believed that the marriage had been arranged, much like those made by the matchmakers of the old days in Greece.

"The family wanted Lisa to have a Greek husband," a friend said. "They wanted him to be from a good family. Kosta was a Greek, he had a good education, came from a good family, and was a handsome guy."

Since Lisa was his only daughter, this was Augustine's first and last chance to give a wedding. He pulled out all of the stops to make it a memorable occasion for Lisa and lavish enough to suit a man of his wealth and prestige. Even Reverend Nicholos Manousakis, who performed the ceremony at St. Demetrios, had never seen such an assembly of the rich and powerful in his church. Kosta's parents flew from Greece to attend the wedding, as did relatives in Chicago.

The wedding reception was held at the Daytona Hilton, a luxurious hotel on the Atlantic Ocean. Augustine had rented several rooms for out-of-town guests and a large dining room for the reception. The reception was impressive even by Daytona Hilton standards. One of the employees called it "unbelievable." Four hundred guests drank champagne while an orchestra played in the gaily decorated room. A reporter from the local newspaper was there to write about it in the Society pages. There was a sit-down banquet for all four hundred guests. An employee at the Hilton said Augustine paid fifty thousand dollars for guest rooms and the reception.

Following the marriage, Lisa rented a condominium apartment in Daytona Beach as home for herself and Kosta. Lisa made it clear to Kosta that he had to be a faithful husband.

"If you ever have an affair," she told him, "I'll leave you and you won't have anything."

Lisa also set down the rules for their financial arrangements. Although they held two joint checking accounts,

18

it was clearly understood that one account belonged to Lisa and the other to Kosta. Lisa didn't write checks on Kosta's account, and he couldn't write checks on hers. The money was kept separate.

"That's the way we ran our marriage," Lisa recalled.

Even though he had no direct access to the Paspalakis money, Kosta lived like a rich man. Lisa paid all of their living expenses, including rent and groceries, and she co-signed whenever Kosta wanted to buy something on credit, such as a new BMW and Jeep Cherokee. Lisa also gave him expensive gifts of jewelry and clothing. Kosta returned to Embry-Riddle to complete his studies but was also put on the payroll at Joyland at a salary of three hundred dollars a week. This relatively small salary didn't come close to paying for his clothes, gold chains, bracelets, and Rolex watch. Kosta's parents occasionally sent him money, but it was only a few hundred dollars now and then. So far as Lisa knew, Kosta didn't have anything except what she gave him.

Once Kosta showed her four thousand dollars and said, "Mom gave me this."

Lisa thought Kosta's mother intended for him to save the money for her, not as a gift.

"They scrimp and save in Greece to hold onto their dollars, because dollars are worth more than drachmas," she said. "It isn't unusual to take money out of Greece. Everybody there has money in the United States."

Several years before she married Kosta, Lisa bought a one-hundred-thousand-dollar life insurance policy on herself that named her brother Dino as the beneficiary. Following her marriage, she told Kosta that she was going to change it so that both he and Dino would be co-beneficiaries in the event of her death. Lisa bought another life insurance policy for two hundred and fifty thousand dollars early in 1988 and told Kosta that she made both him and Dino equal beneficiaries. The information never registered with Kosta. He believed that he was the sole beneficiary of both policies.

Although he craved money, Lisa noticed that her husband had absolutely no aptitude for finance or business. He didn't understand business and had no interest in financial management. Kosta frequently thought of what Lisa called "get-rich-quick schemes," but he didn't grasp even the fundamentals of finance. Where inheritance laws were concerned, his mind was a blank.

Lisa explained Kosta's ineptitude concerning business and inheritance: "Kosta doesn't have a very good concept of financial affairs. He doesn't understand anything about that. Put it this way—he wouldn't realize what he could get and what he couldn't get. I could see him thinking that he'd get everything. That's the way Kosta is. He just doesn't think that way."

After Kosta received his master's degree from Embry-Riddle, he went to work at Joyland and was put in charge of the video games. He collected hundreds of dollars in quarters each day from the machines and had access to cash from other activities at Joyland. While the revenue from every other aspect of Joyland boomed, the cash flow from the video games dropped.

Kosta had little interest in helping run Joyland. His consuming passion was for guns of all kinds, explosives, military tactics, weaponry, and uniforms. Kosta spent hours reading gun magazines, comic books about guerrilla warfare, and *Soldier of Fortune,* a magazine published for mercenary soldiers and others with an interest in military weapons and tactics. Gradually, he began to accumulate a small arsenal of handguns and rifles. He carried a handgun all of the time and kept another one in his car. There were always several loaded guns in the bedroom. Kosta slept with a loaded handgun under his pillow and two or three others on his side of the bed. Sometimes he placed two high-powered rifles loaded and ready to fire between himself and Lisa when they went to bed.

"I have them to protect us." Kosta told Lisa.

Lisa didn't think much about it, because she knew guns were Kosta's hobby. A longtime friend, Peter Kouracos, shared the same interests as Kosta, and she thought Kosta's behavior might be a normal thing for men. She described her husband as being a "Rambo" type of person.

Kosta often disappeared for hours, but Lisa never questioned him about where he went or what he did. It wasn't in her nature to be possessive or to keep her husband on a tight leash. She didn't ask about his unexplained absences, and he didn't volunteer information. Besides, she was too busy running the businesses to pay much attention to Kosta's unexplained dalliances. She had no reason to be jealous even though she realized that Kosta didn't love her all that much.

Augustine was being treated for coronary artery disease, and his health was precarious. Lisa worried about her father, and she had other problems, too. The beach property along the Atlantic Ocean had attracted multimillion dollar companies. Expensive high-rise hotels had been developed along the beach, and there was pressure from the city council to upgrade the Boardwalk. The city had built an expensive auditorium on Atlantic Avenue across the street from the beach to attract conventions and cultural attractions in order to generate revenue. Although the auditorium was farther south than the Boardwalk, the hoodlums and thugs spilled over into the area. Smaller businesses such as Joyland, which had choice locations, were threatened with expensive renovations that could drive them out of business.

There were numerous gift shops, small restaurants, and other enterprises on the Boardwalk that were operated by private owners, many of them from the Greek community. They were under pressure by the city to improve the Boardwalk, which meant they could be burdened with expenses that could break the backs of their businesses. Like most entrepreneurs, the merchants were fiercely independent and had a difficult time unifying to create a strong front to protect themselves from the onslaught. Lisa helped them form a coalition to combine their strength, convincing them that they could only survive by presenting a unified front.

21

"Lisa was the business brain of the Boardwalk," Peter Kouracos said. "Without her the other merchants couldn't agree on anything. They were constantly arguing. She was the force that held them together."

Lisa's brains and leadership presented a strong front that allowed the small businessmen to keep from going bankrupt. Doing that and running Joyland and the other family businesses took considerable time and energy. Kosta did little to help. He thought of one get-rich-quick scheme after another but had no idea of how a business had to be run. Worse, he had no interest. He became increasingly interested in guns, military tactics, and similar things. At Joyland and at home Kosta spent hours reading comic books on guerrilla warfare, soft pornographic magazines, gun magazines, and *Soldier of Fortune*.

To Lisa's dismay, he gravitated toward the Boardwalk transients, composed of a hodgepodge of thieves, robbers, pimps, prostitutes, con men, and other lowlifes who prowled around looking for a fast buck from unwary tourists.

"Every whore and bum on the Boardwalk knows you," she complained. "My father has worked here since 1960, and he doesn't know any of them, but all of them call you by name."

Kosta had little to say about this in the early part of their marriage, but Lisa knew he had the young hoodlums on the Boardwalk thinking that he was rich and powerful. It was obvious to her that he enjoyed their admiration.

"You're trying to impress the wrong kind of people," Lisa told him.

Kosta paid no attention. His interest in the Boardwalk guttersnipes and things military were more than a passing fancy. He longed to work for the Federal Bureau of Investigation or the Central Intelligence Agency and thought he could earn huge sums of money by becoming a professional assassin. He applied for employment to both agencies but was turned down. The rejections did nothing to diminish his passion. He accumulated more guns and weaponry, and spun elaborate tales about his adventures as a professional assassin that captivated the impressionable young transients on the Boardwalk. He always carried a gun and enjoyed moving his jacket just enough to show that he had one. Kosta gained a reputation as being a dangerous man who would kill an enemy in the blink of an eye.

He had plans to make money that he had never discussed with Lisa or anyone in her immediate family. One of his plans concerned their murder, but that wasn't the first thing on his agenda. Kosta conceived dozens of ways to make money without doing any work. The master's degree from Embry-Riddle had prepared him for a job that would pay good wages, and he was married to a rich wife who doted on him, but this wasn't enough for Kosta; he longed to be a heroic figure like those in his comic books. He wanted money and power, and he wanted to kill.

2

Kosta met Peter Kouracos a few weeks before he married Lisa. They were introduced by a vice president in charge of a local branch bank at a breakfast meeting at the International House of Pancakes in Daytona Beach Shores, just south of Daytona Beach. Kosta and the banker shared an interest in guns and so did Peter Kouracos.

Kouracos was very much interested in guns, armaments, and military tactics, just as Kosta was. The banker thought that the two men should be introduced. Kosta and Kouracos hit it off immediately.

The Paspalakis and Kouracos families had been acquaintances for years, and Kouracos had known Lisa since they were both children. They both had graduated from Seabreeze High School in Daytona Beach, and Kouracos said that their relationship was like a brother and sister. Lisa remembered that she was never really very close to Kouracos.

"He was Kosta's friend," Lisa said.

Regardless of how Lisa and Kouracos viewed their relationship over the years, Kosta and Kouracos became very close. The friendship between the two men grew stronger as they got to know one another better. They shared stories about guns and military tactics and discussed their philosophies about living in a hostile world. Their ideas fit together like hand and glove.

"I like to think of myself as a Survivalist," Kouracos said to police. "I thought he had Survivalist thinking."

Survivalists, generally speaking, believe that individuals should be prepared to survive any adversity, including nuclear war. There are Survivalist training courses based on military techniques, and adherents of the philosophy believe in having guns and money hidden for use in an emergency. Survivalist learn about guns, guerrilla warfare tactics, foraging for food, and how to survive any adverse situation, including the aftermath of Armageddon. Groups in various parts of the country don military gear from time to time and play war games to hone their fighting skills.

Kouracos came from an entirely different background than Kosta. Kosta had grown up in Greece while Kouracos had been reared in an affluent Greek family in Daytona Beach. Kouracos had made a name for himself as an active campaign worker for various Republican candidates who ran for local, county, state, and national offices. In 1978, while he was still in college, Kouracos headed the unsuccessful gubernatorial campaign for former U.S. Representative Lou Frey.

Kouracos had an impressive set of credentials: he had served as vice-chairman of the Young Republicans, president of the Helenic Educational Progressive Association, and was a member of the Junior Chamber of Commerce. He was seen as a young man whose political star was ascending; if he didn't achieve elective office he would most certainly be a power broker. He had already achieved a degree of power and prominence, but he was a long way from being a kingmaker.

Part of Kouracos's political clout came from the fact that his parents, Louis and Lydia Kouracos, were major financial backers of political candidates, as was the Paspalakis family. Kouracos enhanced his political stature by earning a reputation as a tireless politician who was willing to tackle the most difficult tasks. He also had a good head for the intricacies of politics.

In addition to his impressive political résumé, Kouracos was a successful businessman. He helped operate his family's South Atlantic gift shop and was a serious investor in the stock market. Kouracos was also an aspiring law student who wanted to become a lawyer to enhance his opportunities in politics and business. This particular goal was as elusive to him as capturing foxfire in a Daytona Beach woods. He studied hard to pass the examinations that would qualify him for law school but had not yet been accepted. Kouracos continued his studies to enter law school while simultaneously pursuing courses to earn a bachelor's degree in business administration. At the time he met Kosta, Kouracos had a license to sell over-the-counter guns such as pistols, shotguns, and rifles.

Kouracos was a twenty-nine-year-old bachelor who had never been married even though his affluence, family name, and political activities made him a prize catch. Kouracos was a good-looking man of medium height, wore expensive jewelry, sported a mustache and thick head of brown hair, and usually wore glasses. Even when he wasn't working, Kouracos preferred to wear conservative three-piece suits that were appropriate for a man who was rich and powerful.

Although he was well-to-do and a major player in local and state power politics, Kouracos liked to think of himself in egalitarian terms.

"I'm a conservative Republican, but I don't look down on people because of their social status," he said.

After their initial introduction over pancakes, Kouracos didn't meet Kosta again until after Kosta and Lisa became engaged. Kouracos considered himself a friend of the entire Paspalakis family, but he quickly became much closer to Kosta. "He was like a brother to me," he said, "but the whole family was like my own family."

Lisa's brother Dino didn't believe that Kouracos was a particularly good friend of the family or of Lisa's. "He was an acquaintance, not the kind of guy you would talk to about private matters," he said. "I can't see Lisa asking him for advice or sharing things with him. Peter was Kosta's friend."

According to Peter Kouracos's police deposition, he and Kosta were together often, and called each other "bro."

They often went shooting together, sometimes at local firing ranges and owned modified semiautomatic weapons. When they went shooting with them, they found remote areas where they could shoot on full automatic.

While they were enamored of guns in general, they were particularly fond of assault rifles. They even made their own rifle and handgun bullets, which takes time and requires considerable expertise.

Both men were excited when Kosta managed to acquire some tracer bullets. Tracers exit a gun muzzle at a lower velocity than a normal bullet and leave a shower of sparks to show the shooter where his other bullets are heading.

Kosta and Kouracos were more interested in the fireworks effect than in the practicality of the tracer bullets. They loaded several AK-47 magazines with regular ammunition and substituted a tracer for every fourth bullet. They waited until it was dark so they could see the tracers before they went into a woods to fire their weapons.

Shooting guns were important to Kosta and Kouracos. They even made a social affair out of cleaning them when they returned to the condominium after an outing to the woods or a firing range. They sat at a kitchen counter with metal cleaning rods, swabs, and bottles of gun cleaning solvent and oil. They cleaned their weapons while Lisa cooked something for them to eat. Lisa was becoming accustomed to having a lot of guns around.

On one occasion, the gun-cleaning ritual could have had disastrous consequences. Kosta and Kouracos were cleaning identical handguns on the kitchen counter. Both guns had the magazines removed and were thought to be unloaded. Kosta got up and went to the kitchen while Kouracos held up one of the pistols.

"Hey, Bro," Kouracos said. "Is this the one that's unloaded?"

"Yeah," Kosta nodded.

"Are you sure?"

Kosta said that he was sure.

Kouracos pointed the gun at the wall and pulled the trigger. The gun went off and blew a hole in the wall. "It was my fault," Kouracos said. "The magazine was out but there was a bullet in the firing chamber."

It was an unusual act of carelessness for a man who had a license to sell firearms.

There were a dozen or so affluent men in the Daytona Beach area who had an almost fanatical interest in guns and who favored the Survivalist philosophy. They borrowed guns from one another all the time, keeping them for months and, at any given time, not everyone knew who had whose gun. In his sworn statement to the police, Kouracos called it "bouncing guns around."

Lisa had never been around guns much. At Joyland her father only carried a gun when he took cash to the bank, and he didn't always have one then. Her brother Dino didn't even like guns. After she married Kosta, he persuaded her to keep a gun in her desk drawer. Kosta kept another gun in his desk, wore another in a shoulder holster, and kept another in his car. Whenever Kosta was at Joyland there were three guns on the premises, two of them his. Lisa had never owned a gun until she met Kosta.

Lisa went shooting with Kosta a few times, but she wasn't much interested in guns and she was too busy working and protecting the small merchants on the Boardwalk to devote much time to that type of recreation.

Sometimes Kouracos accompanied Kosta to remote areas late at night. Kosta carried metal containers, military ammunition boxes, or waterproof bags. Often, he wore camouflage combat gear and carried a trench shovel, military flashlights, wore bandoleers of bullets, and a samurai sword across his chest.

Kouracos drove Kosta to where he wanted to go, then Kosta would give him instructions to let him out.

Kouracos would stop the car, Kosta then heading into the woods with his containers after telling Kouracos to drive away and come back at a designated time. Kouracos was to switch the headlights on and off so that Kosta would recognize him. Kouracos took Kosta on various forays at different wooded areas in and around Volusia County. Kosta would enter the woods with containers, but he returned without them.

"I never questioned what was in the containers that he buried," Kouracos said. "I thought it was Survivalist thinking."

Kouracos sometimes stopped at Joyland to talk with Kosta or say hello to Lisa. He frequently showed up at lunchtime, and the three of them would eat together; if either Kosta or Lisa was absent, Kouracos had lunch with the one who was left. Kouracos became much more of a presence in Lisa's life after she and Kosta married than he had been previously.

The two men and Lisa often watched videotaped movies at the condominium. Kouracos had an extensive library of videos, and he would usually bring one over, because both he and Lisa disliked the movies that Kosta rented. According to Kouracos, his telephone would ring and Lisa would be on the line.

"We've watched all of our videos," Lisa said. "Why don't you get one of yours and pop on over?"

"Okay."

They both knew that if Kosta rented a video, it would be something gory with so much blood and guts that Lisa and Kouracos would have to leave the room.

"His taste in movies was notoriously hideous," Kouracos said. "I just hate to watch any movie he picks out. They're really terrible. Vietnam movies, freak shows, and monsters. He picks out all kinds of weird stuff."

Watching the movies at the condominium was an event. Lisa was a good homemaker in addition to being a businesswoman. She cooked delicacies that took time and effort. They ate while watching the movies. Usually such an evening didn't end until two or three o'clock in the morning.

Sometimes Kosta was the first to cave in. Since Lisa didn't have to get up early in the morning to open Joyland, she and Kouracos would talk about business, politics, and other things of mutual interest for a while after Kosta went to bed.

"She liked to stay up and drink a few Lite beers and talk," Kouracos said.

Kouracos sometimes escorted Lisa to nightclubs because Kosta didn't like to go out and party at night. Lisa loved to dance and have a good time. She wasn't the type of woman to go out by herself, but she worked hard and she liked to blow off steam by dancing and having fun with friends. None of that was for the seemingly unemotional Kosta.

"Kosta was a deadbeat when it came to that," Kouracos said. "He just didn't like going out to nightclubs."

But Kosta didn't mind if Kouracos took Lisa out. He knew it was innocent.

Kosta's obsession with guns didn't bother Lisa, but there were other quirky things about her husband that did. She couldn't understand why a man with a master's degree in aeronautical engineering spent hours reading comic books about guerrilla warfare. His drawer at Joyland was jammed with comic books and they were scattered about at home. Kosta devoured *Penthouse* and *Playboy* in addition to *Soldier of Fortune*. Kosta liked to prop his feet up on his desk at Joyland, fiddle with a pistol he kept there, and leaf through the magazines.

Kosta showed little emotion — except anger. Once he became so angry with Dino and Lisa at Joyland that he picked up a chair and slammed it against a desk so hard that the desk broke in half.

The fact that Kosta read comic books, skin magazines, and daydreamed about being an assassin didn't keep Kouracos from being his best friend. Kouracos, being a political pragmatist, also recognized the fact that Kosta was a member of a powerful and important family.

Kosta mentioned that he wanted to be an assassin, but Kouracos thought that was nothing more than excessive enthusiasm about being a Survivalist. As Kosta and

Kouracos became closer, Kouracos thought that their interest in guns, military tactics, and guerrilla warfare should be carried a step further. He thought of the Survivalist training centers.

Kosta agreed that it was a good idea, but nothing came of it. But not attending a formal training school did nothing to diminish their fervor for guns and other military weaponry. Kouracos stated to the police that he had upgraded his firearms license to allow him to sell top-of-the-line guns such as AK-47 semiautomatic assault rifles, a military weapon used by Russian and Chinese infantrymen.

Kosta acquired an AK-47 and an Uzi, but not from Kouracos, and studied his pamphlets and gun magazines to make them fully automatic. He worked hard at it, and once succeeded by using a piece of nylon string to alter one of the AK-47's mechanical functions.

According to Kouracos, Kosta told Kouracos about his success, and Peter was impressed but also afraid that his friend would get into trouble if he was caught firing an automatic weapon, so he loaned him his gun dealer's license, thinking that it would protect Kosta in case he was ever caught. Kouracos further reported to the police that it never occurred to him that letting Kosta use his license was illegal, although he later admitted, it was stupid.

Besides trying to make guns fully automatic, Kosta experimented with ways to make silencers, which are also illegal, for his handguns and rifles.

Each new gun fed the passion that burned in Kosta to be a soldier of fortune. He still hoped that he could become an assassin for the Central Intelligence Agency. Kosta assembled a large and varied number of weapons, including such things as hand grenades and C-4 plastic explosives, which were manufactured exclusively for military use. He acquired a Samurai sword with a camouflage sheath, camouflaged military uniforms, a crossbow and arrows, and an Uzi automatic machine pistol, another weapon manufactured for military use. Because they are compact and lay down such a rapid field of fire, Uzis are often carried beneath the jackets of Secret Service agents who protect the President and other high-ranking officials. Like the AK-47, an Uzi can be legally purchased in the United States if it isn't automatic, but pamphlets on how to make it automatic are easy to find.

Kosta liked to put on camouflage uniforms, strap on his Samurai sword, and go for late-night forays into lonely, wooded areas. He buried some of his arsenal and other equipment in military ammunition boxes, making notches on trees so that he could find them later.

"Kosta was caught up in this adolescent James Bond fantasy world," an acquaintance said. "Most guys have it when they're teenagers, but they outgrow it. Kosta's obsession just kept getting stronger."

Kosta had daydreams about torture and making money implementing some of the schemes that he read about in *Soldier Of Fortune* and his comic books. He thought of ways to make money with a minimum of effort, and he fed on the admiration and fear he created among the young Boardwalk hoodlums.

In May 1987, Lisa's cousin flew from Greece to visit the United States. Kouracos described him as a compulsive gambler. Kosta had finished his graduate work just a few months earlier and was thinking of ways to make big money and operate on the fringes of the law.

"Kosta wanted to be rich," David Damore said. "But that wasn't enough. He needed the admiration of the community. He needed to be a hero."

Constantinos Paspalakis opened a door for Kosta to take his first step. He told Kosta where he could make a lot of money with a small investment and little effort. Constantinos had a contact in Milan, Italy, who would sell Kosta at least one hundred thousand dollars in high-quality counterfeit one hundred dollar bills for twenty cents on the dollar.

Kosta was excited by the prospective deal. Constantinos passed counterfeit without any trouble. According to

Kouracos, Kosta drove with Lisa's cousin to his family's gift shop, parked his car, and called him outside. Kosta was in high spirits. Kouracos knew that Constantinos had spent a week at the casinos in Atlantic City, New Jersey, before he arrived in Daytona Beach.

Kosta showed Kouracos several crisp, new one hundred dollar bills.

"Look at this," Kosta said.

Kouracos looked at them.

"What do you think?" Kosta asked.

Kouracos was puzzled. They looked like regular one hundred dollar bills to him.

"They're counterfeit," Kosta said. "Constantinos brought them over. He knows where I can get a lot of it."

Kouracos became wary. It was one thing to think like a Survivalist and have an interest in firearms, but counterfeiting was illegal. He listened as Kosta told him how Lisa's cousin had successfully passed many of the bills at the Atlantic City casinos and other places in the United States.

Kosta told Kouracos about the source in Milan and how much the bogus money would cost. But buying the counterfeit wasn't the major problem Kosta had; the hard part, which wasn't really that difficult, would be converting the counterfeit by having people buy things that cost less than one hundred dollars and receiving good money in change.

Kosta said he could use some of the Boardwalk transients to pass off the counterfeit. He said he could recruit a small army to convert the bogus money into good currency.

After he showed Kouracos the good quality counterfeit, Kosta showed him a few bills that were obvious misprints.

Kosta never directly asked Kouracos to get involved, but he hinted at it. Kouracos backed off. He wanted to make his position clear.

"Hey, Bro," he said, "I don't want to be involved in anything illegal."

Kosta said okay and drove off with Constantinos.

According to Lisa's sworn statements, she knew that her cousin had aroused Kosta's interest in counterfeiting and didn't like it. She knew that it was just the type of get-rich-quick scheme that would appeal to Kosta. It also fit the image Kosta had of himself as a man who could operate outside of the law.

By their own admission, neither Lisa or Kouracos reported the scheme to the police.

On February 18, 1987, less than a month before Constantinos Paspalakis arrived from Greece, Kosta and his father-in-law rented a safe-deposit box at a Barnett branch bank with Kosta listed as a signatory. Augustine had authorized access to the safety box, but Kosta was the only person who ever used it. The time frame is not certain, but some time shortly before the visit, Kosta borrowed ten thousand dollars from Augustine and Mary Paspalakis. Lisa's parents didn't tell her that they had loaned the money to Kosta.

In June, just a month after her cousin returned to Greece, Kosta told Lisa that his sister was sick, and he had to visit her in Greece. Instead of going to Greece, Kosta bought an airline ticket and flew to Milan where he bought at least one hundred thousand dollars in bogus one hundred dollar bills for ten thousand dollars in good American currency. He smuggled the counterfeit into the United States without getting caught by customs.

Kosta was elated by his acquisition, but Lisa was distressed, she later told police.

"Don't tell Peter," she begged Kosta when he returned with the counterfeit. "I would really be embarrassed if he knew about this."

Kosta was too excited to follow Lisa's advice. He met with Kouracos, opened the trunk of his car, and showed him stacks of one hundred dollar bills wrapped in plastic. The trunk was jammed with money. Kouracos guessed that it amounted to at least one hundred thousand dollars.

"It was an awful lot of money," he said later to the police.

Immediately after he smuggled the counterfeit into the United States, Kosta recruited Vasilos "Bill" Markantonakis, a house painter, and his wife, Barbara, to help him launder it. Their job was to travel throughout Florida, Georgia, and the Carolinas, using the one hundred dollar bills to make small purchases and receiving good money in exchange. Kosta paid them a percentage of the good money they received and kept the rest.

Bill and Barbara Markantonakis had no trouble passing the fake one hundred dollar bills, and Kosta accumulated tens of thousands of dollars in good currency from the counterfeit operation and accumulated more weapons, ammunition and military gear.

He put thousands of dollars in containers and buried them at various places in the woods, along with silencers that he had acquired for some of his guns. Kouracos often accompanied Kosta as a driver on his nighttime forays to bury things. Kosta usually wore his camouflage uniform, a black beret, and was heavily armed.

In spite of Lisa's admonishment for Kosta to keep quiet so she wouldn't be embarrassed by the counterfeiting, rumors spread rapidly in the Greek community. To most people it was beyond belief. Kosta wasn't that kind of man, and why would he be involved in such a thing when his wife's family had so much money and gave him almost anything he wanted? They knew nothing of Kosta's obsessions or that he was becoming a figure of adulation and fear along the Boardwalk.

Lisa kept her mouth shut about her husband's dealing in counterfeit. She didn't go to the police because she loved him and didn't want him to be arrested, but she expressed her feelings to Kouracos.

"I'd like to disown my cousin for this," she said. "He's put my marriage in jeopardy with this counterfeit scheme."

On April 11, 1987, Kosta, Lisa, and Peter went to the Jai Alai fronton in Daytona Beach. Jai Alai is a fast game but is so repetitive that most people find it boring to watch after seeing their first two or three games. The main attraction at the fronton is parimutuel gambling, which is operated under a state license. Gamblers can choose from an assortment of bets, just as they can at horse races or greyhound races.

While Kosta, Lisa, and Kouracos were watching the game, Kosta got up.

"I'm going out," he said. "I'll be back in half an hour, okay?"

Peter and Lisa sat through the game and Kosta didn't return. An hour passed and Lisa started to get worried. A while later Kosta came back but didn't tell them why he had been gone so long. Lisa wouldn't have liked the truth: Kosta had tried to pass off one of Constantinos's counterfeit one hundred dollar bills and was caught. He had spent the time being grilled by a security officer employed by the fronton. Kosta bluffed his way out of the situation, claiming he didn't know the bill was counterfeit.

The counterfeit bill was given to Mike Pritchard, an agent from the U.S. Secret Service, along with a report stating that it had been passed by Kosta, but saying that Kosta didn't know it was counterfeit. Kosta wasn't considered a counterfeiting suspect because he was part of a wealthy family, and the counterfeit bill could easily have been passed off on him. Nevertheless, the counterfeit bill, along with details were recorded by the Secret Service.

This narrow scrape with the law didn't change Kosta's plans to continue counterfeiting. The large amount of counterfeit that he had represented seed money for much larger plans.

3

Augustine Paspalakis died in November 1988 during the Greek Festival, the most exciting event of the year for the Greek community in Daytona Beach. Doctors said that Augustine died almost instantly from an aneurysm, a ruptured artery. Augustine had been treated for coronary problems, but his sudden death left his friends and family devastated.

Mary, his widow, Lisa, and Dino were in a state of shock and grief. Kosta gave Lisa more attention than usual, but she noticed again how stoic he was. Lisa didn't see him shed a single tear or even look as if he might be grieving for his father-in-law.

Kosta's inability to show emotion bothered Lisa. If somebody died, as her father had, he would simply shrug his shoulders and say, "Oh, well . . ." Once, Kosta's father had brain surgery in Greece, and Kosta never telephoned or wrote to learn the results, let alone offer any comfort to his mother.

He shrugged and told Lisa, "If it happens, they'll call." Lisa was left with the impression that Kosta didn't really care one way or the other.

Lisa had noticed Kosta's lack of emotion on other occasions. When two of their friends in Tampa were splitting up, the man was particularly devastated. Lisa tried to help both of them out of their emotional labyrinths, but Kosta was no more responsive than a statue. Lisa was aggravated by his cold attitude.

She asked him, "If I died, would you cry?"

"Of course," Kosta answered.

But Lisa didn't know what to think; she had never seen tears in her husband's eyes and nothing seemed to faze him.

Kosta seemed to go through the motions of a concerned man, but it was if he was acting a part without any real feeling behind it. Lisa said that she sometimes thought he was scary "because he didn't seem to have a conscience."

Following Augustine's death, Lisa and Kosta moved into the house on 2500 Halifax Avenue. Mary and Dino had separate bedrooms, and Kosta and Lisa shared the large bedroom at the end of the upstairs hall. Kosta brought several handguns, military flashlights, a heavy-duty Mag flashlight used by police officers, and high-powered rifles into the bedroom. He also had a scanning radio that picked up forty channels of radio communications from area police and fire departments, as well as Emergency 911 calls.

The house on Halifax Avenue gave Kosta room to create a machine tooling shop. He bought metal tooling equipment and set about the task of making silencers for handguns and his automatic weapons. He also used the equipment in an attempt to make the semiautomatic assault rifles and pistols that he had acquired fully automatic. The first floor in back of the house, facing the river, was a recreation room. Kosta used it to make bullets by the hundreds that he used in his guns.

Augustine left Joyland, Circus Gift Shop Inc., and the Circus Gift Shop building and land in a trust to be administered by Mary, Lisa, and Dino. It wasn't a secret and no one made any attempt to hide details from Kosta. Such things simply didn't register with him. The way the trust was set up, if one member of the family died, that share would remain in the trust to be administered by the survivors. Lisa realized that her husband believed that the businesses and the house had been left equally to

38

her, Dino, and her mother. The intricacies of a trust were beyond Kosta's grasp.

In addition, Kosta thought Lisa owned a third of the expensive home on Halifax Avenue when it actually belonged only to his mother-in-law. Lisa and Kosta jointly owned a duplex valued at seventy-five thousand dollars that had a sixty-thousand-dollar mortgage on it. They were having a home built in Ormond Beach which would be valued at about $282,000 when it was completed.

Kosta had made half of the down payment on the duplex and the Ormond Beach home with money that he borrowed from banks, for which Lisa had cosigned.

Kosta thought that if Lisa died accidentally, he would receive seven hundred thousand dollars from her life insurance policies, her share of the businesses, and her share of other property, plus all of her jewelry and expensive personal possessions.

The truth was far from what Kosta believed. The money he would receive from insurance in the event of Lisa's accidental death was only half of what he thought it would be. Although Lisa had intended to drop Dino as a beneficiary from one of her life insurance policies and leave it all to Kosta, she never got around to doing it. Lisa had not made out a will and, under Florida law, Kosta would have inherited her estate. Lisa's estate consisted primarily of her personal items and the equity in the duplex and the house she and Kosta were having built. The bulk of her wealth from Joyland and the other family businesses would have remained in the trust to be administered by Lisa's mother and brother. Kosta had no claim on it whatsoever.

While the rest of the family tried to deal with their grief after Augustine died and keep the family businesses operating, Kosta moved ahead with his own plans. Kosta used some of the Boardwalk hoodlums that he had drawn into his inner circle to pass some of the counterfeit one hundred dollar bills he had bought in Italy. But he never told them the money was counterfeit.

Kosta had other plans besides counterfeiting. He wanted to establish a burglary ring, a group of armed robbers capable of knocking off banks and armored cars, a gun-running operation, a drug ring, run a prostitution ring, operate a ring of car thieves for insurance fraud and various other schemes. The most important thing on his list of goals was to create a group of assassins, which he thought of as the Hunter-Killer Club.

This would be a group of people who could prove they were capable of committing cold-blooded murder. Kosta envisioned making hundreds of thousands of dollars through the Hunter-Killers. The minimum charge for a murder — or assassination, as he thought of it — would be ten thousand dollars and could go up to one hundred thousand dollars depending on how difficult the job was. Kosta, as the ringleader, intended to contract each murder, assign the assassin, and receive a hefty percentage as his share.

Kosta wanted his Hunter-Killers to be protected from one another in case they were caught. Each member would murder an "expendable" person, such as a Boardwalk transient without a job or family in the area, while the murder was taped by a video camera. The videotapes of the murders would be passed around among various members of the Hunter-Killers with no one knowing who had which tapes. If anyone went to the police, the videotape of that person committing murder would be handed over to the authorities. It was a check-and-balance system that Kosta believed would work.

Kosta kept this idea to himself. He knew that the people he could recruit that would satisfy him were among the Boardwalk hoodlums. Although many of the whores and thugs knew him by name, Kosta had no real way to establish contact with them. He needed an operational base and someone who could steer prospective killers his way.

Kosta managed to make a few contacts on the Boardwalk, but he was prevented from developing his operations because he had no place to use as headquarters. In addition, his position at Joyland—although he was often gone and worked little when he was there—restricted his activities. Kosta needed his own operation on the Boardwalk to be near the hoodlums who would be his functionaries.

Although he didn't understand the financial apparatus that Augustine had left behind and believed that he would receive a third of the Paspalakis fortune if Lisa died—in addition to her life insurance policies—Kosta wasn't satisfied. He wanted it all. He planned to have Mary and Dino killed so that Lisa would inherit everything. Then he intended to kill Lisa and gain complete control of the Paspalakis family wealth.

4

Deidre Hunt moved to Daytona Beach in early September 1989 and in a matter of weeks the twenty-year-old Massachusetts native was a Boardwalk celebrity. She was beautiful, alluring, exuded a smoldering sexuality, and was dangerous. The Boardwalk transients who flocked around Deidre used words such as *hypnotic* and *magnetic* to describe her. A few called her "a bitch" or "a banshee"—but never to her face.

Deidre was followed by a group of young thugs wherever she went.

Tony Calderone, a friend of Kosta's who'd had sex with Deidre, said, "It was like watching a group of ducklings following a mother duck."

She was a natural leader of the crowd that walked a tightrope between petty and violent crime.

The Boardwalk and Deidre were much alike: cheap and tawdry, but hinting at more promising attractions. The Boardwalk is a microcosm of Daytona Beach, a city that caters to thundering automobiles, motorcycle clubs, and Spring Breakers with little on their minds except sex, booze, drugs, and rock 'n' roll. Though the town rolls out the red carpet for Speed Week (when the Daytona 500 is run), Biker Week, and Spring Break, there is little support for culture. More often than not the residents stay away from the beach during those events, when the smell of exhaust, beer, and suntan lotion taints the breezes sweeping in from the Atlantic Ocean.

Fort Lauderdale, a city a little farther south, used to be the favored place for Spring Break. That city cracked down because of all the damage the "breakers" did and slammed the door in their faces. Daytona Beach, hungry for money, immediately put its nets out to capture the Fort Lauderdale rejects and even advertised itself as a Spring Break town with "The World's Most Famous Beach."

The tourists are easy prey for the petty thieves and con artists who hang out on the Boardwalk at all times but especially during the few months that encompass Speed Week, Biker Week, and Spring Break. There are thieves who specialize in purse snatching and picking pockets. Male and female prostitutes abound, to be bought singly or in combos for orgies. Many naive partiers are enticed outside a nice bar by a pretty face and an alluring smile to be beaten badly by someone hiding in the shadows to steal anything valuable. Deaths occur every year.

The city and the merchants have tried in vain to improve the Boardwalk's image so that local middle-class families will visit the attractions there instead of running in the other direction. Their success has been underwhelming, and the locals stay away in droves.

Most of the businesses along the Boardwalk are run by honest, hard-working people. There are always a few shady characters in any tourist area, and the Boardwalk is no exception. There are tawdry spots on the Boardwalk such as pool halls, beer joints, video game arcades, novelty shops, and smoke-filled nightclubs where young men and women with hungry eyes and voracious appetites look for action. There are bars that feature topless dancers that the street people refer to as "titty bars," joints with male strippers, and places where male and female homosexuals hang out, such as an area near a Holiday Inn dubbed "Fag Hill."

Even the local people don't know the metamorphosis that occurs in Daytona Beach every twenty-four hours. By day it's a decent enough town when measured by the standards of a nation where violent crime runs wild. But from midnight on the thugs and drug dealers dominate the area.

The local newspapers bury stories of murder, rape, shooting, and assault on the inside pages with small headlines unless it happens to be a sensational story. News of crime could damage the economy by preventing tourists from visiting the area for fear of being mugged — or worse.

The sand along the Atlantic shore is so fine that it looks like light brown confectioners' sugar. During the three theme weeks, tanned bodies wearing as little as possible gleam with oil as they broil like hot dogs under the Florida sun. On the outer fringes of the beach, automobiles, sand buggies, and other assorted vehicles cruise back and forth, stereos blaring, while kids lean out and wave beer cans. Young women show off naked breasts and young men moon the crowds with bare behinds.

It was the perfect place for Deidre Hunt, who was known on the Boardwalk as Dee or Cherri. Deidre was five feet, two inches, had smoldering brown eyes, black hair that rippled below her shoulders and a knock-out figure. Everything about her reeked of sexuality except for an occasional bubbly laugh that made her look like an innocent fourteen year old instead of a streetwise hard case.

Deidre's sexual allure was complemented by a mind that could calculate mathematics almost as fast as a computer. This was all the more amazing because she had dropped out of school in the ninth grade and had been on drugs and alcohol since she was a child. But the assets that catapulted Deidre to prominence were her ability to get people to do anything she wanted, her beauty, and her sexual appetite for both men and women.

"She loved to show off her figure," said J.R. Taylor, who had fallen in love with her for a while. "She pranced around in the skimpiest bikinis she could find. She thought she was just the prettiest thing on the Board-

44

walk. There was something haunting about her."

Another person who knew Deidre said, "She was sleazy but beautiful. She wasn't anybody who could be ignored."

Detective Greg Evans of the Daytona Beach Police Department said, "She was the queen of the Boardwalk, no doubt about it. All of the street people looked up to her as some strange kind of role model."

Deidre didn't arrive in Daytona Beach to the sound of trumpets. She followed John Beauvier, a boyfriend from New Hampshire, who promptly left her and headed back north. But Deidre had hot-footed it to Daytona Beach not just to be with her boyfriend but because of a close call with the police: an attempted murder charge, and possible complicity in a separate murder-for-hire case.

When Beauvier beat her up and returned to New England, Deidre moved into a trailer with two young men. One of them was twenty-year-old Mark Kevin Ramsey. An aunt, who lived in Maitland, Florida, came to visit Deidre and was appalled at the squalor in which Deidre and the two men lived.

"I didn't see how people could live like that," she said. "It was nothing but filth."

Deidre was down, but she wasn't out. She moved fast. She knew all of the tricks of surviving on the streets and she was a supreme confidence woman.

"Deidre is a fine actress," said Teja James, who knew her well. "She can become whatever the situation requires."

Deidre's rapid ascendance to stardom on the Boardwalk would come as no surprise to people who knew her reputation. Although she was just twenty, Deidre had been on the streets for years.

Deidre was born in South Weymouth, Massachusetts, the illegitimate daughter of Carol Ann Hunt, on February 9, 1969. Carol Ann was an emotionally disturbed alcoholic who abused her unwanted daughter. Adding to Carol Ann's dislike of her daughter was the fact that

45

Deidre had been born with crooked feet and had to wear metal braces on her legs until she was ten years old.

Deidre and her mother lived in poverty. Carol Ann moved from one public housing project to another, living on welfare payments. Sometimes Carol Ann would become so emotionally distressed that she would sit for days and do nothing. If Deidre wanted anything to eat she had to fend for herself. Deidre's mother would alternate between trying to control everything her daughter did or completely ignore her. Frequently Carol Ann would abandon Deidre and her brother, who was a year younger, and telephone one of her sisters to tell them what she had done.

"Come and get them," Carol Ann would say. "I don't want them anymore."

At other times, Carol Ann would drop the kids off at an aunt's house and drive away. Later she would call, "They're in your yard and so are their things. You'll have to take care of them."

Tough kids in the public housing projects made fun of Deidre's braces, but she fought back. Deidre had a naturally tough streak in her that was exacerbated by cruel treatment. She didn't stay on the receiving end very long. By the time she was in the second grade she was already taking drugs. She started to have sex when she was in the fourth grade. In short order, the bullies were won over by her toughness and sexual favors.

By the time Deidre reached her teens, she had been kicked out of the homes of four aunts and uncles because of their inability to control her.

"She always went out with the lowlifes," one of them recalled. "Those were the choices she made."

Carol Ann, who had been in and out of psychotherapy for years, did a complete flip-flop when Deidre reached fourteen and let her daughter do anything she pleased. Carol Ann was far from being an exemplary mother. She allowed Deidre to drink alcohol, use drugs, and have live-in boyfriends. Although absurdly permissive, Carol

Ann apparently had moments of concern about her daughter. She told Patricia Jackson, a family friend, "That girl is headed for trouble."

By most standards Deidre was already in trouble. She took drugs. She got drunk. She had sex with both men and women. She fought and argued and screamed like an alley cat when something displeased her.

"Deidre was pretty and worldly bright," Patricia said. "She seemed to be a magnet for trouble, but the boys loved her."

Before reaching her teenage years, Deidre developed an obsession about meeting her father. She wrote to him, and her letters were returned unopened. When she telephoned, he hung up. "Deidre didn't want anything from him," an aunt said, "she just wanted to be acknowledged. She was totally rejected by him."

A life of poverty in public housing projects with a bitter, resentful mother and a father who rejected her gave Deidre a tough outlook on life. She knew nothing of love and family stability, and managed to survive by doing to others before they did it to her. Inside, she teemed with bottled-up emotions just waiting to explode, longing for love, acceptance, and attention. At the same time, she developed an amoral philosophy: she knew right from wrong but simply didn't care. What made her feel good was right; anything that displeased or hurt her was wrong.

"There wasn't any nurturing in that (Deidre's) household," said Catherine Divine, an assistant county attorney in Boston. "She grew up in poverty, and her mother had psychological problems. She started using drugs in the second grade. I'm sure that it was all part of an attempt to escape the pain of her life."

By the time she was twelve, Deidre had turned from an ugly duckling with crooked legs into a full-breasted girl with haunting dark eyes that were far too old and knowing for her age. Even though she wore braces on her teeth, her smoldering dark eyes and aura of sexuality captured the interest of boys who seemed irresistibly drawn to her. Deidre, hungry for attention, eagerly accepted their proposals for sex and learned that it was not only an avenue for pleasure but a way to earn money.

Deidre was dating grown men by the time she was twelve. Carol Ann said Deidre was raped by a man in his thirties when she was just eleven. There is no record of the alleged rape because Carol Ann, who had a strong dislike of the police, didn't report it.

By the time she reached the ninth grade at Goffstown High School in Manchester, Deidre concluded that she didn't need formal education to make her way in the world.

"She was very bright, but she never applied herself," an aunt said.

Deidre's sultry looks, lust for recognition, and ability to earn money with her body turned her away from traditional schooling and classmates who were far less worldly wise. So she quit school and had live-in boyfriends at her mother's apartment, who also had live-in boyfriends. Deidre began what Patricia called a career as an "adventuress." She looked for drug-induced highs, sexual excitement, approval, and money. In spite of being tough and, as a psychiatrist later put it, "without a conscience," Deidre had almost irresistible charm. She laughed and joked, soothed and petted. The next moment she might be screaming in someone's face.

Deidre was drawn toward a tawdry area in Manchester known as the Combat Zone. The most notorious strip is along Elm Street, which is crowded with gin joints that serve watered-down drinks, prostitutes, topless dancers, pimps, and whorehouses disguised as antique shops. The Combat Zone attracts riffraff and students from Yale who look for adventure and quick drug and sexual fixes.

The Yale bluebloods drive up and down Elm Street looking for prostitutes. If they see one they like, they slip an intermediary money and ask, "Is she safe?" But most of the time, the prostitutes wait like predators in bars such as the Pink Pussycat and Charlie's, and when they spot a prospect, they move in close, flashing cleavage and thigh, whispering the age-old question: "Want to have a good time?"

If the prospect says yes, the prostitute writes her name on a slip of paper, along with a time and place to meet. This is a cautionary measure to protect the girls from undercover vice squad police and dangerous characters. Straight sex was forty dollars, a half and half, more commonly known as a "suck and fuck" was thirty-five dollars, and a specialist in S&M, golden showers, or domination might get five hundred dollars. A hand job in the back seat of a car or a dark alley would go for ten dollars. An energetic girl could earn six hundred dollars a night, four thousand two hundred dollars a week—tax free.

The Combat Zone is notorious for its outrageous characters, but Deidre even stood out in this crowd. She prowled the usual lascivious dives and gained center stage. Deidre danced topless, flirted as a bar girl, and worked as a prostitute. Deidre would go off with any man who asked her, abandoning the usual precautions.

A blond prostitute who was also one of Deidre's lovers worried about Deidre because her girlfriend sometimes returned from a date with lumps and bruises.

"Guys would come over to the table and say, 'Come on, let's go,' and I would tell her, 'Dee, don't do it. You don't have to go.' But she would go anyhow."

One of Deidre's girlfriends in the Combat Zone was Bridgette Riccio, a prostitute who sometimes became involved in confidence schemes and theft. Bridgette, a tall blonde, was enthralled by the petite brunette with the smoldering eyes and braces on her teeth that made her smile almost angelic in its innocence.

Bridgette became one of Deidre's lesbian lovers and partners in sex orgies for money. She wasn't Deidre's only girlfriend. Deidre had several lesbian affairs, most of them with slim girls who had natural or bleached blonde hair. Money wasn't the only thing that attracted

Deidre to bizarre sexual activities; she had a huge sexual appetite for both men and woman, and was willing to try anything once.

"Deidre was obsessed by sex in any form," Bridgette said. She was consumed with passion. We were friends and lovers, but it was a very sick relationship."

Deidre's outrageous behavior made her a star in the Combat Zone by the time she was sixteen. Cars filled with young men from Yale or elsewhere drove up and down Elm Street chanting her street name: "Cher-ri! Cher-ri!" Deidre loved the attention. During her time in the Combat Zone, Deidre tattooed a small black butterfly on her right shoulder.

Most of the time Deidre lived in flop houses on Elm Street with boyfriends or girlfriends. Often she stayed at her lovers' apartments. Ironically, she was drawn back to Carol Ann from time to time and lived with her mother in rundown public housing projects. Carol Ann generally ignored anything Deidre did.

An exception came when Deidre arrived with a boy-friend and two blond lesbian lovers. Carol Ann opened a bedroom door and found all four of them. According to Deidre's two girlfriends, only Deidre and her boyfriend were in bed making love while the two girls "just hung out" in the same room. Nevertheless, the scene so en-raged Carol Ann that she screamed, slapped her daughter, and ordered all four of them out of her house.

During the visits to her mother's house, Deidre's atten-tion was still focused on the Combat Zone, where her daredevil attitude and sexual escapades kept people buzz-ing.

"She wanted to be recognized, even if it was for some-thing bad," Bridgette said. "Dee always had to be the cen-ter of attention. She'd do anything to be in the spotlight."

Deidre moved step by step from prostitution to more malevolent activities. She seemed intent on exploring the darker side of human nature. Deidre increasingly be-came friendly with people who were involved in theft, mugging, burglary, armed robbery, and murder.

During this time, Deidre became fascinated with guns. She brought them home and played with them as if they were toys. Deidre told Bridgette that she had killed several people.

"The first time's the hardest," Deidre said. "After that it gets easier." Once, when Bridgette was feeling depressed, she contemplated suicide.

"I don't want to live any more," Bridgette sobbed. "I want to kill myself."

"Why don't you?" Deidre asked.

"I'm scared."

"That's all right," Deidre said. "I've got a gun. I'll do it for you."

The matter-of-fact manner in which Deidre offered to kill her snapped Bridgette out of lethargy at once.

"I think she actually *wanted* to do it," Bridgette said. "I don't think she would have blinked."

Bridgette gradually followed Deidre into darker realms. Deidre's need for drugs and sex became more pronounced, and the pent-up rage from her earlier years caused her to become volatile; Deidre would explode into a rage without warning. Her need for attention became greater, and she was no longer content to have her stardom restricted to the Combat Zone. Deidre wanted a bigger audience and concocted a scheme that she hoped would generate a furor, giving her wide publicity in newspapers and on television. Just after she turned seventeen, Deidre told Boston police that she had been kidnapped by two men who drove her to New York and raped her.

"Dee had hoped for headlines," Bridgette said, "but the police didn't believe her."

The Boston police had records of Deidre's arrests for prostitution, and even when she reported the fake kidnapping she bragged that she was a star in the Combat Zone. Surprisingly, Deidre agreed to take a polygraph test, which convinced the police that she had invented the kidnap-rape story. Deidre was fined one hundred dollars for making a false report and released.

The lower she moved into the abyss, the better she seemed to like it. She ran through strings of male and female lovers and associated with thugs. But she still had the ability to charm people in the upper middle class. One of them was her attorney.

"She seemed like a nice young lady," said Jean-Claude Sakellarios, her attorney in Manchester. "I think she's a little simplistic. She has a sort of street intelligence, but she's also subject to domination."

If Deidre needed more excitement to satisfy her darker nature, Bridgette was a willing follower. They consumed large amounts of alcohol and experimented with various types of drugs. This combination of chemical experimentation reached its apex on July 5, 1987, when they had a party at Bridgette's apartment where everyone got stoned on beer and LSD. The beer and the hallucinogenic drug left Deidre and Bridgette craving additional excitement when the party broke up.

Later that night they drove to a park on the outskirts of Manchester where Veronica Rudzinski, a twenty-nine-year-old woman, sat in her car and listened to the radio while she waited for a friend to arrive. It was a dark night, and Veronica couldn't clearly see the face of the woman who suddenly appeared at the car window.

"Got a light?" the woman asked.

Veronica reached into her purse for a lighter, lit it, and saw another woman pointing a gun at her. Veronica grabbed the gun and struggled, but the woman pulled it free. Veronica was shot four times. One bullet hit her arm and the other three struck her body.

Deidre and Bridgette fled, but someone in the park wrote down the license number on Bridgette's car and called for help. Veronica was rushed to a hospital and survived the gunshot wounds, which had been made by .25 caliber bullets. Deidre and Bridgette were found, along with the .25 caliber semiautomatic pistol that had been used to shoot Veronica. They were arrested and charged with attempted robbery and attempted first-degree murder.

Deidre and Bridgette tried to incriminate each other.

Deidre had the advantage of having been around criminals who had told her about the plea-bargaining system, and she used it to her advantage. The police didn't know which of them had shot Veronica and had charged both with attempted first-degree murder. Deidre told prosecutors that she would testify that Bridgette, her lover, had done the shooting, if she could plead guilty to a lesser charge. The prosecution agreed, and Deidre entered a plea of guilty to being an accessory to attempted first-degree murder. Bridgette was stuck with the charge of attempted first-degree murder.

America's criminal justice system is overloaded so that the wheels grind slowly. Deidre spent six months in jail after she had pleaded guilty, but it was time to loaf, not do time. Deidre read historical romance novels and attended alcoholic rehabilitation sentences that were ordered by the court as she waited for Bridgette's trial and her own sentencing.

On the day Bridgette went to trial, Deidre was kept outside of the courtroom until she was to testify. Veronica, who had recovered from her wounds, took the witness stand and was asked by the state to identify the woman who had shot her. Veronica looked around, her eyes resting only a moment on Bridgette's face.

"I can't," she said. "She's not here."

The state had no choice but to dismiss the charges against Bridgette.

Veronica accompanied the prosecutor to his office and stopped short when she saw Deidre.

"That's her!" she said. "That's the one who shot me!"

The prosecution had already made the bargain with Deidre and was stuck with it. Deidre, rather than finding incarceration painful, seemed to be exhilarated. She had been in the headlines numerous times. Her release from jail provided another opportunity to take center stage.

Deidre applied makeup and used fruit juice to pat on her long dark hair to hold it in place. Somehow she managed to acquire a pink satin dress, and when she was released from jail to meet her grandmother and some friends, she moved with the bearing of a queen, shoulders back, head held high, glowing with pride.

Deidre seemed to view the event on the jail house steps as a "coming out." Certainly it marked a new phase in her life: she had outwitted the law and was firmly established as one of the Combat Zone's most dangerous people. They sought her company and she looked for them. Deidre and a nineteen-year-old thug named Anthony Pfaff met one another and Anthony confided a secret: he had been hired by Kenneth Johnson to kill Johnson's wife, Sharon.

Deidre knew about the plot to kill Sharon, but police dismissed the idea that she might have been involved in the scheme, even though Deidre would boast later that she was a participant. Whether she was involved or not, Deidre acquired considerable knowledge concerning murder for hire.

On February 9, 1988, Anthony bought two cases of beer and some marijuana to celebrate Deidre's nineteenth birthday. Anthony flashed large amounts of money which he told Deidre had come from his income tax refund. Deidre probably knew better. Police investigators said later it was part of the advance payment Anthony had received to kill Sharon Johnson.

Sharon, who was seven months pregnant, was brutally murdered at a construction site on July 28, 1988. Police said that Anthony Pfaff and Jason Carroll repeatedly stabbed Sharon while her husband watched, taunting her as she was being killed. After the pregnant woman had been stabbed numerous times, she was strangled. Anthony, Jason, and Sharon's husband, Kenneth, were arrested and charged with first-degree murder and other charges stemming from the gruesome slaying.

Deidre was questioned by the police several times to see if she had been involved in the murder. The police were unable to establish a link of any kind between Deidre and the murder. Nevertheless, Boston became too hot for Deidre, and, when her then boyfriend John Beauvier moved to Daytona Beach, she followed him, anxious to get out of town.

After Beauvier beat her up and went back north, Deidre gravitated to the Boardwalk and found the kind of people she was used to.

"They recognize each other," said Daytona Police Chief Paul Crow. "All they have to do is make eye contact."

5

Kosta often went to lunch at Arthur Treacher's Fish and Chips when he was putting in his time at Joyland. The fast food restaurant, which is part of a national franchise, was owned by Tony Calderone and was within easy walking distance of Joyland.

Calderone, thirty-nine, was a heavy-set man, a little less than average height, with a head of thick dark hair and an olive complexion. He looked, dressed, and acted rich. Besides owning the seafood franchise, Calderone was the owner and manager of Artie's Pub, which was located on Highway A1A, the street that runs along the Atlantic Ocean and the Boardwalk in Daytona Beach.

Calderone had never been in serious trouble with the law, but he was a man police kept an eye on. He had been caught with a small amount of cocaine, but the stash was only enough for personal use, not enough to make him a dealer.

Kosta and Calderone first became acquainted in February 1989 when Calderone was having video games, a pool table, jukebox, and cigarette and candy vending machines installed at his two restaurants. The machines and pool table belonged to ABC Vending, which Calderone thought was owned by Kosta and a man named Dominick. Later on Calderone learned that Dominick was the machine mechanic at Joyland and that Lisa owned ABC. The agreement was that Calderone and ABC would split the proceeds from the games and vending machines fifty-fifty.

Calderone also had a passion for guns. He chatted with Kosta while the machines were being installed and when the topic of guns came up they found a mutual interest. They developed a friendship in short order. Most of Kosta's friends outside of the Greek community, where he was considered an upstanding citizen in spite of the rumors that he was involved in counterfeiting, were passionate about guns, explosives, and other kinds of weapons.

One day, Calderone showed Kosta a 9-millimeter Brown that he owned.

Kosta said, "I like this gun. Do you want to see my collection?"

Calderone said that he would, and Kosta showed him three pistols.

"Those are nice," he said.

"Can I keep this gun for a week?" Kosta asked, referring to Calderone's Browning.

Calderone hesitated. "Well, Kosta, I've got to have a gun around the restaurant."

"I'll loan you one."

Calderone agreed, and Kosta loaned him a gun that Calderone thought was "a piece of shit," but he didn't pay much attention because he kept the gun in a briefcase. Two weeks passed and Calderone saw Kosta again.

"Where's my gun?" he asked. "I want it back."

"No, I've got to have that gun."

"Why?"

"For political reasons."

"What the hell does that mean?"

"A banker friend of mine wants that gun very much. I'll get you another gun."

"No," Calderone said. "Get my gun back."

"It's too late I already gave it to him."

"Okay, Kosta, fine." Calderone was exasperated. "Give me a gun. I don't want this piece of crap."

57

Calderone wasn't to receive another gun from Kosta for several months. As time passed, it dawned on Calderone that giving Kosta his Browning was "à pretty stupid thing to do." The gun was registered in his name, and, if it was used in committing a crime, it would immediately be traced to him.

Sometimes Lisa joined Kosta for lunch and eventually met Calderone and his wife, Sheila. Lisa was cordial, but she didn't develop a close friendship with either of them.

In April, Kosta asked Calderone if he would be interested in becoming a partner in a business he wanted to open on the Boardwalk.

"What kind of business?" Calderone asked.

"A pool hall. We can lease the property from my uncle and remodel it."

"Who else is in on it?"

"Dominick."

Calderone was interested, but he was in the process of selling his two restaurants and planned to return to his old job of selling cars. He told Kosta that he wouldn't have time to work at the pool hall.

"That's okay," Kosta said. "Dominick and I will run it but split the money three ways."

The deal sounded good to Calderone. He gave Kosta six thousand dollars as his share of the business.

Lisa was against the pool hall from the moment Kosta mentioned that he planned to start his own business. Kosta didn't mention that Dominick and Calderone were his partners. Instead, Lisa said, "He made it sound like he was borrowing the money from Angelo Katsouleas."

Angelo was a student at Florida State University in Tallahassee. He had been Kosta's best friend in Chicago when Kosta attended undergraduate school in Lockport. Angelo had been an undergraduate student with Kosta, and now he wanted to move to Daytona Beach. Lisa didn't understand the complicated tale that Kosta told her, but she didn't like the idea of a pool hall. She believed that Angelo received money from relatives in Greece and that he had a rich, childless aunt who gave him money. Lisa considered Angelo "a real straight-laced type of guy."

Kosta ignored Lisa's protests, leased a location on the Boardwalk, and started to remodel it as a pool hall that served beer, pizza, and sandwiches named Top Shots. Besides giving him a headquarters from which to operate, it had another big advantage. It was located at the opposite end of the Boardwalk from Joyland, far from the attention of his wife and brother-in-law.

Calderone didn't like the way Kosta went about remodeling the leased space that was to become Top Shots.

"Kosta did everything in a half-assed sort of way," he said. "He tried to do things without getting the proper licenses. Dominick would try to do it right, and Kosta would say, 'I'll take over this deal. I can do it because I know somebody in the licensing department.' He tried to circumvent the whole system and wound up getting us a lot of fines."

Calderone didn't like the people that Kosta hired to work at Top Shots when it opened on June 25, 1989. One of them was Mark Kevin Ramsey, a Boardwalk transient who had a string of convictions for various misdemeanors. Ramsey skimmed money from sales at Top Shots from the day it opened as did the other employees.

Calderone visited Top Shots as a customer and said that the pool hall seemed to be managed by people about as efficient as the Keystone Cops. The record keeping was a joke; there was no system and no control. Kosta didn't even bother to keep receipts for income or outgo.

"I need more money," he told Calderone. "I got to have more money."

"You need to run it like a business," Calderone replied. "You need control."

59

"I need money."

Calderone abandoned his plans to go back to selling cars. According to him, he went to work at Top Shots to protect his investment while simultaneously trying to close his two restaurants.

He said he told Kosta, "Look, I invested six thousand dollars. I need to make money off of it. I'm not rich."

Kosta just shrugged.

A few days later, after Tony saw other problems at Top Shots, he talked to Kosta again.

"This is getting a little bit old for me," he said. "I have to leave and close my businesses because there's nobody watching the store."

Calderone left, finished closing out his accounts at the restaurants, and prepared to become a car salesman. Kosta, who had been without Calderone's help for a while, approached him.

"Hey, I got a deal for you," Kosta said. "I'll get you out of the business. We'll sell your partnership."

"Fine, I'll do it."

"How much?"

"Six thousand dollars. That's exactly what I put in. Give it back to me."

"I'll give it all back."

Kosta told him that his "cousin," Angelo, was coming in from Chicago and would buy out his share. In a few days Angelo arrived and gave Calderone three thousand dollars in cash and a check for three thousand dollars.

"You're out," Angelo said. "We'd appreciate any help you could give us with the books, the receipts, and all that stuff."

Calderone said he would be glad to help make the transition. The sale of his share of Top Shots was completed in July. He learned that Angelo bought Dominick's share of the pool hall the same month.

By the first of September Calderone was making plans

once more to start selling cars. Kosta came to see him again.

"You know, I'm having trouble running the place," Kosta said. "Angelo doesn't want to work, and I don't have the time to do it. Would you run the place?"

"No," he said. "I've got better things to do for one hundred and fifty dollars a week than come down and watch your bar."

"We'll make you a partner again, okay?" Kosta said. "You'll be just like a partner except that you don't have to put any money in it. You'll still get a third of the profits."

Calderone accepted the deal. He became the manager of Top Shots but there were different versions to the role he actually played. Calderone insisted that he did nothing illegal and had no plans to do anything against the law. According to Deidre Hunt and her girlfriend Lori, that wasn't quite the case.

6

Mark Kevin Ramsey had only been in Daytona Beach a few weeks before he met Kosta Fotopoulos. Ramsey was a 21-year-old from North Carolina. Nothing about him or his appearance was remarkable; he was six feet tall, slim, with long brown hair, and wore a beard and mustache. He was cut from the same mold as scores of other transients who prowled the Boardwalk.

For a week or two after he arrived in Daytona Beach, Ramsey worked as a grease monkey at a Jiffy Lube garage. His supervisor considered him a good employee until Ramsey started hanging out at the Boardwalk. Once Ramsey found the Boardwalk and easy pickings there, he was off and running.

"He'd skip a day or two and then show up," his supervisor said. "Then he just stopped coming in. He was okay before he got tied up with that Boardwalk crowd."

Ramsey became a hustler, pimp, petty thief, and a male prostitute, among other things. He liked the riffraff that lived on the edge, and he found a home among them. Ramsey snatched purses, blind-sided older people and stole their money and jewelry, then ran away. He was constantly in and out of jail on charges of theft. He had never spent time for a felony, although he claimed that he had once killed someone. Whether that was true or not is doubtful; Boardwalk transients routinely claimed they had committed murder at one time or another.

Ramsey was in Top Shots a few days before Calderone became the manager. Kosta was interested in Ramsey's criminal background. He hired Ramsey as a bartender and told him, "I might have other jobs for you that will be financially beneficial."

One of Ramsey's best friends was Teja Mzimmia James, a good-looking, husky black teenager from Brooklyn. Teja came to Daytona Beach during Spring Break in 1989 and never left. He lived with his father in Holly Hill, a small town adjoining Daytona Beach, and sometimes helped him hang dry wall. Teja was six feet tall and at age nineteen had a reputation for being a tough guy, able to handle himself with the roughest crowds.

"If they know you're going to get violent, they don't throw much shit at you," Teja said.

Teja fought a lot to maintain his reputation, especially with new arrivals who had to be taught the harsh ways of the Boardwalk social hierarchy. Teja talked tough, too, bragging about more serious crimes and claiming that he had committed murder although he wasn't sure that he had. Once he had a serious fight in Brooklyn and bludgeoned a man with a club. The man didn't get up, and Teja thought he was dead. Teja was happy enough to "beat the shit" out of someone for pleasure or profit, steal, pimp, burglarize, and commit other assorted crimes.

Teja started to hang out at Top Shots when Ramsey became the bartender.

He saw Kosta occasionally at Top Shots but never talked to him. Teja had also seen Kosta at Joyland when he worked there for three days a few months earlier. He didn't know Lisa except by sight, but he liked her, and in the three days he was at Joyland his street sense took in the whole layout of the place. Like the other transients on the Boardwalk, Teja believed that Kosta was rich and that Lisa worked for him.

63

Calderone considered Ramsey a punk, but he'd do donkey labor, such as hauling beer coolers from one end of the Boardwalk to the other for the minimum wage. Calderone thought Ramsey was "a messed-up kid" who seemed to look at Kosta like a father or a big brother.

Ramsey's "good" qualities, however, didn't justify his stealing so far as Calderone was concerned. Since he couldn't make an impression on Ramsey, Tony took Ramsey into Kosta's office.

"He's ripping us off," Calderone said. "You need to fire him."

"I swear to God, I never took a penny out of that register," Ramsey replied.

"The goddamned money never made it to the register, did it, Ramsey?" Calderone replied.

"No, it didn't."

"That's okay," Kosta said. "He'll pay it back."

Calderone was stunned. Kosta and Ramsey grinned at him, and Calderone walked out of the office.

"Kosta didn't do a thing about it," Calderone said.

Other people who regularly visited the pool hall noted that Kosta had what they thought of as a fatherly interest in Ramsey, at least for a few weeks. They knew that Kosta was involved in much more than running a pool hall and that Ramsey was involved in at least part of the operation.

Teja was at Top Shots in September when one of the customers went into a drunken rage. Ramsey told the drunk that he had to leave.

"Make me," the customer said defiantly.

Ramsey could probably have handled the man, who was so drunk that he could hardly stand, but he was afraid of breaking probation and being sent back to jail. Ramsey turned to Teja.

"Throw him out, okay?"

"Sure." Teja walked up to the man. "You got to go, man."

"I ain't taking shit from a goddamn nigger," the man said and spat in Teja's face.

Teja hit the man with a right cross, followed by a left hook. The man went down, staggered to his feet, and started for the door. Ramsey had called the police, and the man was arrested almost as soon as he stepped outside of Top Shots.

Kosta was standing at the entrance to his office and saw the fight.

"You handle yourself pretty good, man," Kosta said. "Do you like to fight?"

"Sometimes."

Kosta took Teja into his office and started to chat, working in a lot of personal questions to find out about his background. Kosta was pleased that Teja had been in scrapes with the law and that he knew about guns. Kosta didn't know that Teja sometimes carried a gun himself, depending on the job he was doing or the neighborhood he was in. Kosta opened his coat enough so that Teja could see that he had a gun in a shoulder holster.

Teja didn't like being around an armed man when he didn't have a gun himself. He was a little nervous about Kosta.

"How would you like to make ten thousand dollars?" Kosta asked.

Teja thought he was joking and laughed. "Sure. Who do I have to kill?"

Kosta's expression didn't change. "We'll see. I need people I can depend on to do jobs for me. I might have some work for you if you're interested."

Teja said, sure, uh-huh, thinking that Kosta was just bullshiting him and left. Kosta told him to stay in touch.

Ramsey talked with Teja later that night. He told Teja that Kosta was involved in counterfeiting and that he was going to blackmail him.

"He's got to pay me or I'll turn him over to the police," Ramsey said.

Teja didn't know what to think. Blackmail was okay as long as you could get away with it. But Teja didn't know what to think of this dude, Kosta. The man had guns.

Yvonne Lori Henderson was six feet tall, had long naturally pale blond hair, blue eyes, and a good figure. The eighteen-year-old girl was striking but not pretty. She still had teenage pimples and usually didn't pay much attention to how she looked, rarely wearing makeup.

Lori was the daughter of Terry Henderson, a respected criminal lawyer in Deland who worked in the Public Defender's office. Lori's upbringing should have prepared her to go on to college after high school and become a part of the mainstream of upper middle America. Instead she headed toward the Daytona Beach Boardwalk, which was about twenty miles from Deland. Lori was rebellious and enjoyed life in the fast lane. She was bisexual and sometimes participated in sex orgies. In September 1989 she lived with a girl named Sheila Rainey.

Sheila came home one night with a petite brunette with smoldering dark eyes and boundless sexual energy named Deidre Hunt.

Lori was immediately captivated by Deidre, or "Dee" as most people in Daytona Beach called her. Deidre was working two nights a week at a topless bar, and Sheila had brought her home to crash. Did Lori mind?

Lori didn't mind at all. Two days later Lori kicked Sheila out and Deidre remained. A few days after that, Deidre went to Top Shots with her former boyfriend, Newman Taylor, better known as J.R., to drink some beer. Deidre's relationship with J.R. had been a stormy affair. The first time they met on the Boardwalk, a month or so previously, they didn't get along. At the time Deidre was living with Kevin Ramsey, another man known only as Chris, a bisexual fifteen-year-old prostitute known as Tiger, and another youngster named Richard Ross, who was a whiz at hot-wiring cars and stealing them.

Although their initial meeting had been a bummer, J.R. and Deidre got along fine when they met at a party where everybody was tripping on acid.

"Hey, you want to go to California?" he asked.

"Why not?" Deidre answered.

"Maybe we just ought to go fuck," J.R. said.

"Yeah."

The next day they moved Deidre's things into an apartment at Beverly Court that J.R. shared with four other young men. Deidre quit her job and became J.R.'s "old lady" for about a month before they broke up. Deidre stayed at the apartment for a while after the break-up, and J.R. still had sex with her, as did the other men, but she was no longer his girlfriend.

Tony Calderone saw Deidre at Top Shots and got interested. He sauntered over and J.R. moved away. (There are different versions of Deidre's relationship with Calderone but this is the one that police believe, part of which was verified by Calderone.)

Deidre and Calderone sat in Top Shots for about two hours drinking beer. Both of them got pretty drunk. Deidre left with Calderone, who said he felt sorry for Deidre.

"The kid said she was down on her luck and didn't have a place to stay," he said. "I wanted to help her out."

Deidre was lying since she was living with J.R. and the four other men but was anxious to improve her status. She did that in short order. Calderone rented a suite for her at Casa Del Mar, an upscale motel on the Atlantic Ocean. Calderone had sex with Deidre on several occasions.

Later that night, after settling in at the motel, Deidre returned to Top Shots where some of her friends had gathered.

"Hey, I got a suite at the Casa Del Mar," she said. "I got it for a week. You all can stay there with me but you have to be out by seven-thirty in the morning. That's when Tony's going to come and check on me."

J.R. asked, "Are you fucking him?"

"No," Deidre lied.

J.R. and a few others went to Deidre's suite and partied until early morning, being sure to leave before Calderone showed up at seven-thirty. When Calderone left, Lori later testified that Deidre went to her place to pick up her things.

"I'm moving into the Casa Del Mar," she told Lori. "Tony's starting a prostitution ring and I'm going to run it. He's paying for everything."

Deidre flashed money in her face. "I've got unlimited money to spend."

Lori was impressed.

"Do you want a job at Top Shots?" Deidre asked.

Lori stated that the implication was that she would work there and be part of the prostitution ring. Lori did work at Top Shots and retained her close friend and lover relationship with Deidre.

Deidre was under the impression that Calderone owned Top Shots and intended to milk him for all he was worth. She thought he was what every street girl or prostitute hopes to find, a sugar daddy who would give her a place to stay and an opportunity to make a lot of money. According to Lori, Deidre said she ran drugs for Calderone as well.

"I'd pick up a bag of cocaine or a suitcase full of money and put it in a coin locker at the bus station," she told Lori. "I never knew who picked it up."

The police investigated Deidre's allegation and could find no evidence that Calderone was involved in drug dealing.

"We found absolutely no evidence that there was any

major drug deals involving Tony Calderone or anyone else at Top Shots," Damore said.

Kosta had been in Las Vegas when Calderone hired Deidre to work at Top Shots. When he returned and saw her, Kosta was interested. At the same time, Tony's interest in Deidre was waning.

"There's this pretty young girl I hired," Calderone told Kosta.

"Well, I want to meet her," Kosta said. "I'm looking for a girlfriend."

Calderone introduced Kosta and Deidre. Their eyes locked and something crackled between them.

"From then on, I was out of the picture," Calderone said.

Kosta began picking up the tab at the Casa Del Mar, but Deidre didn't tell the people who partied at her suite that things had changed. They still had to be out of the suite by seven-thirty in the morning. The person who was most immediately affected was Tony Calderone.

"Deidre was fascinated by people with money and power," he said. "When she found out that I didn't have either one, it didn't take her long to switch me off."

Calderone said that didn't bother him because he wasn't interested in Deidre any longer. But occasionally he felt like having sex with her.

"I'm going to see Dee tonight," he told Kosta.

"No, you're not."

Calderone thought Kosta was kidding. "Why not?"

Kosta flashed his gun and gave him a flat look. "Because you're not."

Calderone knew that Kosta was serious. "Okay, man, it's not worth it to me."

"He seemed to be insanely possessive and jealous about her," Calderone said.

Calderone noticed a major change in Deidre once she became Kosta's mistress. He thought that he had been kind to Deidre by getting her a place to stay when she said she was down and out. Now Deidre seemed to despise him.

"She had total resentment toward me," he said. "A total animosity. I mean, she hated my guts. Why, I don't have any idea. I never did anything bad to that girl. I never did anything but try to help her, but she turned on me like I was a piece of shit."

Calderone noticed that Deidre became cockier and that the sleazy bunch that constituted the Top Shots clientele looked to her as their leader. If she said go, they went. If she said jump, they asked how high.

"It was the craziest goddamn thing," Calderone said. "She would say, 'Let's go to this bar' and everyone would follow her. She was like the Pied Piper. If she told them to beat somebody up, they beat them up. She was the leader."

Deidre had leadership qualities of her own, but her real power came from the common knowledge that she was Kosta's mistress. All of the Top Shots people were a little afraid of Kosta. Deidre seemed to be more than Kosta's lover; she seemed to be his top sergeant. When she spoke it was as if Kosta himself was speaking.

7

At Top Shots, Kosta cultivated young Boardwalk hoodlums. Deidre, who knew more than Kosta could ever hope to learn about living on the streets, was a magnet. She drew the street people by the dozens. The Godfather-type role Kosta played at Top Shots had many forms. He loaned money to people, but they didn't know it was counterfeit. Sometimes Kosta would give one of the borrowers two one hundred dollar bills and say, "Here's two. I want four back." That meant they had to turn a profit, usually by selling dope or stealing something. Once they accepted the conditions, they would be pressed hard to pay Kosta double what they had borrowed. But sometimes Kosta was a benevolent loan shark. He would hand over two hundred dollars and simply say, "You owe me." That meant they had to be available when he wanted them to do something illegal. Kosta used the favor as leverage.

Gus Moamis got out of jail on September 25, 1989. He was flat broke, but he knew Deidre and considered her a friend he could count on. He headed directly for Top Shots.

"I'm busted," Gus said. "I need something."

"We'll take care of you," Deidre answered.

Deidre gave Gus something to eat and some beer, then took him to an apartment Kosta had rented for her on

Atlantic Boulevard. Some other friends arrived and they played touch football in her yard.

When the game was over, Deidre told Gus she was going to take a shower. Gus waited until the water was running for a while, then took off his clothes and stepped in with Deidre.

"Hey, what are you doing here?"

"What do you think?"

They lathered one another and "did a lot of kissing," Gus said. Kosta had warned Deidre not to have sex with any men except him, but this was a condition Deidre would not accept even though she promised Kosta she would be faithful. Gus played with Deidre's breasts, kissed her navel, her abdomen, and between her legs. Deidre did the same for him. Then they went to bed and had sex.

"You've got to be gone before seven-thirty in the morning," Deidre told him. "That's when Kosta comes. You don't want him to find you here. You don't want this man mad at you."

Gus left before Kosta arrived, then went to Top Shots later that afternoon. He didn't know what Kosta looked like. Deidre served him beer, and Gus saw three men talking on the Boardwalk in front of Top Shots. He thought they were cops. Two of the men left, and the other came into the bar and headed directly to Gus.

"How you doing?" Kosta asked.

"Man, you're cop, and I don't want to talk to a cop," Gus said.

"I'm not a cop."

Deidre came over. "That's Kosta."

Gus wasn't sure. He still thought Kosta might be a policeman.

"Look, what will it take to prove that I'm not a cop?"

"I don't know."

Gus went to a table with Kosta and talked with him for

an hour or so, guarding his answers because he still thought Kosta might be a policeman. Nevertheless, he told Kosta about his criminal record because the police already had that. He wasn't giving anything away. Kosta seemed impressed.

"I want you to do something for me," Kosta said. "Come on."

Gus followed Kosta into his office and sat down. Kosta put one thousand dollars on his desk.

"I want you go down to the Bellair Plaza and pick up a Z-28," Kosta said.

He told Gus where the sports car was parked and that the keys were inside.

"If you go down there, pick up the car and bring it back to me, the thousand dollars is yours."

Gus knew that he was stealing the car because no one would pay a thousand dollars just to have a car picked up. Gus didn't mind, and he wanted the money. He found the car where Kosta said it was, drove it back, and received ten one hundred dollar bills from Kosta. Gus didn't know what happened to the car, but it was just the beginning of a series of car thefts for him.

After a while, Gus realized that the car thefts were part of an insurance scam. People would visit Kosta, tell him where the car was, then Gus, Teja, or somebody else would pick it up. The keys were always in the car or hidden nearby. The stolen automobiles were always expensive, and they weren't ordinarily delivered to Kosta for disposition. Kosta's car thieves usually drove the car to an out-of-the-way spot, poured gasoline on it, set it on fire, and watched it blow up. The car owner collected from his insurance company, Kosta received a cut, and paid Gus and the other car thieves a thousand dollars.

Kosta paid them in counterfeit, but they didn't know it until much later. When he looked back, Gus realized that it was the kind of thing Kosta did. He knew that Kosta used him and others to pass counterfeit bills in exchange for real money. Sometimes Kosta handed someone a one hundred dollar bill and said, "Go get me a six pack of Budweiser."

"That's one of the ways he changed the money," Gus said.

Kosta also pocketed legal currency from Joyland and Top Shots and replaced it with counterfeit.

Gus wasn't sure at the time that Kosta used counterfeit to pay him or the others for the car thefts even though he was aware that Kosta was passing the counterfeit in numerous ways. In the process Kosta accumulated a large amount of legal tender. Kosta often had large sums of money on his desk.

"There would be stacks of twenties, fifties, and hundreds," Gus said.

Deidre always had hundreds of dollars and spent it freely. She bought clothes and enjoyed giving money to her friends. Deidre never seemed to run out of money. She even paid J.R. twenty-five dollars each time he kissed her and additional money to have sex with her. Paying J.R. was just a game Deidre played; she gave him money any time he wanted it, but she also harbored a secret grudge against him because he had dumped her.

Gus asked Deidre where she got her money. She just smiled and said, "Guess."

Gus persisted.

"I got it from Italy," Deidre told him.

"They [Kosta and Deidre] would sit in the back office and examine the bills, and most of the time it was hundred dollar bills," Gus said. "I didn't know if it was real money or not. There were a few fifties, twenties, and stuff, but mostly hundreds. I just came out and asked Dee one day, 'Is that counterfeit?' and she said, 'Yes, it's counterfeit.' They would just sit there and look at the bills."

Gus bought a gram of cocaine from Kosta the second day he was out of jail, but that was the last time he had to pay for drugs. He said Kosta had access to large amounts of cocaine and gave it to Gus whenever he wanted some. According to Gus, Deidre was Kosta's intermediary in selling cocaine at Top Shots.

"People would come in, you know, and say, 'Hey, does anybody have any coke?' Then somebody would go tell Dee and she would bring it out and sell it to whoever wanted it."

Gus had been told that Kosta was running a prostitution ring from Top Shots, and he saw enough to make him believe it. Gus noticed men dressed in expensive suits and ties stop at Top Shots and leave with Lori, Tiger, a classy-looking prostitute named Holly Ayscue, or one of the other girls who was available. Sometimes they would even go out with Deidre with Kosta's approval; he didn't mind her getting paid for sex or sleeping with her lesbian lovers.

Deidre paid no attention to Kosta's orders concerning her sex life. She had dozens of male lovers, along with her lesbian lovers, and did combinations of both men and women. Gus spent a night with Deidre again shortly after he had stolen the first car for Kosta. Kosta didn't show up that morning but J.R., Richard Ross, and two young men Gus didn't know came over.

"How would you guys like to make some quick money?" Deidre asked them.

They were all for it.

Deidre told them that Kosta knew about a hotel room on the beach that was worth robbing. She told them the room number, what was in it, and gave them directions she had received from Kosta on how to do it. They followed Kosta's directions, as relayed by Deidre, and pulled off the robbery. Deidre told them they would find two movie cameras, some jewelry, money, and a Rolex watch. When they broke into the room that was exactly what they found.

"Everything was exactly where Dee said it would be," Gus said.

This was the first in a string of motel and hotel burglaries that Gus and others committed for Kosta, but it was almost always Deidre that gave the instructions. Gus said Kosta always knew who would be registered in which room, when they would be out, and what would be in it. Sometimes Kosta gave the orders himself.

"He would say, 'Go rob room 202,'" Gus said. "He would know exactly what was in the room and when it would be vacant. We'd bring the shit back to him and he would sell it to different people who came into Top Shots."

Gus said that burglaries were committed at the La Playa, Howard Johnson, Holiday Inn Surfside, Marriott, and other hotels and motels along Atlantic Avenue. Sometimes the thieves simply reached behind the counter and got the key to the room they robbed; at other times they were told where the room key was buried or hidden.

"We were busy," Gus later stated to the police. "We hit cars every day and motel rooms every day. There was prostitution, robbery, car theft, drugs, and counterfeiting out of Top Shots. If a guy came in to pick up Lori, Dee, or Holly Ayscue, Tony knew all about them. He knew their names, their Social Security numbers, where they worked, where they were born, where they lived, what kind of car they drove. He knew everything about them."

After Gus had stolen and blown up nine cars for the insurance scam, Kosta called Gus into his office. Gus had only been out of jail for six days. He had slept with Deidre that same night and was afraid that Kosta had found out. Kosta had something entirely different in mind.

"That was when he asked me to kill Lisa," Gus said.

Kosta sat behind his desk wearing a gun in a shoulder holster.

"Have a seat," Kosta said. "Want a beer?"

"Sure," Gus said.

Kosta had beer brought to them, and they sat around drinking and chatting. A weird thing that Gus and his friends had noticed about Kosta was that he seemed to be unemotional. Nothing seemed to rattle him or excite him. Kosta laughed occasionally, but it didn't seem natural.

Except for the times his temper flared up, then he was like a raging bull.

They were working on their third beer when Kosta leaned forward and looked hard into Gus's eyes.

"Do you think you could kill somebody?" Kosta asked.

Gus said, "I don't know. Maybe if the money was right."

Kosta leaned closer. "How much would it cost for you to kill somebody?"

"I ain't got no idea."

"Name a price."

Gus laughed. "I don't know. About a hundred thousand dollars."

Kosta picked up a briefcase from the floor and put it on the desk. He opened it up and Gus's eyes almost popped out. It was filled with money.

"You're serious, ain't you?" he asked.

"Yes. There's seventy-five thousand dollars here."

The briefcase remained open on the desk, but the conversation became a game of cat and mouse. They discussed the ways Gus would kill someone: take them out in the woods and shoot them, drown them, strangle them, anything. Kosta described detailed plans on how he would kill someone, but Gus was only half listening:

his eyes were jumping from the seventy-five thousand dollars in cash to the gun in Kosta's shoulder holster.

"There was seventy-five thousand dollars looking me in the face," he said. "If I had had a gun right there, he wouldn't have had the money no more, the way I looked at it."

Gus tried to figure out how to get the money then and there and, realizing that he couldn't, tried to get Kosta to tell him who he was supposed to kill, but Kosta dodged the question and countered with one of his own.

"Well, if you were going to kill someone, how would you do it?" Kosta asked again.

"We just talked about that," Gus said.

"I want to give you a little time to think about it," Kosta said. "If you want to do it, the money is here. You get half of the money before and half of it afterwards."

Gus left Kosta thinking that he would do the job. He really wanted to do it and get the seventy-five thousand dollars, and he realized that he only had two choices: either kill whomever Kosta wanted killed or be killed himself.

"Kosta was the kind of person that if you are doing something for him and he feels threatened in any way by knowing you're not doing it, you have got to be taken out of the picture," Gus said. "You either had to leave town or do what he told you to do. My Dad was in the Mafia, and Kosta worked the same way. If Kosta felt threatened by you, he would take you out."

Gus spent the night with Deidre after Kosta had asked him if he could kill someone. They had sex, then Deidre took a shower. Gus was sitting on the bed when Deidre came out of the bathroom naked.

"Did Kosta talk to you?" she asked.

"Yes."

"Well, did you tell him yes or no?"

Gus realized that Deidre knew all about Kosta's plan

78

to have someone killed.

"Do you know who it is?" he asked.

"It's Lisa."

Gus was interested in the job Kosta offered him, and he thought about the seventy-five thousand dollars that was on Kosta's desk. He was ready to talk to Kosta some more, but he got caught while committing a motel burglary for Kosta the next day and had to cool his heels in jail.

8

Tony Calderone had an impossible job when it came to managing Top Shots. Not only was Ramsey stealing from the pool hall, so were Lori and Deidre. The business was barely staying even but Kosta didn't seem to care.

Calderone told him, "We've got to do something about this stealing. I'm working cheap and I need bigger profits so I can get my cut."

Kosta just shrugged and told him not to worry.

Calderone had more to worry about than just the way the employees were stealing from Top Shots. Kosta insisted on keeping a gun behind the bar, and Calderone didn't think that Ramsey, Lori, or Deidre should have access to a gun, especially Deidre. She was known to go crazy when she got her hands on a gun. Calderone made his misgivings known to Kosta and warned him that somebody might freak out and shoot a customer for nothing.

"We need it for protection," Kosta said. "If somebody tries to rob us, you could shoot them dead and you'd be scot-free."

Calderone began moving the gun to the back office whenever he came to Top Shots. He also staggered his visits to the pool hall, hoping that he could keep Deidre, Lori, and Kevin off balance enough to cut down on their stealing. It didn't work and neither did his efforts to keep the gun from behind the bar. Each time he moved the gun away, Kosta put it back. And the stealing continued. Fi-

nally, Calderone realized that the only one who [could give]
orders and expect to have them followed was [Kosta.]
he didn't care about the stealing or the possibil[ity that one]
of the hotheaded employees might shoot a cus[tomer.]

Calderone saw a different side of Kosta when [he came]
to work at Top Shots than he had noticed when they had
first met at Arthur Treacher's. First, Kosta fell head over
heels in love with Deidre, which was something that
Calderone couldn't understand.

"I always thought of Kosta as a respectable businessman," he said. "He had a beautiful, wealthy wife and was
part of a powerful family. I couldn't understand why he
would risk having an affair with this girl from the streets."

Kosta was irrationally jealous where Deidre was concerned. He gave orders that no one was to see her unless
he was present. He threatened to kill any man who had
sex with Deidre, and he had terrible temper tantrums. He
yelled at people, smashed things, and was quick to pull his
gun. People were afraid to disagree with him.

Kosta had his hand in so many illegal pies that it was
hard to keep track of them. Even in hindsight Calderone
and others saw so much occur in such a short time that it
made their heads spin. Kosta gathered street toughs
around him that had been recruited by Deidre, and he
had long, secretive meetings with her. Kosta started to reveal things about himself, which was unusual, because he
usually placed great emphasis on secrecy.

"He kept his mouth shut," Gus Moamis said. "Kosta
didn't want people to know what he was thinking or planning. Once you knew what he was up to you either had to
go along with it or you would be dead. Kosta didn't want
any witnesses."

In spite of being secretive about what he was doing at
any given time, Kosta had a need to boast about the things
he had done in the past. He also wanted to impress
Calderone with the fact that he was a dangerous man capable of killing anyone who crossed him. He told

81

erone that he was a commando assassin and that he
videotapes of himself killing people.

"Do you want to see them?" Kosta asked.

"No," Calderone said.

"I have torture tapes, too," Kosta said. "You can see them if you want to."

Again Calderone said that he didn't.

Kosta continued to tell Calderone and others about his background.

"He said he was trained as a commando in Greece," Calderone said. "I never asked by whom. I just walked away from that ignorant talk."

The younger, more impressionable people that Kosta had gathered around him, with Deidre's help, heard long stories. Kosta told them that he had been trained by Israeli terrorists and that he was an assassin for the Central Intelligence Agency.

"I never know who the guys are who ask me to do a job," Kosta said. "They tell me to kill someone and we make tactical and financial arrangements."

How much money Kosta made by being an assassin was a question that frequently came up.

"Anywhere from ten thousand dollars to one hundred thousand dollars, depending on how difficult the job is," Kosta said.

Kosta showed them a "letter of deniability" with a letterhead from the Central Intelligence Agency. He said the letter was proof that he was a CIA assassin and that, like the premise of the old television show "Mission Impossible," the CIA letter could be used by the CIA to prove that it had no knowledge of his assassinations. What Kosta actually showed them was a letter from the CIA rejecting his request for employment.

Calderone thought Kosta was "full of shit" and switched off his hearing when Fotopoulos started bragging. The younger people, already in awe of Kosta because of his wealth, guns, BMW, and money, believed him — at least in part. Kosta shared more with Deidre than the others, and she saw a way to profit from being an integral part of Kosta's life.

Deidre believed Kosta's claim about being trained by Israeli terrorists and that he was a hired assassin. Kosta gave her details that convinced her his stories were true. He told Deidre that when he entered a foreign country for an assassination job he was always given an AK-47 assault rifle, which lays down a deadly field of fire but which is not very accurate, and picked up a weapon suitable for assassination that had been planted for him near the target.

Kosta told her that he was given an AK-47 in case he was captured. That way, he said, his captors would think he was a terrorist rather than an assassin because an assassin would use a more accurate weapon than an AK-47.

Kosta showed Deidre many of his weapons, large caches of money, and grenades, and promised to teach her how to swallow her tongue to kill herself "in case you're captured and don't want to be tortured."

Kosta told Deidre that she could be rich and powerful, just like he was, if she could prove that she could kill. In addition to all of the money he had in counterfeit and real cash that he had buried, Kosta showed her ten thousand dollars that he kept in the trunk of his car.

Deidre had street smarts, but she had always been poor. She longed for more, and she was receptive to Kosta. He was a man she thought she could control and hang onto his coattails to go as high as he could take her. She wanted to use him until he was of no further use to her.

Kosta told her about his Hunter-Killer Club, and that he was the head of a group of assassins who made hundreds of thousands of dollars on contract killings. Kosta said that the assassinations were usually political and not very dangerous but that a person had to prove himself, or herself, to be admitted to this elite Hunter-Killer group.

He outlined the club to her, namely that one had to kill

someone while the murder was videotaped as a safeguard to prevent members from going to the police.

Deidre was the first one of Kosta's circle of Boardwalk hoodlums to hear about the Hunter-Killer Club. It excited her. Deidre saw it as a way to get money and power, which she badly wanted now that she saw how Kosta lived. Kosta asked her if she could kill someone.

"Yes," Deidre said, and told him about the shooting of Veronica Rudzinski in New Hampshire.

Kosta told Deidre that, as much as he loved her, they could never be together as long as his wife was alive.

Kosta asked her again, "Do you think you can kill someone?"

Deidre told him again that she could.

Kosta nodded. "You have to become a member of the Hunter-Killer Club to prove it. Then you can take over the responsibility for killing my wife."

Calderone didn't know anything about the plans Kosta had to kill his family, but only a few weeks after he started running Top Shots Kosta started to make plans to commit armed robberies.

"I'm going to rob an armored car," Kosta said. "I'll use Teja and J.R. I've got the guns and bullets."

Or, he would say, "I'm going to knock off a McDonald's."

Kosta said that it was easy to rob a bank and outlined his plans to Deidre, Teja, J.R., Lori, and Matthew Chumbley, a nineteen-year-old drifter.

"You have to have a good getaway driver and car," Kosta said. "Then you need a sniper to pick the cops off when they arrive. You have two guys go in and do the robbery and two guys covering them. That's how you knock over a bank."

Kosta outlined various plans to Teja, J.R., Ramsey, and Chumbley. Each of them was supposed to be involved in one scheme or another.

Calderone said, "I just shook my head. I just couldn't believe the guy talking all of this bullshit."

Deidre moved out of the Casa Del Mar into a room at the Southern Sands Motel, which was also along Atlantic Avenue, and then took up residence in a house at 935 Schulte Street. Kosta paid for all of Deidre's living expenses and also gave her money. He'd also forbidden her to have sex with anyone else and that he would kill any man he caught her sleeping with.

Deidre not only continued sleeping with whom she chose, but also had people stay over every night to drink, take drugs, and have sex. The only restriction she put on them was they had to be gone before seven-thirty a.m. when Kosta arrived. Deidre was firmly entrenched as Kosta's girlfriend and as a partner in Kosta's criminal activities and didn't want to jeopardize her chances of getting rich.

J.R. bragged, "Deidre's in love with me. Kosta's jealous because he knows I can get her back any time I want to."

9

Matthew Chumbley, also known as Mike Cox, was a 19-year-old thug who had hitchhiked from Kentucky to Daytona Beach because "that's where the tourists are and they're easy pickings."

Chumbley was a thief, burglar, male prostitute, pimp, and mugger. He claimed that he had killed a man and never backed away from the boast even when he was questioned by police. He just refused to comment on it. Chumbley was also a ripoff artist, a small-time dope dealer, a con man, and he didn't mind hurting people. His favorite theater for operations was the Boardwalk.

He boasted, "I would hide against a wall, wait for people, then jump out and beat the shit out of them with a two-by-four, rob them, and get the hell out of there."

Chumbley shacked up with friends, slept in abandoned buildings, behind closed restaurants, and in alleys. He was often rousted by police for loitering. On his arrest sheets, Chumbley listed his address as "the streets of Daytona Beach."

With a record for male prostitution, soliciting for prostitution, larceny, burglary and illegal trespass, he was five feet, ten inches tall, had a husky build, and walked with his shoulders in an insolent slump. People who heard his voice without seeing him were sure that he was black. His brown hair was permed into curls and bleached blond on top, with longer, brown hair down his back.

Chumbley had been a drug addict since he was fourteen years old. Homeless, living by thievery and deceit, he was almost a stereotype of Daytona Beach's Boardwalk transients.

He was in Daytona Beach about three weeks before he ventured into Top Shots. It was late in September 1989. He parked himself on a bar stool and started to drink beer, hoping to meet Kosta Fotopoulos or Deidre Hunt. The word was out that Kosta and Deidre were into heavy-duty money and always had jobs for reliable people. Sometimes big money. Chumbley, who had lived in poverty all of his life, was looking for the pot of gold at the end of the rainbow.

He met Deidre and Kosta in time, but there was nothing memorable about the encounter. Kosta put him through the usual informational drill. Chumbley was immediately impressed by Deidre, whom he found "haunting and sultry."

He needed money to feed his drug habit. He used all types of drugs, but the one he preferred was crack cocaine. His normal weight was 175 pounds, but he was emaciated because of his drug addiction. Most of the time he didn't want to eat, and, even when he was hungry, he spent his money on crack instead of food.

Chumbley had become part of the inner circle around Kosta and Deidre. He liked being tough and bragged about it. He was proud of the illegal things he did and got a kick out of telling Marjeanne, his girlfriend, and the other Top Shots regulars about them.

Kosta liked him because he was "expendable."

In the privacy of his back office at Top Shots, Kosta continued to hold court, dispense favors, assign jobs, and tell stories. Kosta was the general and Deidre was his chief lieutenant. She was the one who had the contacts and personality to bring in the kind of people that Kosta wanted.

The young people there were much alike and were comfortable with one another. They had hard-scrabble lives and did whatever they needed to do in order to survive. Kosta was an enigma to them. He was rich and powerful, but he seemed to prefer their company over that of the Daytona Beach elite. More than one of them said that they looked at Kosta almost as a god.

Feuds notwithstanding, they generally got along well except for the tension between Ramsey, Deidre, and Kosta which developed just before Ramsey was fired in late September. At the time Chumbley became part of the group, no one except Kosta, Deidre, and Ramsey knew why the strain existed. Even though there were obvious problems, Ramsey still joined in the sex orgies that were held at various times.

Kosta didn't participate in the orgies. He was fixated on Deidre to the point of obsession.

Kosta was thirty, which made him at least ten years older than most of the others in the group, and he was married to a rich woman. He had convinced the young people that both he and his wife were rich. They were impressed because he always carried huge sums of cash that made their eyes bug out.

He always carried a pistol and liked to point it at people. Sometimes he pulled the trigger. Kosta was the only one who knew the gun was unloaded when he did this and thought the reactions of people were hilarious. Those on the receiving end of his joke didn't think it was very funny, considering the fact that Kosta told them he had killed at least a dozen people.

Deidre loved talking about her days as a Combat Zone prostitute and recounting how people would drive up and down Elm Street chanting her name. An aura of power surrounded Deidre in addition to the fact that the group knew she spoke for Kosta when he was absent.

No one loved Deidre's murderous stories more than Kosta. They were kindred spirits who both wanted money, adulation, and power. Both of them were fascinated with guns, murder, and torture. Kosta and Deidre seemed intent on outdoing one another in describing their past adventures. They also spurred one another on to make the present and future even more exciting and bloody than the past.

A person who knew Kosta and Deidre said that when the two met it "was like pouring gasoline on a fire."

10

Tony Calderone continued to complain about the situation at Top Shots. Deidre snubbed and humiliated him, the employees skimmed money, there was little if any bookkeeping, and he was supposed to get a third of the profit from the pool hall.

Lisa Fotopoulos and her brother Dino Paspalakis knew nothing of these things, but Dino wondered why a man like Calderone would manage Top Shots. Calderone was well-off financially; he had sold his two prosperous restaurants, lived in a comfortable home, and drove an expensive Jaguar automobile.

Why, Dino wondered, would Calderone manage a poolroom for one hundred and fifty dollars a week?

Dino was of medium height, soft-spoken, immaculately groomed, and dressed well. He was a gentle man who abhorred violence. He had never warmed to Kosta and considered him "a liar and the biggest con man in the world." Dino knew that his sister and mother loved Kosta, and he kept his misgivings to himself.

Dino and Kosta were almost exact opposites. Kosta was cold and unemotional while Dino was warm and empathetic. Kosta bragged about how macho he was while Dino presented himself as concerned and understanding. He hated Kosta's guns but never complained about them or the munitions that Kosta brought to Joyland and into his mother's home on Halifax Avenue where Dino lived, too.

Dino and Lisa both disliked the clientele at Top Shots and stayed away as much as possible. Kosta had attracted exactly the kind of people that Lisa had told him he would, not knowing that this was precisely what Kosta wanted. Although Lisa and Dino disliked Top Shots, Kosta was family, and they both stopped in occasionally. Dino met Deidre, who was still using her Boston street name of Cherri, when she was a waitress there. She made an unfavorable impression on him.

"She had an unusual thing that she did," he said. "She had a tip bucket that she used every time she served a drink. She would put the tip bucket next to the person like a big hint."

If people didn't tip or gave what Deidre considered an insufficient tip, she would insult them.

On one of his unannounced visits to Top Shots, Dino saw Kosta and Deidre playing pool. Dino didn't have any idea that Deidre was Kosta's mistress but they seemed to be much too familiar with one another. This upset Dino. He kept the incident to himself, but he didn't think that Kosta was behaving like a proper husband.

Dino shared Lisa's concern about the clientele at Top Shots. He saw Teja James there, who was obviously on good terms with Kosta and Deidre, even though Teja had been fired from his job at Joyland.

"I never liked him because he was a bum off the Boardwalk," Dino said. "Teja had a reputation for being a tough guy. I didn't hire him. Teja was telling people that I was giving him mean looks and didn't like him being there."

Dino tried to be friendly with Deidre even though he didn't like her. Once he went with a friend to the Ocean Club and saw Deidre sitting with another girl about fifteen years old who was another regular at Top Shots. Dino and his friend, Bill Sayers, joined them to be polite.

It was an almost surreal experience for the two men.

"They got into a real strange conversation about Ouija boards and stuff like that," Dino said. "The fifteen-year-old girl said she was pregnant. Bill and I looked at one another and thought it was time to get out of there."

Lisa sometimes went to Top Shots after she had closed Joyland to wait for Kosta so they could go home together.

She had several conversations with Deidre Hunt while she visited Top Shots, never dreaming that the street girl was having an affair with her husband. Or helping plan her death. Deidre was the type of person Lisa tried to avoid.

Deidre wouldn't allow Lisa that luxury when they were both in Top Shots at the same time. Deidre plopped down on a bar stool or chair at Lisa's table.

"What does it feel like to be filthy rich?" Deidre asked.

Lisa saw envy in Deidre's eyes and dodged the question.

Deidre looked at her ring and asked, "Is that a real diamond? Is that a real Gucci purse?"

"That girl's a tramp," Lisa told Calderone. "She has no class at all."

"I know," Calderone agreed, but he didn't tell Lisa that Deidre was her husband's mistress.

Lisa didn't like encounters with Deidre, and the girl made her feel strange. Whenever Lisa entered Top Shots, Deidre seemed to stand at attention, like a soldier, then began talking about the plans she had to attend college and to get a license selling real estate.

Lisa said the feeling she had sometimes was not so much envy from Deidre as it was to actually trade lives, to *be* Lisa.

"I've never had that feeling before from anyone," Lisa said. "It was weird. She was very envious of me. She wanted to be me."

Calderone noticed the same thing. He had heard Deidre say, "God, I wish I was her."

"She envied more than Lisa's money and jewels," Calderone said. "She envied the fact that Lisa was a real lady and that she wasn't. She never could be. You can put perfume on a pig, but you still have a pig."

Deidre and Kosta's other Boardwalk friends knew that Lisa was wealthy, but they thought that Kosta owned Joyland and everything else that actually belonged to Lisa and her family. Lisa never embarrassed her husband by telling his friends that it wasn't true. But Deidre's probing got on Lisa's nerves, and she phrased her sentences in such a way to hint that she was the one with the money. Lisa alluded to the fact that her father had owned Joyland and gave Deidre a general idea of how things really were without actually saying it outright. "Any halfway knowledgeable person would have been able to figure it out," Lisa said.

Lisa despised Top Shots. She had tried to persuade Kosta from the very beginning not to open it. She knew nothing of the criminal activities that were directed from there, but she noticed that the pool hall attracted an increasing number of thugs and hoodlums, especially after Deidre started to work there. "The crowd was really, really bad in there," Lisa recalled.

She told Kosta that he ought to close it down. Her husband gave her warning looks, and Lisa didn't press further. Lisa was a strong person, but she had begun to discover Kosta's anger. She didn't like to admit it, but she was a little afraid of her husband.

Another disturbing and embarrassing aspect of Kosta's business was that the police were often called to Top Shots. There were frequent brawls at the poolroom. The Paspalakis family was respected in the community, and the fact that police were called to her husband's business caused Lisa considerable embarrassment.

Another difficulty in Lisa's relationship with Kosta was that he often stayed out all night after Top Shots opened. There was no reason that he should check in and out, but sometimes Lisa called Top Shots during working hours just to say hello. But beginning in September 1989, when Deidre started working at the pool hall, Kosta was increasingly hard to find. Lisa called Top Shots when he was supposed to be there only to find out that he was gone and no one knew where he was.

Still, Lisa didn't pry.

Once Lisa got exasperated when Kosta came home late and asked, "Where were you?"

"I was talking to the cops," Kosta said. "Ask them."

"Oh, come on, now. I'm not going to ask them. Really."

Lisa wasn't about to embarrass herself by calling them to see if her husband had been at the police station.

"You need to close that place because it's causing a lot of problems," Lisa told Kosta. "No only on the Boardwalk but with me and you. You really need to close it."

"It's none of your business," Kosta snapped.

"Yes, but if I divorced you right now, you'd have nothing."

"I'll look into it," he said.

Lisa didn't know whether he would or not.

Calderone, on the other hand, had started to worry about Kosta's relationship with Deidre. Deidre seemed to become obsessed with the idea of being Lisa within days of becoming Kosta's mistress.

"She admired Lisa for the things that Lisa had, the fine jewelry, the manicured fingernails," he said. "Lisa was very much a lady, and Dee thought if she had the same things she'd be like Lisa. Dee was fascinated with power and money."

In spite of Lisa's aversion to Top Shots, she sometimes helped Kevin Ramsey when he had been left in charge and inventory came in. This simple task was too complicated for Ramsey, and he would telephone Lisa at Joyland to ask for advice on how many kegs of beer and other provisions he should buy. Lisa would go to Top Shots and take care of the business.

Ramsey wasn't a friend, but Lisa didn't feel uncomfortable with him. Except for her brief visits with Deidre and others at Top Shots, Lisa had no other contact with the poolroom clientele. Neither did her brother Dino.

They both knew that it was a trouble spot on the Board-walk, but neither of them had any idea of what was really happening at the pool hall.

Almost as soon as Kosta met Deidre, he told her about his plan to get the Paspalakis fortune by killing everyone in the family. Kosta's plan was to kill Lisa's mother, Dino, and finally Lisa, leaving him as the lone heir. Deidre had no qualms about helping with the murders because she believed they would make her rich. Kosta said he would marry Deidre when Lisa was dead.

Kosta wanted several layers of insulation between himself and the murders so that none could be tied to him. Deidre's role was to pick out potential killers and get them to Top Shots where Kosta could evaluate them. Deidre knew that Kosta planned to kill the people he hired after they had successfully completed their assigned murders.

The plan, which Deidre helped refine, was to make the murders look like accidents or robberies. Kosta hadn't put a great deal of thought into the "accidents," but he wanted to personally kill whoever he had hired to murder Lisa or his in-laws during the "robberies" or "burglaries."

"Dead men tell no tales," he said.

Deidre was a willing participant and suggested that J.R., Chumbley, Teja, and an 18-year-old named Bryan Chase were likely candidates. Chase wasn't considered violent but Deidre thought he could be manipulated to commit murder. Although Chase was not violent, he was a naive country boy who was way out of his league among the Boardwalk crowd. Deidre believed he could be forced to commit murder if he was scared enough.

Kosta periodically called prospective murderers to his back room at Top Shots to assess their willingness to kill for money. Chumbley had already made a point of telling Kosta that he would murder if the price was right.

Gus Moamis had said he would contract to commit

murder, but he had been caught during a burglary and was in jail.

Teja was summoned to Kosta's back office at Top Shots so that Kosta could sound him out. "There are three guys in a warehouse in Port Orange," Kosta said. "They've got a couple of hundred thousand dollars in cash and some cocaine. I want you to kill everybody there and bring me the cash. You can do whatever you want to with the dope."

"Sure," Teja said, thinking that Kosta was full of bullshit.

Kosta said he would provide an Uzi.

"Uh-huh," Teja said. "Sure, I'll do it."

Teja thought this was just talk, but he later found out that there really was a big dope operation at a warehouse in Port Orange. When Kosta didn't follow through with plans for the killing raid, Teja asked him about it.

"It was the wrong place," Kosta said. "I had the wrong license plate number."

"Oh."

"Well, how much would it take for you to kill someone?" Kosta asked.

"About ten thousand dollars," Teja answered.

Kosta and Deidre filed away Teja's willingness to commit murder.

Kosta probed J.R.'s feelings about murder at the house Fotopoulos had rented for Deidre. Besides Kosta, Deidre, and J.R., Lori Henderson was also there and heard the conversation. They were sitting at a table in the kitchen, and one of J.R.'s friends was taking a shower. Although J.R. had been Deidre's boyfriend, Kosta didn't mind him being around her when he could keep an eye on them.

The conversation around the table was normal at first, then Kosta said, "I've killed a lot of people. There's nothing to it."

Sooner or later, it seemed, Kosta always got around to bragging about the people he had killed. J.R. had a reputation for being a tough guy on the Boardwalk, and he wasn't fazed.

"Yeah, I know."

"I was just kidding when I told Dee there was a tape of me killing someone," Kosta said.

J.R. didn't say anything. He didn't want Kosta to know what he was thinking.

"I like the way you fight," Kosta said.

"You kill people and you like the way I fight. So what?"

Deidre sat on the couch, intensely interested, but saying nothing. J.R. wanted to act like he wasn't impressed one way or the other.

"You're a tough guy," Kosta said. "I'd like to pay someone ten thousand dollars to have someone killed so I can inherit some money. Would you do it?"

"Sure, I'll do it."

J.R. pressed for additional details, but Kosta cut him off. He wouldn't say another word about it. He wouldn't talk about deals. He simply cut the subject off.

"It was pretty obvious that he wanted me to kill somebody," J.R. said. "I figured it must be his wife or somebody or a relative."

It was also obvious that Deidre was a major part of Kosta's plan for murder.

Kosta visited the house regularly, usually arriving between seven a.m. or eight a.m. He went into a bedroom with Deidre and had sex. Lori knew that they sometimes watched his videotapes and once, after they had been unexpectedly interrupted by Gus Moamis, Deidre gave her a locked ammunition box to take to Kosta at Top Shots. Lori made sure that she was out of the house if Deidre happened to be absent during Kosta's regular visiting hours.

Kosta not only had sex with Deidre at the house, he took numerous nude photographs of her posing like the models he saw in the *Playboy, Penthouse,* and the other porno magazines he looked at. She was photographed with her legs apart, her labia open to expose the clitoris. Kosta also photographed Deidre cupping her breasts and squeezing her nipples. He carried them around and showed them to people.

Kosta was both physically and emotionally enthralled by Deidre. She was a sexual adventuress who was willing to try anything, and more often than not, enjoyed it. Deidre captivated him with her sexual allure, toughness, and proven ability to shoot someone. Kosta relished her sordid background, especially the violent aspects.

11

Kosta felt comfortable discussing his plans with Deidre. She listened to his schemes and embellished them, giving them a sharper edge. Deidre helped him pass counterfeit, was enthusiastic about becoming a hired killer, and had no qualms about the prospective murder of Kosta's wife and in-laws. Or the murder of the people who they expected to carry out the contract killings.

Kosta took Deidre on several shooting expeditions in the woods to teach her how to shoot better and to become familiar with different types of guns. He told her about the money he made as an assassin and showed her checks for large amounts of money that he said were payments for killing people.

Deidre was not just a willing student about guns, she was fascinated by them as much as Kosta. She started reading Kosta's gun magazines and studied the articles and advertisements in *Soldier of Fortune*.

"It's good to know about guns," Deidre told Lori. "Kosta's got a lot of them."

Kosta gave Deidre counterfeit and good currency, paid her rent and all expenses. She often made shopping excursions and returned with hundreds of dollars worth of clothes. Having lived in poverty all of her life, Deidre was intoxicated by the good life she was living and looked forward to having one that was even more luxurious.

"I want money," she told Lori and her other friends. "I love money and power, and I'll kill to get it. I'm going to become an assassin like Kosta."

The couple had watched at least one videotape that showed a man being severely tortured. The torturer wasn't shown but Deidre said his voice sounded exactly like Kosta's. Kosta proved his indifference to pain by talking with her while holding the coals of a lighted cigarette against his inner arm. He held it there for at least five minutes and his expression never changed.

"You have to learn how to deal with pain," he told her.

After the first step, killing someone while having it recorded on videotape, the prospective Hunter-Killer member was given a black beret. The second step was to select someone as a target, hunt him down, and kill him without leaving a clue.

Deidre was excited about the prospect.

Once, when he knew his wife and in-laws would be away from home, Kosta took Deidre to the expensive, three-story house on the Halifax River. Deidre had to hunker down in the car to avoid being seen by the neighbors until Kosta pulled into the garage. Once inside, Deidre's eyes almost popped out of her head.

"You see how I live," Kosta told her. "You can live the same way."

There were only three obstacles in the way: Mary, Dino, and Lisa.

Both Kosta and Deidre mentioned the Hunter-Killer Club to Lori, Teja, Gus Moamis and Kevin Ramsey. J.R. wasn't told. Lori considered it frightening and Teja thought it was interesting and perhaps a way to make money. Ramsey liked the idea and was eager to join.

Gus Moamis thought it was similar to organized crime.

"He made it sound like a real big deal," Moamis said. "The way he told it, it sounded like organized crime with secret pledges and everything."

Tony Calderone heard about it and said he thought the Hunter-Killer Club was another one of Kosta's pipe

100

dreams, perhaps a fantasy gleaned from one of his comic books. Calderone was more concerned about Kosta's increasingly reckless behavior with Deidre than he was with a make-believe group of assassins.

"They [Kosta and Deidre] were doing things out in the open, throwing caution to the wind," he said. "I thought, here's a guy with a beautiful, rich wife, and he's risking everything for a street girl."

Calderone told Kosta, "Man, she's nothing. You can lose everything."

Kosta smiled. "No, I won't. I'm a perfect husband."

Calderone tried again. "She could get a divorce and you wouldn't have anything."

"Greek men don't divorce their wives."

Calderone was still uneasy, but he said nothing more.

Kosta continued to collect weaponry for himself and plan the elimination of Lisa and his in-laws. He bought Deidre a handgun that she threatened to use at any real or perceived slight, regardless of how minor. Her friends were scared to be around Deidre when she had a gun.

"You didn't want to be around Deidre when she had firearms," Teja said. "She would go crazy when she had a gun."

Deidre pulled the gun in the blink of an eye. Once she walked by a bus stop with Teja and Lori. A man sitting on a bench whistled at her.

Deidre whirled around. She didn't like it and told the man so.

"Yeah, well you're ugly anyhow," the man retorted.

"I'm going to kill you for that!"

Deidre pulled out the gun, and it was all Teja and Lori could do to restrain Deidre while she tried to shoot the man.

"I'm going to kill him!" she screamed. "I'm going to kill him!"

They managed to get Deidre away before there was any

shooting, then calmed her down. But Deidre was dangerous and volatile when she had a gun. When her pet cat had kittens, the playful offspring aggravated her. She found a sack and put the kittens in it, tied it shut, and took them out into the backyard.

"What are you doing?" Lori asked.

"I'm going to take them out and shoot them dead," Deidre replied.

Lori and Teja protested, but Deidre was in no mood to listen to reason, and she was too dangerous to argue with. Deidre took the bag of kittens outside and shot at it until all of the kittens were killed.

Deidre talked more about all of the people she had killed and the people she planned to kill. She enjoyed talking about murder, and she played with the gun as if it was a toy. Deidre seemed anxious to fulfill the requirements to become a member of Kosta's Hunter-Killer Club.

Kevin Ramsey had a loud argument with Kosta in late September. Calderone heard it through Kosta's closed door at Top Shots, but he couldn't make out the words. But Kosta was obviously furious, and, when the argument was over, Kosta fired Ramsey and told him never to come back to the poolroom.

Several rumors about the argument circulated. Ramsey told Teja that he had tried to blackmail Kosta and had threatened to go the police regarding his counterfeit operation unless Kosta paid him off. J.R. heard that Kosta had kicked Ramsey out because he had threatened to start his own prostitution operation.

No one except Kosta and Ramsey knew for sure what the argument was about, but it was clear that in the aftermath Ramsey was frightened.

Lisa knew Ramsey only from the times she had helped him with the inventory at Top Shots and was surprised when Ramsey showed up at Joyland and entered her office.

"Is Kosta here?" he asked.

"No."

"Well, can I talk to you?"

"Yeah, sure," Lisa said. "I'll meet you in the snack bar."

Ramsey was waiting when Lisa arrived.

"I think somebody's going to kill me," he said.

"Why?"

"It has to do with drugs or something," Ramsey said. "I think it's somebody in Daytona Beach."

Lisa listened in surprise as Ramsey spun a tale about how he had been involved with drugs and that the people he had worked with had concluded that he was an informant. He seemed scared. Lisa couldn't believe he was telling her such a story.

"I'm not the kind of person that you tell that kind of stuff to," she said.

Lisa launched into what she said was a lecture.

"Look at the kind of people you hang out with," she said. "You need to get yourself out of that crowd."

"Yeah, but somebody's trying to kill me."

Ramsey and Lisa were still talking when Kosta walked in.

"Well, there's Kosta," she told Ramsey. "Why don't you go talk to him about it?"

"No. I don't want to get Kosta involved," Ramsey said, and left in a hurry.

Kosta told Deidre that Ramsey was trying to blackmail him about the counterfeit operation. Deidre was furious because she didn't want her plans to become rich and powerful jeopardized by anyone. Kosta was her ticket to a better life.

"I want you to kill him," Kosta said. "I'll record it on videotape. It will be your first step to becoming a member

103

of the Hunter-Killer Club."

Kosta also told her, "This will prove that you can kill. Then you can take the responsibility for having my wife killed."

Deidre agreed to kill Ramsey and listened to Kosta outline the plans. Ramsey, who had taken Deidre in to live with him for a few days when she was having a hard time, believed that his former lover was still a good friend. Kosta told her to meet with Ramsey and say that he had a job for him.

"Tell him the past is the past," Kosta said.

Deidre told Lori that she was going to kill Ramsey.

"Why do you want to kill Kevin?" Lori asked.

"He's expendable, and he's been blackmailing Kosta," Deidre said. "I'm going to join the Hunter-Killer Club. Besides, I hate him."

Deidre met Ramsey on the Boardwalk on the afternoon of October 3, 1989.

"Kosta wants to see you tonight," Deidre told him.

Ramsey was hesitant.

"He isn't mad at you anymore," Deidre said. "He wants you to do a job for him."

Ramsey told Deidre that he would meet her that night.

"Kevin believed that Deidre was his friend," J.R. and Teja said. "He trusted her. He didn't think Kosta would do anything to him with Deidre around."

That evening Ramsey was troubled when he talked with Robin Berghdorff, his live-in girlfriend. They were inside the trailer Robin was buying. Even though he trusted Deidre, Ramsey was still afraid.

"I think I'm going to be killed or hurt real bad," Ramsey said. "I learned too much about Kosta's business."

"You ain't got nothing to be afraid of," Robin told him.

"I was selling drugs for Kosta," Ramsey said. "I know

about the prostitution ring at Top Shots, but I don't know who's behind it."

Ramsey said that he had recruited Tiger and set her up in a motel room to work for him as a prostitute.

Ramsey started to cry. "I'm afraid of Kosta," he sobbed. "I'm really afraid."

Nothing Robin said consoled him. Ramsey wept for almost a solid hour, then pulled himself together, and headed for the Boardwalk to meet with Deidre.

Lori was with Deidre on the Boardwalk, waiting for Ramsey. Deidre became increasingly agitated as time passed and Ramsey didn't make the rendezvous.

"If he doesn't show up, we'll have to find someone else to kill," Deidre said.

"Who?"

"Tiger. She's expendable, too."

Tiger's real name was Cindy Bennett. She was fifteen years old and already pregnant at the time. Lori waited with Deidre for quite a while and neither Ramsey or Tiger showed up.

Deidre was about to give up when Ramsey arrived. She was angry with him for being so late.

"Let's go," she snapped. "You've kept Kosta waiting."

Lori stayed behind as Deidre and Ramsey left the Boardwalk. Kosta waited for them in his black BMW. He gave Ramsey a friendly greeting.

"I've got a job for you, man," Kosta said. "Do you want it?"

"Aren't you mad at me?"

"No. That's over and done."

"Then I'm in," Ramsey grinned.

Deidre got in the front with Kosta, and Ramsey sat in the back. Kosta told Ramsey the job he had in mind might involve enemy gunfire.

"You need to know what it sounds like," Kosta said. "You need to know what it's like to be shot at."

"Yeah," Ramsey said. "God, I'm hungry. Can we stop and get something at a 7-Eleven?"

"We don't have time," Deidre said.

"I'm starved."

"Goddamn it! You can eat later."

"I'm out of cigarettes, too," Ramsey said. "Let's stop and get something to eat and some cigarettes."

"Later!" Deidre snapped.

Ramsey continued to beg them to stop so he could get a sandwich and cigarettes. Deidre was furious with what she felt was whining but tried not to show it. She was sure that if they stopped Ramsey would flee.

It was about three a.m. and pitch black when Kosta drove into a remote wooded area east of Daytona Beach, not far from the Strickland Shooting Range. The area was filled with scrub palmettos and weeds. It was dark and lonely, accessible only by a small dirt road that was almost impossible to see by a person who didn't know it was there.

The three of them got out of the car.

"We're going to tie you to a tree and fire bullets at your feet," Kosta said. "You don't have to worry. We're not going to shoot you."

"Is that all there is to it?" Ramsey asked.

"Right."

"God, I'm hungry," Ramsey said.

"You can eat later," Kosta said. "We've got to get some stuff out of the car. Look around and make sure there's nobody around to hear the gunfire."

While Ramsey searched the area to insure their privacy, Kosta and Deidre went back to the car. Kosta opened the trunk. He took out some rope, a Mag flashlight, an AK-47, a video camera, and a .22 semiautomatic pistol with a silencer.

"I was so mad at him I wanted to kill him in the car," Deidre said. "Let's kill the son of a bitch and get it over with."

Ramsey smiled when they returned with their equipment. He grinned as they tied him to a tree, assuring him once again that they were going to shoot bullets at his feet. They told him that what they planned to do was part of the initiation into the Hunter-Killer Club. Ramsey nodded and told them how hungry he was.

After Ramsey was tied up, Deidre took the .22 semiautomatic pistol with the silencer and Kosta started the video camera.

"Is this okay?" she asked.

"No, move this way."

Deidre moved and the Mag flashlight shone in her face.

"Don't shine that shit in my eyes!" she snapped.

Ramsey, tied to the tree, grinned.

"Okay," Kosta said.

Deidre pointed the pistol and fired three rapid shots that struck Ramsey in the chest. When the first shot struck, Ramsey's face twisted in agony. He lifted his left leg and screamed, "Oh, God!" and kept on screaming as two additional bullets struck him, then he slumped.

Deidre walked to Ramsey without hesitation or instructions, grabbed a handful of Ramsey's hair, lifted his head, and fired a bullet point-blank into his left temple. Ramsey's blood spattered onto her jeans and sneakers. The entire videotape took fifty-seven seconds. The murder took about forty seconds.

Ramsey was still twitching in death throes as his body sagged against the ropes even after Deidre shot him in the head.

"Damn!" Kosta said. "I knew this would happen."

He walked to Ramsey and fired the AK-47 into his head, blasting off a chunk of the young man's skull.

Kosta put the remaining rope, video camera, and guns

107

back into the trunk of his car and drove back to town with Deidre.

"I was so pissed off at him whining about stopping for something to eat and cigarettes that I almost shot him in the car," Deidre said.

"Yeah, well, it's too bad in a way," Kosta said. "We should have gotten him something to eat. It's too bad that he had to die hungry."

"Yeah," Deidre said. "What a bummer."

They parted company in Daytona Beach. Kosta kept the weapons, video camera, and videotape. Deidre kept her shoes and jeans, which were spattered with Mark Kevin Ramsey's blood.

12

Kosta was afraid that both Deidre's and his telephones had been tapped and had worked out a code system so that their telephone conversations couldn't be recorded. The code was a five-digit number, the first number designating the telephone location, and the other four numbers denoted the hour and minute in military time. For example, Kosta might call Deidre and say, "Five thirteen fifty." That meant Deidre was to be at location five at 1350 hours military time, which translates to 1:50 p.m.

The day after they murdered Kevin Ramsey, Kosta telephoned Deidre's house and spoke in numerical code. She went to the appropriate public telephone and waited for his call. When it came, Kosta said he wanted to see her.

Kosta picked her up in his car and she crouched down so no one could see her as they drove away.

"Lisa's got friends and relatives all over town," he said. "They'd get suspicious if they saw me driving around with a pretty young girl."

Although Kosta was afraid Deidre's telephone might be bugged, he wasn't concerned about eavesdropping devices in her house. He drove there and they went inside.

"You looked like you really enjoyed that last night,"

Kosta said. "How would you like to kill my wife for ten thousand dollars?"

Deidre had not balked at the murder of Mark Kevin Ramsey, and she wasn't upset at the prospect of Lisa's murder. She just didn't want to do it herself. Too many people knew that she was having an affair with Kosta, and she considered the job too risky.

"I don't want to kill Lisa," Deidre said. "I'll help you."

"Good. You've got the responsibility for killing her. I want you to find someone to kill her. J.R. and Matt are expendable. Offer ten thousand dollars."

"J.R.'s a good choice because he says he killed someone before."

Kosta told Deidre again about the insurance policies that Lisa had.

"We're building a new house in Ormond Beach," Kosta said. "When I get the money, Lori and Teja can live there with us."

Deidre, who had caught a glimpse of how Kosta lived in his mother-in-law's house, was intrigued. She told him that she had enjoyed killing Ramsey.

They talked more about plans to have Lisa killed. Kosta told her that he had no intention of actually paying someone to kill Lisa. The money was just the bait. What Kosta intended to do was wait until the assassin murdered Lisa, then he himself would kill the murderer. Kosta said he might have the assassin shoot him in the arm before he killed the murderer.

"It will make me look like a hero," he said.

They agreed that Deidre should approach J.R. and offer him ten thousand dollars to kill an undesignated woman. Kosta wanted J.R. to go to Joyland, stage an attempted robbery, and kill Lisa. J.R. would be told to take Lisa's jewelry and run to make it appear as if the

110

murder had been committed during a robbery.

The real plan was for Kosta to step out of a rest room and kill J.R. after he murdered Lisa. There would be no witnesses, and he could say he shot J.R. in self-defense. Kosta told her, "I love you," and left.

Deidre thought of the money and the way she would live after Lisa was dead. She also thought of the videotape that Kosta had of her killing Ramsey. She wanted to believe that Kosta loved her, but she wasn't sure. Deidre decided to see J.R. as soon as possible to ask him if he could be paid to commit murder.

After she and Kosta parted, Deidre was in a state of high excitement. She wanted to tell Lori all about how she had killed Ramsey and the plan to kill Lisa. She had saved the shoes and jeans that were spattered with Ramsey's blood. Kosta had told Deidre to keep the murder a secret, but Lori already knew that Ramsey's murder had been planned.

That evening Deidre was at the Great Barrier Reef nightclub when Lori came to meet her. Lori's boyfriend, Teja, had gone to the Beachcomber, another club that wasn't far away. Deidre was flushed with excitement.

Deidre grabbed Lori. "Oh, oh, I've been waiting for you. I have to tell you about this."

Deidre took Lori outside, and they sat on a bench. Deidre described the murder in detail and told Lori how anxious she had been to do it. She told Lori that she had wanted to shoot Ramsey in the car and was impatient with Kosta to get the video camera ready.

"I asked him, 'Are you ready yet?' " Deidre said.

Then she described the shooting. "After the first shot, he just made a loud, excruciating scream like I

111

had never heard before," she said. "I shot him three times, and he was still moving, so I grabbed him by the hair and blew his brains out."

Lori listened to the details and noticed that, in addition to being excited, Deidre seemed scared. "She was acting real weird," she said.

"I'm going to be an assassin and make a lot of money," Deidre said. "Kosta videotaped the whole thing. Would you still like me if I became an assassin? Would you still speak to me? Could we still be friends?"

"I guess we could."

Deidre said that Ramsey was still twitching after she had shot him in the head and that it made Kosta mad.

"He took his gun and gave me a leather jacket so I could catch the cartridge, and then he shot Kevin in the head," Deidre said.

"Why did you have to catch the bullet?"

"Kosta said it was something that was easy to trace."

"It doesn't seem right that he would be videotaping you," Lori said. "It seems awful strange to me."

"Oh, no. He loves me," Deidre said. "He's doing this for me. He wants to help me."

Deidre showed Lori a black beret that Kosta had given her that morning and explained that she had completed the first step to become a member of the Hunter-Killer Club. When she finished her stalking task, Deidre said she would receive a silver insignia with the letters HK to wear on the beret.

"Kosta wants me to have his wife killed," Deidre said. "If she gets killed, he receives seven hundred thousand dollars in insurance."

"This is getting pretty weird for me," Lori said.

Deidre explained that she and Kosta would hire someone to kill Lisa by offering them ten thousand dollars. But Kosta would never pay the assassin because he intended to kill whomever murdered Lisa.

"Where's Teja?" Deidre asked.

"At the Beachcomber."

"Look, can I stay at your apartment tonight?"

"No," Lori said. "This is too crazy for me."

Lori left Deidre and went home with Teja and told him everything.

"That's crazy," he said. "Kosta's crazy."

Lori told Teja how Deidre had pulled her outside of Top Shots the night before and told her, "It's tonight. He's going to have me kill someone tonight."

"He wants her to hire someone to kill his wife so he can receive her insurance money," Lori continued.

"Who's she going to get?"

"She said she'd try to get J.R. Kosta doesn't like him anyway."

"Yeah, but he's your friend."

"I'll warn him that he won't get out of it alive."

"We know too much," Teja said. "You know what Kosta does to people who know too much."

Lori was already terrified of Kosta. "Are you afraid of him?"

"Damn right I am."

"Deidre's just using Kosta to get ahead," Lori said. "She'll drop him if he doesn't do the right things for her."

"Not if she's telling the truth," Teja said. "He's got that videotape."

Kosta finally had the wheels in motion to kill Lisa, but things turned sour on his counterfeiting operation. Bill and Barbara Markantonakis had been arrested by the U.S. Secret Service for passing counterfeit currency. They had entered a plea of innocent and were out on bail. They contacted Kosta, who told them to meet him on the Boardwalk.

According to his police deposition, Peter Kouracos rode with Kosta when he went to meet Bill and Barbara, but he remained in the car. Kosta, as usual, was carrying a gun in a shoulder holster. He told Kouracos to let him know if anybody showed up.

Bill and Barbara were nervous as Kosta approached them. They already knew that Kosta had deadly plans. In June 1987 Kosta had offered Bill fifty thousand dollars to kill his father-in-law. Bill had refused the offer. Augustine died less than six months later.

In April 1988, with Augustine out of the way, Kosta tried to hire Bill for twenty thousand dollars to kill his brother-in-law, Dino. The same month Kosta upped the ante and offered Bill another eighty thousand dollars in cash and forty thousand dollars in jewelry to kill Mary Paspalakis, his mother-in-law. Bill wasn't a killer and turned all of the offers down. But he and Barbara knew that Kosta was dangerous.

Kosta asked if they had implicated him in the counterfeit operation. They told Kosta that they had not.

"If you do, I'll kill you," Kosta told them.

Kosta told them that Augustine had not died a natural death, but that he himself had had him killed. Kosta boasted that he had formed a group of professional murderers who had already killed eight people. His criminal enterprises, he said, included prostitution, burglary, car theft, drug dealing, gun running, robbery, and money laundering.

Kosta handed them just under five thousand dollars in cash and ordered them to return to Greece. It would be next to impossible for the United States government to have them extradited to stand trial. That would prevent them from testifying that Kosta was the kingpin behind the counterfeiting operation.

"If you come back or testify against me, I'll kill you," he warned again.

Bill and Barbara took the money and caught the first flight to Greece.

Peter Kouracos's feelings were hurt when Kosta opened Top Shots without telling him. The two friends had considered going into business together on several occasions. Once they considered buying a business that dealt with surplus ammunition, but nothing ever came of it but talk.

Kouracos was a successful investor and gave Kosta tips on buying and selling stocks and bonds. Kosta started with a portfolio worth two thousand dollars.

"He followed my advice and turned it into ten thousand dollars," Kouracos said.

Believing that Kosta thought of him like a brother, Kouracos was bewildered about being left out of the plans for Top Shots.

"He kept me in the dark for three weeks before he opened Top Shots," Kouracos said. "I was upset and said, 'Why didn't you ask me?' "

The point was not worth arguing about because Kouracos held a grudge against the people who owned the property Kosta leased. Kouracos admitted that he would not have become involved because of that. Nevertheless, the two men had become even closer friends. Sometimes Kouracos visited Top Shots alone, dropped in with Lisa, and occasionally went there with Dino, but none of them liked the poolroom because of the low-class clientele.

While Kosta planned murder, robbery, and mayhem, he continued to improve his standing in the upper crust of Daytona Beach society, thanks to being a member of the Paspalakis family. Kouracos was a member of the Halifax Masonic Lodge and persuaded Kosta to join, too. He also encouraged Kosta to take an interest in politics by joining the Young Republicans. This latter affiliation inadvertently led to Deidre later becoming a bright, if brief, star in the highest circles of Daytona Beach and Volusia County politics.

Kouracos met Deidre on his visits to Top Shots, although he said he didn't get to know her very well. "She seemed like a nice personality at the time," he said.

He had noticed Deidre's uncanny ability to calculate mathematics in her head. That was the first thing that impressed him, although he didn't fail to notice that Deidre was pretty and sexy.

Cochairman for the reelection of Bud Asher to the Daytona Beach City Commission, Peter was obligated to attend the victory celebration at campaign headquarters in mid-October. Unfortunately, he didn't have a date.

Two days before the election, he approached Kosta and asked about taking Deidre to the party. He was concerned about taking a barmaid to a gathering of powerful politicians and their supporters.

"Do you think I should take her?" he asked.

"I don't know why not," Kosta replied.

Kosta gave Deidre several hundred dollars, which she spent buying appropriate clothing, getting her hair done, and having a manicure. Deidre wanted to look good because Kosta and Lisa were going to be at the celebration, too.

When Kouracos went to pick up Deidre, the woman who had killed Kevin Ramsey a few days earlier, she

116

was beautiful and radiant, obviously excited about an opportunity to mingle with some of the richest and most powerful people in the area.

Kouracos and Deidre arrived as the party was already in progress, though the votes were still being tallied. Deidre amazed everybody by looking at the results from the precincts and calculating them with incredible speed.

Deidre was at her best. She was bright, beautiful, and bubbly, and her eyes sparkled. She was sexy but smiled in a way that made her look like the very picture of innocence. She captivated people, including Councilman Asher and his wife, Dawn.

"She's really effervescent," Asher said.

Kouracos noted that Deidre and Dawn had conversations that were punctuated with laughter. "Dawn liked her," Kouracos said.

The party moved from city hall to Asher's house about nine p.m. The change of location did nothing to diminish Deidre's ability to take the spotlight. Asher said, "She's the life of the party."

The evening ended with Kouracos being embarrassed. Among other things, the Ashers had served long loaves of French bread that had been made into enormous sandwiches. The guests sliced off a piece of the sandwich that was of manageable size. When Kouracos told Deidre he wanted to leave, she ran up to Dawn.

"Can I take some food with me?" Deidre asked.

Dawn said it was fine.

"Oh, yeah," Deidre said loud enough to be heard by almost everybody there. "I'm going to take one of those big sandwiches down and slice it into pieces and sell them for a dollar apiece at Top Shots."

Kouracos was appalled. When they were in the car,

117

he said, "I would have no problem with you being charitable and feeding the poor on the Boardwalk. But I have a serious problem with you selling them for a dollar apiece."

"Oh, I was just kidding," Deidre said.

There was another election party that Kouracos had to attend, and he thought of Deidre as a date. Kouracos didn't want to have sex with Deidre, but he was a little surprised that she didn't even flirt with him.

"She didn't give me a second look," he said. "I didn't want to do anything with her, but she just tuned me out. I'm not a bad-looking guy, and women usually show some kind of interest. Deidre just flat out gave me the cold shoulder."

Nevertheless, Kouracos took Deidre to another election party. He said it was largely because of her ability to do mathematics so quickly.

"She was excellent at calculating arithmetic," he said. "At city hall, I had her calculate the vote totals. She was absolutely great at that. It's not that I can't add myself, I just can't do it as fast as her."

Kouracos watched Deidre shine among the area's elite and concluded that she was a social climber.

"She reveled in the idea of being around members of the city commission," he said. "She liked rubbing elbows with the rich and the powerful. But I thought, 'If this girl wants to better herself, I don't have any problem with giving her a taste of what this is like.'"

Kouracos noted that on both occasion that he took Deidre out, she wore new clothes, had her hair done, was carefully made up, and had her nails manicured. "She looked very nice," he admitted.

About two weeks after Councilman Bud Asher's victory celebration, the city councilman telephoned Kouracos to say he was having a Halloween party.

"Bring that girl who was with you on election night," Asher said. "She was the life of the party."

The party was scheduled to start at Asher's house and move to Razzles, a nightclub on Seabreeze just a block from the Atlantic Ocean. Peter begged off.

Deidre and Kosta were already in a frenzy of activity by then. Kosta's plan to kill Lisa and his in-laws was falling apart due to a telephone call Dino had received from Greece. Kosta and Deidre were frantic.

13

Dino Paspalakis got a telephone call from Bill Markantonakis in mid-October.

Bill told Dino that he was involved in Kosta's counterfeiting operation, had been arrested, posted bond, and skipped bail by returning to Greece.

"Kosta's out to kill you and your family," Bill warned him.

Dino wasn't fond of Kosta, but he didn't believe Bill's accusation even though Bill tried hard to convince him.

"It was such a ridiculous accusation," Dino said. "How can you believe it?"

Later Dino, Kosta, and Lisa were in the office at Joyland together.

"Bill Markantonakis called from Greece," Dino said. "He told me you plan to kill all of us."

Kosta laughed and shrugged it off. Although Dino didn't believe Bill, he was left with niggling doubts.

Following Ramsey's murder and Bill's warning to Dino, Kosta initiated a whirlwind of activity. Both time and circumstances had turned against him in his plan to inherit the Paspalakis fortune. Now his goal was to have Lisa killed as soon as possible for the life insurance benefits.

Kosta had ordered Deidre to keep Ramsey's murder

a secret and had started a rumor that Ramsey had stolen a pickup truck and moved to Orlando. That was what Robin Berghdorff, Ramsey's former girlfriend heard. Robin was now dating Bryan Chase, a gentle eighteen-year-old farm boy from Cleveland, who had been befriended by J.R.

Killing Ramsey had intoxicated Deidre. She strutted, filled with demonic energy. She was bursting with a need to brag to all her friends about what she had done. In just a few days she could no longer keep it all inside. J.R., Lori, and Teja were at her house.

"Have you seen Kevin around lately?" Deidre asked.

"No, come to think of it, he hasn't been in town lately," Teja said. "I wonder where he went. His girlfriend told me he went to Orlando."

"No, he isn't," Deidre said. "He's still in Daytona."

"Where is he?" Teja asked.

"He's dead."

Teja still wasn't sure that Deidre had killed Ramsey, even though Deidre had already told Lori. J.R. didn't know what to think.

"Stop joking around," Teja said.

"No, I killed him."

"Yeah, right, Deidre."

Lori was in another room and Deidre called her. When Lori arrived, Deidre said, "Tell them that Kevin's dead."

"Yeah, he's dead," Lori said.

"I killed him out in the woods," Deidre said. "I killed him and Kosta made a videotape. I'll show you."

Deidre left the room and came back carrying a pair of white tennis shoes that were spattered by dark markings and a pair of jeans with stains on the legs. "That's where his blood splattered," Deidre said.

J.R. and Teja admitted that it could be blood, but that didn't prove anything. It could be blood from an animal or some other kind of stain.

Deidre wanted Teja and J.R. to believe her. She related the entire episode for them, as she had done previously for Lori, then asked: "Do you know what it feels like to grab somebody by the hair and blow their brains out? It feels good!"

"She acted like she had really enjoyed it," J.R. said later.

Kosta also seemed to be bursting with a need to talk about Ramsey's murder and his plans for killing Lisa. He asked Tony Calderone to go for a walk with him on the Boardwalk. "My wife's aunt just opened a shop in the Marriott," Kosta said.

"That's pretty expensive," Calderone said.

"They've got money. Lisa has a lot of insurance."

Calderone thought that it was a strange thing for Kosta to say.

"What would be a good way to kill someone?" Kosta asked.

Calderone said, "I don't know."

"Do you have a boat?"

"No."

"Too bad," Kosta said. "A perfect way to get rid of someone would be to take them out and shoot them, put chum in the water to attract sharks, then throw them overboard. The chum would draw sharks to eat the body, and you're home free."

"I guess if you're going to do it that would be a good way."

Calderone didn't like the way Kosta's mind seemed to be working. Here Kosta was, married into money, a member of a powerful family, a guy who had everything. Calderone thought that Kosta was throwing it all away because of his obsession with Deidre.

"You know, this girl could bribe you," he said of Deidre. "She could do anything to you."

"She could never do anything because I have a tape of her killing somebody."

Calderone had heard Kosta talk of torture videotapes and videotapes of himself killing people. Kosta reminded him about those tapes, and Calderone became more than a little bit uneasy.

"I've got a tape of Deidre killing Kevin," Kosta said. "Do you want to see it?"

Calderone was chilled to the bone.

"No," he answered.

Calderone wasn't sure whether or not Ramsey had been killed, but he decided to keep his mouth shut for the time being.

"I felt pretty guilty about it," he said. "I introduced them [Deidre and Kosta], but I didn't know what they would do. They were getting kind of hot and heavy, and I kept seeing them just doing stupid things, just ignorant, stupid things that I thought would wind up getting him in trouble with his wife, causing him to have a divorce or marital problems. He was very blatant about the things he did, always thinking he was making a secret of it when everybody knew what was going on. He was leaving a trail behind him like bread crumbs, flaunting it with Deidre."

Kosta's plans became even more tangled when Bill and Barbara Markantonakis returned to the United States and were immediately nabbed by the U.S. Secret Service in Syracuse, New York. They told Secret Service Agent Mike Pritchard that Kosta was the counterfeiting kingpin and that he had threatened to kill them if they implicated him in the operation.

Pritchard launched an investigation to gather evidence against Kosta and Peter Kouracos for counterfeiting and witness tampering.

Kosta immediately tried to cover his tracks. He had already buried counterfeit and good currency, and now he was pressed to hide all of the counterfeit while he was busy trying to have Lisa killed.

Kosta put counterfeit in ammunition boxes and in a cylindrical metal container that had once contained Pepsi-Cola syrup. Events goaded Kosta into feverish activity. He had Peter Kouracos drive him into the woods so that he could bury ammunition boxes, metal containers, and waterproof vinyl bags.

Kouracos wasn't concerned about Kosta's behavior since burying things wouldn't have been unusual for a Survivalist. Besides burying various containers, Kosta made forays into the woods to dig things up. Sometimes he had to go back with a metal detector because he couldn't find his secret burial places. Even with the metal detector he sometimes returned empty-handed.

Kosta arrived unexpectedly at Calderone's house during this period at one a.m. He was dressed in combat camouflage fatigues, a beret, a utility belt, and carried a Samurai sword in a camouflaged sheath across his chest, an assault rifle, and a holstered pistol. He looked like he was going to war.

"I need you to go with me someplace real quick," Kosta said.

Calderone's wife and son were asleep. "Where are we going?"

"Just down the road. We'll be right back."

"Kosta, it's one o'clock in the morning."

"I swear, we'll be back in ten minutes."

Calderone said he thought that Kosta just wanted to talk with him. He was doing a lot of covering up for Kosta concerning his affair with Deidre. Calderone dressed and got in Kosta's black BMW.

"What's the deal?" he asked.

Kosta didn't say anything, he just kept driving. And

driving. He drove to a remote wooded area northwest of Daytona Beach, then stopped the car and got out.

"Drive around for a while and pick me up in thirty minutes," Kosta said.

"What are you doing here?"

"I got something buried here and I've got to get it."

"What's buried?"

"I'll tell you later."

"God, this is crazy."

Calderone got out of the car to get behind the wheel and was immediately besieged by mosquitoes. Kosta jumped out, jangling his Samurai sword, guns, and other military gear attached to his utility belt.

"These mosquitoes are going to eat you alive," Calderone said.

Kosta ignored the comment. "Drive around for thirty minutes, then come back down and blink the lights so I'll know it's you."

Calderone started to drive around and immediately noticed that the gas tank was almost empty. He didn't know if there was even enough to get to a filling station. Finally he decided to attempt to drive to Ormond Beach. He bought gasoline there and headed back to where Kosta was. Forty-five minutes had passed since he had dropped Kosta off.

Calderone pulled over and blinked the lights once. He waited for a long time in the darkness and Kosta didn't appear. Calderone started to drive on and blinked the lights again. The second time Kosta leaped out of the woods.

"He was like some kind of friggin' Ninja idiot," Calderone said. "He jumps out of the bank of the woods in front of the car. It scared the shit out of me. I didn't know what it was. I slammed on the brakes and, sure enough, it was him."

"I'll have to come back," Kosta said. "I didn't find

125

it."

"What were you looking for?"

"Machine guns, explosives, and counterfeit," Kosta said.

Calderone said this was the first time he had heard Kosta mention counterfeit. It was a weird morning, and he was glad when he got back home and Kosta left.

14

After Deidre agreed to find an assassin for Lisa, she approached the subject bluntly at her house with J.R. He was tempting fate again by spending the night with Deidre.

They sat on the bed naked, talking. "Kosta wants to kill his wife," Deidre said. "He wants you to do it."

"How much does he want to pay?"

"One hundred thousand dollars."

"Okay. I'll do it."

"I'll have to talk to Kosta."

"You're always saying Kosta wants you to do this and Kosta wants you to do that," J.R. said. "Everything Kosta says comes through you."

The conversation somehow managed to turn into an argument. Deidre was still angry at J.R. because he had dumped her. Now he gave her another reason to be sore at him.

"You think you're the best-looking thing on the Boardwalk," J.R. said.

This struck a nerve with Deidre.

"J.R., all of my life I thought that I was ugly, and I really believed that I was ugly. It wasn't until I was fourteen that I was convinced that I was even pretty. When I compare myself with the women that are down here, I will give myself credit before them."

Deidre's feelings were hurt because she thought that she never flaunted her good looks and sex appeal. She told herself that she had never looked down on anyone and had always tried to help people when she had the opportunity.

The argument resulted in J.R. refusing to show up at a meeting with Kosta to plan the details of Lisa's murder. During that time, Deidre moved into another house because Kosta had failed to pay the rent on the one she lived in. Deidre had two housemates now, a man named Larry and a girl named Shannon Simpson, who didn't like Deidre.

Deidre contacted J.R. again. He visited Deidre at the house, but this time he took a girlfriend. Deidre, Larry, Shannon, J.R., and his girlfriend were all in the living room. Deidre was sprawled on a couch reading a magazine called *Guns*. She showed J.R. a picture in the magazine.

"That's the gun Kosta's getting me," she said. "Kosta wants me to kill his wife."

J.R. was surprised that Deidre would say something like that in a roomful of people.

Days later, J.R. drove to Virginia with his brother, and it was about two weeks before Halloween when he returned. He was on the Boardwalk with his brother when Deidre saw him. Lori and Teja accompanied her. Deidre ran up, threw her arms around J.R., and gave him a kiss.

"Where have you been?"

"Virginia, to see my folks."

"Let me talk to you," Deidre said, pulling him away so that only Lori could hear what she told him. "Kosta wants to pay you ten thousand dollars."

"For what?" J.R. asked.

"For killing a lady."

"Yeah? Who am I supposed to kill?"

Deidre said that Kosta wanted to meet him the next afternoon behind Popeye's, a fast-food restaurant specializing in fried chicken.

"He wants you to shoot her in the head five or six times,"

Deidre said.

Deidre said she would give him additional details at Popeye's and bring him an untraceable gun to commit the murder.

J.R. agreed to do the job and to meet Deidre later.

Deidre and Teja left, but Lori stayed behind to tell J.R. that she had been present when Kosta and Deidre made plans to have Lisa killed. Lori told him that Kosta intended to kill the person who murdered Lisa.

"Whoever kills Lisa is going to die," Lori said. "I don't want you to be the one."

J.R. was supposed to hide behind a restaurant until Dino left Joyland to take money to the bank, then go in and kill Lisa. He was supposed to take Lisa's jewelry, rifle through some drawers to make it look like a robbery, then Kosta would step out of an office.

"Kosta's going to hand him the money," Deidre told Lori, "and when J.R. reaches out to take it, his guard will be down. That's when Kosta's going to shoot him dead."

Deidre had moved once again and now lived in an apartment. Kosta still paid all of the bills and gave her spending money. Kosta thought that the apartment provided them, with more privacy, although he still thought their telephones were bugged; they continued to use the code system when they were away from one another and needed to communicate.

Kosta drove to Deidre's apartment and told her that she needed to get a gun for J.R.

Deidre asked Lori if she knew anyone who had a .22 caliber pistol. Lori said she knew a guy who had one, but when they went to his apartment he wasn't home. Then Lori remembered someone else who had a gun and Deidre drove to that apartment. He wasn't home either, but Lori remembered that he had a shotgun, not a handgun.

Deidre telephoned Kosta to tell him about her problems and said the only firearm she might be able to get was a shotgun.

"That would be perfect," Kosta said.

"There's no way he could hide it," Deidre said. "It's too big."

"No, no. It's perfect."

Deidre and Lori renewed their search for Lori's shotgun-toting friend but couldn't find him. Deidre tried everyone that she and Deidre knew, frantically trying to find any kind of gun. She wasn't particular any longer. But in spite of her efforts, she came up empty-handed. Finally, Lori and Teja accompanied her to a Pic 'n' Save store where Deidre bought a plastic Uzi machine pistol, a toy handgun, and a kitchen knife with an eighteen-inch blade.

Deidre, having been unsuccessful in acquiring a gun, had improvised. Her plan was to have J.R. use one of the toy guns to force his way into Lisa's office at Joyland, then stab her to death. The plan collapsed when J.R. didn't show up to get the knife and the details. Deidre didn't know that Lori had warned J.R. that Kosta intended to kill him. Deidre relayed the bad news to Kosta.

"Damn it!," Kosta said. "You'll have to get somebody else."

"I don't know who to get."

"Get somebody expendable."

Deidre thought of Matthew Chumbley. Kosta said Chumbley would be perfect because he had no home, no job, and no relatives in Daytona Beach. Chumbley also had a criminal record. Kosta didn't think the police would think much about Chumbley's death, especially while committing a "robbery." Kosta told Deidre to get in touch with Chumbley and proceed with the plan that same day.

"That's too soon," Deidre protested.

"I want her dead today," Kosta said.

Deidre told Lori that Kosta wanted her to get Chumbley to kill Lisa. They went back to the Boardwalk and looked but couldn't find him. Deidre became frantic. Telling Kosta that she had failed again scared Deidre, and she was relieved when she finally located Chumbley. But it was too late to kill Lisa that day.

Deidre, who knew that Kosta had already approached Chumbley about a proposed hit, talked briefly to him on the Boardwalk.

"Do you want to make ten thousand dollars?" she asked.

"Who do I have to kill?"

"Well, it might be a lady," Deidre said. "I can't tell you right now. I have to talk to somebody first."

"What gives you the idea that I would do anything like that?"

"Because you've tried to buy guns before."

"Okay, I'll do it."

Deidre told him to meet her at nine p.m. at the Great Barrier Reef, then she contacted Kosta. Kosta agreed to hire Chumbley and said the plan would be the same as it had been for J.R. But this time, Kosta said he would provide Chumbley with a .38 caliber pistol.

Deidre met Chumbley at the Great Barrier Reef Pub. They both got a beer and Chumbley ordered something to eat after they sat down at a booth.

"You can make ten thousand dollars a week by killing people," Deidre told him.

"What are you talking about?"

"Kosta has a Hunter-Killer Club," Deidre said. "It's a group of professional assassins."

Deidre explained how a person could become a member of the group.

"It's mostly political assassinations," Deidre said. "People very high up in the government are involved. Even if you get caught, the most you can get is three or

131

five years."

Chumbley thought that the Hunter-Killer Club sounded glamorous. She told him how she had taken the first step to gaining acceptance by killing Ramsey.

"Nobody liked Kevin, anyway," Deidre said. "You never hear anybody say anything good about him. They say he's gay and alcoholic—just no good."

The idea of making big money appealed to Chumbley. They both drank a lot of beer as they talked and got pretty drunk.

"I've got half a million dollars in a Swiss bank account," Deidre said as the beer loosened her tongue and fired her imagination. "Kosta put it there for me."

They drank and talked some more.

"Kosta thinks our phones are tapped," Deidre said. "We have to talk from phone booths."

"Well, what's this deal?"

Deidre said she would give him a .38 caliber pistol to use in the murder when she met him the next day at one p.m.

"What's the deal?" he asked again.

"You have to go to a business on the south side of the Boardwalk," Deidre said. "There will be a lady there. Kill her. You have to shoot her. A guy will come out of the restroom and give you ten thousand dollars. You shoot that person in the shoulder so it won't look like he was in on it."

Deidre was vague about where the shootings would take place and who he was supposed to kill, but Chumbley figured out that the victim would be Lisa and that the murder would take place at Joyland.

"Is Kosta the one coming out of the restroom?" he asked.

"Yes," Deidre said. She gave him a glazed look. "You can kill him if you want to. I don't care."

Chumbley knew about Deidre's affair with Kosta and

132

thought she was just trying to look tough by showing that she didn't care if Kosta was killed, too. He knew she didn't really mean it because without Kosta she had nothing.

Chumbley wanted the ten thousand dollars, and he had a vision about what he would do with it. He intended to spend it all on crack cocaine, go up on the Boardwalk pier, and play Santa Claus by "throwing it to all of the peons" down below.

Deidre told Chumbley once more that she would give him a gun that was untraceable.

"I want a silencer," Chumbley said.

"That's too hard. I'd have to dig it up."

"Out of the ground?"

Deidre just grunted and kept talking. Chumbley's hunch that she was faking her indifference about Kosta's death proved to be true.

"You're only supposed to kill the lady," she told him. "Just wound Kosta in the arm to make it look like he tried to stop it."

Deidre told Chumbley she could record the killing on videotape if he wanted to start the process of becoming a member of Kosta's Hunter-Killer Club. Chumbley thought she was out of her mind.

"I didn't think she was for real," he said.

Chumbley had mixed feelings about the Hunter-Killer Club, but he had a strong interest in killing Lisa for ten thousand dollars.

"I want the money before I kill the lady," he said. "I want to see the money on the counter when I walk in. I won't do it unless I have the money first. I want to see the money when I walk in."

Deidre contacted Kosta, who told her it wouldn't be a problem. He said there would be stacks of paper covered with counterfeit to make it look like the money was on display when Chumbley walked into Joyland. It wouldn't matter if he used good currency anyhow, he said, since he

133

intended to kill Chumbley before he got the money.

Deidre reported back to Chumbley and told him the money would be stacked up on a table where he could see it when he went into Joyland to kill Lisa. They agreed to meet the next day with Kosta and fine-tune the plan.

"I really wanted to do it," he said.

In the meantime, Chumbley was broke and tried to burglarize a house. He was caught that same night and was in jail when he was supposed to see Kosta and Deidre the next day.

15

Deidre didn't know that Chumbley had been arrested, and spent several hours looking for him when he didn't show up for their appointment. Finally, Deidre abandoned her search. She met Lori and Teja, dropped both of them off at her apartment, then called Kosta from a telephone booth. She spoke a numerical code and they both hung up. A short while later, the telephone rang and Deidre answered.

She told Kosta that she hadn't been able to find Chumbley and couldn't think of anyone else.

Kosta told her that Chumbley had been arrested for burglary, but that didn't change his mind about having Lisa killed. The only question was who was going to do it.

"I want her dead today," Kosta said. "What about Teja?"

Deidre told him that Teja might do it, but the plan would have to be changed if Teja agreed. Teja couldn't be killed, Deidre said, because she didn't want to upset Lori, who was her best friend and sometime lover. Kosta said he understood, and assured her that Teja wouldn't be hurt. In fact, Kosta said, he would make it a point not to be at Joyland when Teja killed Lisa.

That sounded okay to Deidre. Kosta said he would meet her at the apartment in a few minutes and would speak to Teja.

Teja had told Kosta during one of their conversations at Top Shots that he would kill someone for ten thousand dollars, but now he had serious reservations. He was an-

gry about Ramsey's murder and had been told that whoever killed Lisa was going to be killed by Kosta. Teja began to think that Deidre and Kosta were too blood-thirsty
for his taste, and he resented the blasé manner in which
Deidre talked about Ramsey's killing.

Deidre enjoyed telling the story of Ramsey's death and
said that it had been "a trip." Teja was annoyed that Lori,
who knew all about the plan to kill Ramsey, had sat calmly
in Top Shots, drinking beer with him, while Ramsey was
being murdered.

Teja had asked Deidre, "Why did you have to kill him?"
Deidre had answered, "Because he needed it."

Teja was tough and knew about guns, but he didn't have
the kind of weapons that Kosta had. Teja had pistols, but
Kosta had automatic assault rifles, hand grenades, and explosives. If it came down to a shootout with Kosta, he
would be outgunned.

Deidre drove back to her apartment, where Teja and
Lori were waiting, and told Teja that Kosta wanted to see
him.

"He's going to come talking to you next," Deidre said.
"What are you going to do? He's going to ask you to work
for him. If you don't, you'll end up like Kevin."

Teja was so afraid of Kosta, that he didn't think he had
much of a choice. But he didn't want to kill Lisa and then
have Kosta blow him away. Deidre assured him that Kosta
wouldn't hurt him because he was Lori's boyfriend. Teja
didn't think either one of them could be trusted, especially
when his life was at stake.

Kosta showed up, and the apartment seemed to fill with
a cloud of menace. He gave Teja a flat stare.

"You know about Kevin," Kosta said. "I don't know how
you know, but I know that you do. You've got two choices.
You can work for me and get paid, or you can go down the
other road."

Teja knew the "other road" Kosta referred to was the

one that Ramsey took. He said, "Man, I'm not going to get killed. I'll work for you."

"Don't leave town," Kosta said, "because I know where your family lives."

Teja's father lived in Deland, just a few miles away, and Teja was afraid Kosta would kill him if he backed down.

"You'll be my middleman and be paid from ten thousand to fifteen thousand dollars," Kosta said. "If there's a problem, I'll refer it to you, and you take care of it."

Teja agreed. He wasn't afraid of being killed the way Ramsey was "because I wouldn't be dumb enough to get in a car with somebody and go out in the woods." Teja also had his own guns, but he didn't tell Kosta or Deidre.

"I want you to kill my wife today," he told Teja. "I'll give you a gun." Kosta outlined the plan that he had previously presented to J.R. and Chumbley.

Deidre said they had not been able to get a gun but had toy guns and a kitchen knife that was two feet long. Kosta said that that would work. He then outlined the plan. Teja was to get a black jacket and a black hat, wait until Dino left for the bank, then force his way inside and stab Lisa.

"Stab her in the back, three ribs up," he said. "That punctures her diaphragm and keeps her from screaming. Then stab her two more times."

Teja was supposed to rifle the drawers and take Lisa's jewelry, then run out of Joyland into the Marriott lobby, discard the hat and jacket, and walk to the car where Deidre and Lori would be waiting for him.

"I'll pay you ten thousand dollars," Kosta said. "I want you to do it this afternoon."

Kosta left, and Deidre tried to assure Teja that nothing would happen to him after he killed Lisa. She asked him if he was willing to do it.

"Yeah, I'll do it," Teja said.

Lori spoke up: "You tell Kosta that if anything happens to Teja, I'm going to get that shotgun and kill him."

Deidre was relieved. She telephoned Kosta and told him that Teja would do the job.

"If anything happens to Teja," Deidre warned, "Lori's coming after you with a shotgun."

That afternoon, Deidre, Lori, and Teja sat in a rented car waiting for Dino to leave. Teja wore a black jacket and hat, and had the knife hidden. Dino usually left at eleven a.m. to make a bank deposit, but eleven o'clock came and went, and Dino didn't come out of Joyland. After noon, the three conspirators got nervous. The plan wouldn't work with Dino still inside.

Deidre started to drive away. "Oh shit!" she said. "How am I going to explain this to Kosta? He's going to be pissed."

After she dropped Lori and Teja at their apartment, Deidre went home and waited. The telephone rang, Kosta gave her a code and hung up. Deidre drove to the designated pay telephone and waited for it to ring.

"What happened?" Kosta asked.

"It got all fucked up," Deidre said.

Kosta was angry that things had gone wrong again.

"He was desperate to have his wife killed," Deidre recalled.

"I want that bitch dead," he said, and hung up.

Kosta's life became even more complicated. He had contracted with three people to have Lisa killed and each attempt had been botched. But in spite of all he had to lose if Lisa divorced him, he started being less secretive about his affair with Deidre. He took her to restaurants, theme parks, gun shows, and he parked his car where it could be seen when he visited her.

Tony Calderone thought Kosta was about to make a mess of things with his marriage. He still didn't believe Kosta's boasts about being Daytona's answer to John

Rambo, and he considered his affair with Deidre ridiculous. Calderone warned Kosta about it several times, but Kosta never listened. —

Deidre didn't pay any attention to Calderone's attempts to get her to break off the affair with Kosta.

"Kosta's good to me," she said.

"Why are you doing this?" he asked. "Why don't you go back to Massachusetts?"

"I couldn't do that. I've got too much to lose."

Calderone didn't know what she was talking about. Besides wanting to keep Kosta from messing up his marriage, Calderone hoped to get Deidre out of Top Shots because her stealing was cutting into his profits.

"That's one reason I was trying to split them up," Calderone said. "My primary concern was that they were screwing around and hurting the business by neglecting it, which was like dipping into my pocket. The other reason is that I didn't think they were right for each other. I hated to see Kosta throw his life away and all that he had with Lisa. I felt that Dee had a stranglehold on Kosta and all of the little derelicts that hung around the Boardwalk. I thought that if she went, they would all go."

Deidre also flaunted her sex life to Calderone. She told him that she slept around a lot. "She told me she had slept with J.R., Teja, and Lori and some other guy at the same time she was sleeping with Kosta."

"They argued a lot," Calderone said. "They were either smooching or fighting. There was no happy medium in their relationship. Kosta didn't want her sleeping with other guys behind his back."

Calderone couldn't fire Deidre, and he couldn't get Kosta to fire her. He was exasperated and confused by Kosta's bizarre behavior.

About a week before Halloween, Calderone was having dinner at home with his wife, Sheila.

"Boy, Kosta is really screwing up," he said.

"How?"

"He's screwing around with Dee Hunt," Calderone said. "He's really messing up his life."

Tony didn't mention that he had slept with Deidre, too, because he didn't want to screw up his own marriage. Sheila didn't ask any questions, and Calderone thought that was the end of it. Sheila had other ideas.

Lisa received a telephone call from Sheila Calderone on October 25. It turned Lisa's world upside down. Lisa recalled it in a deposition:

"You better start watching your husband," Sheila said. "You better put a private eye on him."

"Well, why?"

"Just do it."

"Come on, you're my friend. Tell me at least what to expect," Lisa said. "I don't want to sit across from some private eye at a brown desk and tell him to follow my husband, and have him come back and tell me this and this is going on. You're my friend. Tell me."

Sheila kept silent.

"Is he having an affair?" Lisa asked.

"Yes, he is."

"Is it somebody from Top Shots? Is it Holly?" Lisa asked. She thought it must be Holly because she thought she was a classy-looking girl.

Sheila said no.

Lisa took a guess, "Is it Deidre?"

Sheila said that it was.

Lisa telephoned Calderone and asked why Kosta would go out with Deidre.

"I don't understand it when he has somebody like you," Calderone replied.

* * *

Lisa was in the car with Kosta the next day and asked him if it was true that he was having an affair with Deidre Hunt. "He started yelling at me and screaming and saying that he can't believe that I am saying these things," Lisa said.

Lisa thought Kosta's outburst was out of the ordinary because he was usually very unemotional. He certainly wasn't unemotional about this development.

"He was screaming at me," Lisa said. She asked him who the woman was.

Kosta wanted to know who told her and assured her he wasn't having an affair.

Lisa didn't tell him who had spilled the beans, but said, "I'll believe you if you say it isn't true."

"It isn't true."

Lisa reminded Kosta that if he cheated on her, she would leave him, thus ending his free ride. Kosta reacted with more shouting.

But she wasn't convinced. "I had made up my mind. I want her out of Top Shots immediately," she told Kosta.

"I have no problem with that."

Lisa told Kosta she didn't want Deidre to know that she had anything to do with her getting fired, since she still wasn't completely sure. She wanted to give her husband the benefit of the doubt.

Lisa went to bed with strong suspicions that Sheila was telling the truth. She was going to watch him closely, but she woke up early the next morning and Kosta was already gone.

Lisa went to one of her stores, thinking that was where he might be. She found Kosta there, and they went to a Home Show together. Afterward, they went back to the store and while Lisa was talking to her brother on the telephone, Kosta disappeared. She checked outside and saw that his car wasn't there. Lisa remembered that she had seen Deidre with Peter Kouracos at Commissioner Bud

141

Asher's party. Kouracos had sort of teased her that Kosta was having an affair with Deidre, she said, and had given her an idea of where Deidre lived.

"That was when I went chasing through the rain after Kosta," Lisa recalled.

Lisa got in her car and drove off in the rain to where she thought Deidre lived. She drove up and down the street without spotting her husband, then she saw Kosta's car pull out of one of the apartments, and she started following him.

Kosta tried to get away. They had a high-speed chase down side streets until Lisa almost had a wreck. She then decided to return to Joyland in the hopes that Kosta would show up eventually.

Lisa was a nervous wreck when she got back to Joyland. Kosta arrived about thirty minutes later.

Lisa asked, "What are you going to say to me now — that it is not true, after I saw you come out of her place?"

Kosta said, "No, it's not true."

"Come on, you're not going to deny it again?"

"Remember the stuff I was burying in the woods? I was looking for it. Remember?"

"Yes."

"Well, I lost all of that stuff and so I went and rented a metal detector," Kosta said. "I left early this morning to look for it. Come here and I will show you."

He took Lisa to his car and opened the trunk to show her a metal detector. He said that Deidre had it, and he had gone to her apartment to get it.

Lisa went back inside Joyland, yelling at him. "I don't believe you!"

Kosta said, "I'm doing it for us, baby."

Kosta said he would prove it to her. He telephoned Deidre's apartment.

"My wife thinks we're having an affair," he said. "I'm calling to explain that we aren't."

He gave the telephone to Lisa.

"I explained to her that employees are a dime a dozen," Lisa said. "She's got to know where I'm coming from, that I'm trying to save my marriage."

Deidre said, "Well, yeah. I don't blame you."

After that, Lisa started behaving in a way that was unnatural for her—she stuck to Kosta like glue. If he said he was going to the 7-Eleven store, she would say, okay, I'll go with you. Her attempts were fruitless, however. She was far too busy at work to be around Kosta all the time.

16

On Halloween, Kosta, Deidre, and Teja talked about killing Lisa. Lori was present but took no part in the discussion. Kosta was even more desperate than before to have Lisa murdered because she had learned of his affair with Deidre. If he didn't act before Lisa divorced him, he would be out in the cold.

In just a few days, Teja said Kosta talked with him almost ten times about killing his wife. Kosta had Teja accompany him when he drove to Daytona Beach Shores to deposit boxes of quarters in Joyland's safe at a branch bank.

Teja saw boxes of quarters stacked up in Joyland's safe-deposit area, but he was more impressed when Kosta took him into a room the size of a walk-in closet. The room was filled with stacks of five, ten, twenty, fifty, and one hundred dollar bills.

Kosta didn't tell Teja who the money belonged to but left him with the impression that it was his. Earlier on the trip over Kosta had opened the trunk of his car and showed Teja a briefcase filled with money.

"This is ten thousand dollars," Kosta told him. "I have it with me all the time. You can have this kind of money if you play the right game."

Teja was impressed with the money. He said that he and Kosta stopped to eat lunch at a fast-food seafood restaurant. Kosta gave him instructions on how to kill Lisa that night at a Halloween party at Razzles, a nightclub on Seabreeze Boulevard about two blocks from the Atlantic Ocean.

He told Teja to wait until Lisa had to go to the bathroom, then repeated his directions for using the knife: stab her in the back, three ribs up so she couldn't scream, then stab her two more times and sit her down in a chair; position her with her head down so that people would think that she has passed out drunk.

At the bank, Kosta let Teja look at all of the money, then took him to a teller's window where he conducted some business. Teja was impressed by the television security.

"Man, it would be impossible for a guy to bring a gun in here," he said.

The clerk said, "Yes, it would."

Kosta whipped his gun out of his shoulder holster, causing the clerk to lose her color.

"No, it wouldn't," he said, then holstered the gun.

Back at Deidre's apartment, Kosta outlined the plans to kill Lisa once more. Deidre and Lori heard them.

Kosta said he thought that Lisa had a private detective following him.

"I want it done tonight," Kosta said.

That same day, Deidre, Lori, and Teja drove to a pawn shop in New Smyrna Beach where Deidre bought a .22 caliber semiautomatic pistol with money Kosta had given her. Kosta wanted the gun to use in a backup attempt if Teja failed to kill Lisa at Razzles. Teja wasn't about to shoot Kosta's wife

145

in front of a few hundred witnesses.

Later, Deidre gave Teja the knife she had purchased at Pic 'n' Save and reiterated instructions on how he was to kill Lisa at Razzles. Deidre was on the telephone with Kosta and was relaying instructions. Teja said he couldn't understand Deidre so he took the phone and talked directly to Kosta.

The plan was still the same. "I was supposed to stab her three ribs up from behind, stab her once more, pull it out, stab her again one rib down, turn it, and bring it out," Teja said. "That would stop all talking, all screaming, all breathing, movements and all."

"Just sit her in a chair, fold her arms in front of her, and lean her head down so she looks drunk," Kosta reiterated.

By now, Teja had heard it so often he could have done it in his sleep.

The Halloween party at Razzles was jammed with about four hundred people. Commissioner Bud Asher and his wife were there. Lisa wore a cowgirl outfit with boots, skirt, and checkered shirt. Kosta wore a black robe and a mask but kept the mask off most of the time. Deidre and Lori arrived with Teja, who carried the kitchen knife draped under a rag so that it couldn't be seen.

Lisa and Deidre caught one another's eye, and Deidre went into another room with Lori and Teja. Lisa was upset about seeing Deidre and was bothered because Kosta didn't stay around her very much.

Lisa said that Kosta wandered far away from her, which was unusual. He wasn't visiting with friends, just roaming around, staying away from her. She went up to him.

146

"Why are you keeping away from me?" she asked. "Why don't you come sit with me? I am your wife."

"I'm trying to win a prize and the judges are up front," Kosta said. "I want the judges to see me."

Teja intended to kill Lisa. To him, it seemed like now or never, or he would be killed himself. He managed to move close to Lisa and hovered there for about ten minutes trying to get up enough nerve to stab her. Once she started toward the ladies' room where he was supposed to kill her, but Teja lost his nerve and walked over to Deidre and Lori.

"Man, I can't do this," he said. "There's too many people watching me."

Deidre said, "I need some money. Go to the bathroom. Kosta's going to follow you, and he's going to give you some money for me."

Teja was worried about going into the bathroom. He was afraid of Kosta. Kosta might kill him in there, he thought.

Kosta gave him forty dollars to give to Deidre and told him again to kill Lisa. He said that he already had a check for ten thousand dollars made out in Teja's name.

Teja gave Deidre the money from Kosta when he left the bathroom. He ordered a beer and saw Kosta about thirty feet away on the dance floor. He looked at all the hundreds of people, and at Deidre and Lori.

"Man, I just can't do this," he said for the second time.

"Oh shit," Deidre said. "Kosta's going to be mad. Oh fuck. Wait right here, I got to talk to him."

Deidre caught Kosta's attention, and he started toward her. This caught Lisa off guard. Kosta wanted to go to the bathroom in the room that Deidre was

147

in, which was farther away than the rest room where they were. Lisa didn't see Deidre, but she knew Deidre was there, and she was suspicious.

"I'm going to the bathroom," Kosta said and started toward the restroom where Deidre was.

"Why don't you go to this bathroom?" Lisa asked. "It's closer."

"No, I want to go to that one."

Kosta headed toward the other bathroom, leaving Lisa bewildered and suspicious.

Teja didn't see where Deidre went but he saw Kosta go into the men's room and went after him. He walked inside, and one of his friends was standing guard outside a closed stall.

"What are you standing there for?" Teja asked.

"Kosta and Deidre's in there."

Then Kosta and Deidre opened the door and came out of the stall.

"What are you guys doing in the bathroom?" Teja asked.

"Don't worry about tonight," Kosta said. "I'll call you tomorrow between eight-thirty and nine."

Kosta went back to the party, but Deidre, Lori, and Teja left in a car Deidre had rented with money Kosta gave her. Deidre had only driven a little way when she got scared. She stopped at a dumpster, wiped the knife so it wouldn't show fingerprints, then threw it away.

"I don't want to get stopped for a traffic violation and have that knife," she explained. "It's pretty obvious we intend to kill somebody with it."

That night, after they had arrived home, Kosta told Lisa that he was going to get up early and be at the shooting range all day.

"Don't make any plans for me," he said.

It was unusual for Kosta to do anything like that, but Kosta was acting strange. Lisa went to sleep.

17

On November 1, instead of going to the shooting range as he had told Lisa, Kosta met Teja behind the Texan Motel on the beach. Teja had driven there with Lori. Kosta got in the car and immediately ducked down.

"What's going on?" Teja asked.

"My wife has a private investigator after me."

They drove to Deidre's apartment where Kosta outlined a plan to kill Lisa at Joyland. It was the same plan that Deidre and Kosta had given to Teja the day before.

Then Deidre and Kosta went into the bedroom and had sex. Teja thought of it as "their little fancy." Teja and Kosta rode back to the Boardwalk with Deidre, but Lori stayed behind. Kosta gave instructions on where Deidre was to drive and pointed things out to Teja.

He showed Kosta where Dino and Lisa parked their cars, and told him when Dino left for the bank. That was when Teja was supposed to go in and kill Lisa. Deidre would park behind Hog Heaven so Teja could see Lisa arrive and Dino leave.

Kosta had Deidre drive through the route he had shown her, park behind Hog Heaven, then drive to Atlantic Avenue, where she would pick up Teja after the murder.

"We more or less went through a dress rehearsal," Teja said.

Kosta told Teja to get Lisa to open the door to the office, hit her in the face with a right cross to knock her back, then shoot her. He told him to be sure and rip Lisa's jewelry off because it was good Greek gold, and he wanted it. The low caliber gun, Kosta told him, wouldn't be heard outside Lisa's office.

The .22 caliber semiautomatic pistol Deidre had brought for him to use jammed after the first shot. Teja had said he would fix it, but couldn't because he didn't have a file that was small enough. Nevertheless, this was the gun he intended to use to shoot Lisa.

Deidre and Lori were both in the car that afternoon at Hog Heaven. They arrived about one-thirty p.m. and waited for Dino to leave and Lisa to come to work. This time Dino and Lisa went through their anticipated schedule. At two-thirty p.m. Teja hid the gun in the pocket of his jacket, got out of the car, walked through the parking lot, crossed Atlantic Boulevard, trudged up the dirt mound at Joyland, then went down the steps and entered Joyland's game room.

Teja knew the layout of Joyland from having worked there. Instead of going to the office where he knew Lisa was, he sat down and started to play a video game where he was a pilot trying to shoot down jet planes.

He was thinking, how can I get out of this? He then went to the bathroom to make sure Kosta wasn't waiting there to step out and kill him, and to take the clip out of the gun. He put the clip in his pocket. There was one bullet in the firing chamber, which was all the gun could accommodate without jamming whether it had a full clip or not.

Teja stuck the gun in his waistband and pulled the football jersey he was wearing over it. He went back

151

and started playing video games again because there was a man hanging around the door to Lisa's office.

When Lisa arrived at Joyland she noticed that the pistol Kosta had given her for protection was missing from her desk drawer. She assumed that he must have taken it to the shooting range.

The man near Lisa's office door left. Teja stopped playing, walked to Lisa's office, and knocked on the door. Lisa opened it. Teja put a hand on the doorjamb in case Lisa tried to run out and said, "Is Kosta here?"

"No," Lisa said.

"Do you know what time he's coming back? I'm supposed to talk to him about a job."

"No, what is it you want?"

Teja said that Lisa noticed the gun in his waistband, looked back up at him, and cringed. She was obviously scared. Teja pulled the gun out and pointed it at her.

"Get back in the office," he ordered.

"No, no, no, no," Lisa said. She was panic-stricken. Suddenly she was on the floor, scrambling between Teja's legs.

"Get up, bitch!" Teja said. "You're going to die."

Lisa got to her feet.

"Get back in the office!" Teja ordered.

Lisa said, "No, *you* get back in the office."

Teja cocked the gun and aimed at her. Lisa ran off through an arcade to a restaurant her aunt had in the Marriott.

Teja put the gun back in his jacket, left Joyland, and went into the Marriott. He discarded the jacket and baseball cap and tried to appear nonchalant. He

152

stopped and talked to a friend, then walked out the Atlantic Avenue exit to meet Deidre. Deidre wasn't there. Finally Teja saw her driving the car back and forth on Atlantic Avenue. Teja hid between two houses and waited until he saw Deidre come back again, then ran out and flagged her down. He got into the car with her and Lori.

"So how did it go?" Deidre asked. "Is she dead? How many times did you shoot her?"

"I didn't kill her," Teja said. "She got away."

"Oh, shit. Now Kosta's *really* going to be mad."

Deidre drove to her apartment and immediately threw herself on the floor and started to beat it with her fists and feet, like a child having a tantrum, screaming at the top of her lungs.

"He's going to make me do it!" Deidre screamed. "Now I'm going to have to kill Lisa!"

In a little while, Kosta telephoned and Deidre answered. "Is she dead yet?" he asked. "How did it go?"

"She—she's not dead," Deidre said. "She got away."

"Oh, shit! Oh, shit!" Kosta said. "I got to deal with this. Now how am I going to deal with this? Put Teja on."

Teja took the telephone.

"You go home and stay there," he ordered. "Don't leave your house until I call you."

Teja took off. He was worried about being picked up by the police and charged with attempted armed robbery.

Deidre had met Bryan Chase, the eighteen-year-old farm boy from Ohio, who was trying to become part of the Boardwalk crowd. At first, Chase stayed with his father, then moved in with Robin Berghdorff for a

153

while after Ramsey disappeared.

"Everybody liked Bryan," Robin said. "He wouldn't hurt a flea. He was just a great big teddy bear."

That was before Deidre seduced him, and he started to hang around with J.R. and other regulars on the Boardwalk. Shannon Simpson and J.R. stayed for a little while at Bryan's apartment when he moved away from Robin.

"Bryan liked everybody," Shannon said. "He was the type that was real shy. He couldn't get a girlfriend."

"I slept with Deidre," Bryan bragged one time.

"Be careful," Shannon said. "I don't like her."

"Oh, she really likes me," Bryan answered. "She wants to come over."

In just a short time, Bryan tried to shed his gentle image and imitate J.R.'s macho attitude. He tried to act tough.

"He got on my nerves because he was acting weird," Shannon said. "He tried to act like J.R. J.R. would be going on, 'Oh, baby, you're so fine.' Then Bryan would do it."

Following Teja's failure, Deidre suggested that Bryan kill Lisa. Kosta still insisted on having Lisa killed that same day. He came up with a plan. Bryan was to park his car outside Joyland and wait for Lisa to leave. Kosta would drive his car and Lisa would follow in hers. Once Lisa was in traffic, Bryan was to intentionally ram into her, get out and walk to her car as if to apologize for the accident, and shoot her in the head as many times as he could.

Deidre took the plan to Bryan, and he agreed to kill Lisa for five thousand dollars.

"Once you agree to this, there's no backing out,"

Deidre told him. "You've got to go through with it."

Bryan said, "Okay."

At her aunt's restaurant, Lisa called the police about the attempted armed robbery and tried to reach Kosta at the shooting range. There was no telephone number that she could find. Lisa stayed at her aunt's restaurant for a while then went back to work at Joyland. Kosta came back about four p.m.

Lisa told him what had happened and Kosta looked puzzled. "Like, 'You poor thing,' " Lisa said.

She tried to describe the man who had attacked her and wondered if Kosta might know who it was. He said he didn't.

Later that evening, two police officers came to the office. Lisa was "really shook up" over what had happened. She was scared. The policemen, who normally patrolled the area, stopped in to talk with her and to see how she was feeling. She described the man to them, and they told her it sounded like Teja James.

Kosta wasn't there and didn't hear Teja's name mentioned. He left Lisa alone at Joyland, and she didn't think that he was too concerned about her.

At that moment, Kosta was talking with Deidre, working out an alternate plan in case Bryan somehow failed to kill Lisa during the "accident." If that happened, Bryan was supposed to wait until three a.m., then break into the house and shoot Lisa in the head while she was asleep. He gave details of how Bryan should break in. Kosta said he would be lying awake with a gun in his hand, and after Bryan shot Lisa with the .22 caliber pistol, he would kill Bryan.

"I'll come out of it looking like a hero," Kosta said.

Deidre and Lori talked with Bryan on the Boardwalk, and Deidre outlined the second plan to him, omitting the part about him getting killed. Deidre told him to break into a window on the second floor and walk to Lisa's bedroom at the end of the hall on the second floor.

She gave Bryan the .22 caliber pistol and told him to shoot Lisa in the back of the head five or six times, then meet her at Krystal's.

Bryan said he would do it.

Lisa was very scared when it was time to leave Joyland. She usually drove home by herself around eight or nine p.m.

"I was scared that night, and I didn't want to go home to an empty house because my mother was out and so was my brother," Lisa said.

Kosta had returned, and she told him how scared she was.

"Why don't we go get a video?" he asked.

Lisa thought that was a good idea, but she was too scared to go from her car to her house by herself. Ordinarily, Kosta didn't escort her home, but this time he suggested that she follow him. They would get the video and then drive home.

Lisa started to follow Kosta, but he took a strange route. The video store they patronized was easy to get to from Joyland, the route having no turns or back streets. But Kosta drove down a few side streets and came to several traffic lights where they had to stop. There were more turns and more stoplights.

"I was following him, and he was turning and going and stuff like that," Lisa said. "I felt like I was being followed, and I was very, very scared."

Lisa thought the same car was behind her all of the

156

time but at a distance. She was so scared that she took a gun she carried in the glove compartment and put it on the seat beside her. When they arrived at the video store, she told Kosta.

"Kosta, I feel like I'm being followed."

He laughed at her. "Oh, you're just being silly."

But when they left the video store and headed home, Lisa still felt like she was being followed.

Bryan Chase met Deidre and Lori at Krystal's. Bryan told her that he had had car trouble and couldn't catch up with Lisa.

"Then you're going to have to go there tonight and do it," Deidre said.

Deidre was furious that Bryan had failed to kill Lisa.

Bryan had time to kill and met J.R. on the Board-walk. He told J.R. that he was going to make five thousand dollars by killing Kosta's wife.

"Man, it's a setup," J.R. told him. "No one who kills Lisa is going to leave the room alive."

"What?"

"Kosta and Deidre made me the same offer," J.R. said. "Lori told me that Kosta's going to kill the guy who kills his wife."

Bryan left J.R. and ambled about. He was afraid that Kosta would kill him if he didn't kill Lisa, and afraid that Kosta would kill him if he did. He wandered around near Krystal's and bumped into Lori.

"I'm going to shoot Lisa in the head, and Kosta's going to jump up and blow my brains out," he told her.

Lori reported to Deidre, who said, "Oh, shit! How

157

did he find out?"

Deidre and Lori looked for Bryan and told him that he had to do it.

"You don't have a choice," Deidre said. "You kill Lisa and get five thousand dollars, or Kosta's going to come after you."

18

When they got home that night, Lisa heard Kosta banging around outside and on the lower floor. The house had three floors, with the main living area on the second floor. The lower floor was the basement and game room where Kosta spent a lot of time making bullets. Their bedroom was on the top floor.

"I heard a lot of racket coming from downstairs," she said. "He was going up and down the stairs, so I went downstairs."

Lisa noticed that the sliding glass door was open, and there was a lot of noise coming from the barbecue area. She looked out and saw Kosta there.

"What are you doing?" she asked.

Kosta told her that he was burying something.

Kosta was always burying things in the woods, but it was unusual for him to bury things around the house.

"Well, hurry up, because I want to watch the movie," Lisa told him.

When they settled down to watch the movie, Lisa's mind wasn't on it. She was still scared about what had happened at Joyland, and she was aggravated about Kosta's affair with Deidre.

Lisa had pretty much made up her mind that she was going to leave Kosta.

"Did you ever go to her apartment?" she asked. "Did you ever take her home?"

159

"I took her to Waves maybe once," Kosta said. He was angry at her for continuing to bring it up. "But I never went with her alone. Her best friends, Lori and Teja, were always with us."

Lisa had seen Lori, but she didn't know who Teja was. She told Kosta that.

"You know Teja," he said. "He's a black guy that's Lori's best friend."

"Well, I don't know him."

Lisa kept talking about a divorce, and Kosta stayed angry. He suggested that they drive down to the Keys on November 4 to meet her cousins. That would give them a chance to get away from things for a while.

Kosta said he would rent a boat, and the two of them would go out on the water. Lisa did not scuba dive or snorkel.

"He was going to go scuba diving or snorkeling or something like that," she said, "and I was supposed to sit on the boat."

Lisa planned to make the trip with Kosta but she still intended to get a divorce.

"You know," Kosta said, when he and Lisa finished watching the movie. "Teja might send his friend over to kill you."

"Why would he do that?"

"So you couldn't identify him."

Lisa didn't think that made sense. Why would a guy facing a charge of armed robbery commit murder so she couldn't testify against him? Why risk the electric chair to protect yourself from a year or two in prison?

"What are you, crazy?" Lisa asked.

"I'm just telling you what I would do," Kosta answered.

The thought frightened Lisa because she didn't know how criminal minds worked. Maybe what Kosta said made sense.

"What are you trying to do?" she asked him. "Scare the hell out of me?"

They stopped arguing and went to bed. Lisa was very scared, but managed to fall asleep. Kosta lay awake holding a pistol, waiting to kill Chase after Chase killed his wife.

Bryan Chase was having trouble breaking into the house. The house had a deep backyard that led down to the river, so he had time and privacy. But the window that he tried to break into wouldn't budge.

He kicked it and punched it and nothing happened. Finally he gave up and went to Krystal's where Deidre and Lori were waiting.

"Did you do it?" Deidre asked.

"I couldn't get in," Chase said. "The window wouldn't break."

"Damn!" Deidre said.

They went to the parking lot and Deidre listened while Chase gave her excuses as to why he hadn't killed Lisa. Deidre was having none of it.

"She was really mad," Lori said. "Here he was supposed to be getting himself killed, and he showed up at Krystal's."

The more Chase balked, the angrier Deidre became.

"You've got to go back and do it," Deidre told him. "If you don't, Kosta's going to kill you."

It was about four a.m. when Chase returned and tried to break into the house again. He had no more luck than he had on the previous attempt. A neighbor's lights went on and dogs started to bark. Chase fled.

The next day Kosta and Deidre talked on the telephone.

"What happened?" Kosta said. "I heard him trying to get in. I was so mad I almost kicked a window out myself."

"He couldn't break through the plexiglass," Deidre said.

"Get him an Exacto knife," Kosta said. "That ought to do it."

Deidre and Lori bought an Exacto knife and a glass cutter and took them to Chase. Deidre told him that it should cut through the plexiglass. Deidre emphasized that Chase had no choice but to do it.

Deidre and Lori drove off, then Deidre remembered that she had forgotten to tell Chase something. She drove back and they found Chase outside of his apartment throwing up.

That same day, Detective William Adamy and two other police officers from the Daytona Beach Police Department met Lisa at Joyland to have her look through a mug book showing the faces of people who had been arrested in the area. None of the photographs had names under them.

Lisa had no trouble identifying the man who had attacked her the day before.

Lisa turned to Kosta. "That's Teja. Isn't that Teja?"

She remembered the previous day that two police officers said the attacker she'd described sounded like Teja.

Instead of answering her, Kosta gave her what Lisa described as a "huffy" look and walked away without answering.

A while later they had to go to Edgewater, which is

about a ninety-minute drive each way. Kosta was behind the wheel. Lisa was wound up about the attempted robbery and her husband's affair with Deidre. They started to argue about Top Shots, but Lisa said they were really arguing about Kosta's affair.

They argued all the way to Edgewater, took care of business, then started to argue on the way back. Then Lisa suddenly realized that Kosta had told her that it was Teja James who had attempted to rob her. She remembered that Kosta wasn't present when the police officers said that the attacker sounded like Teja and that no name had been mentioned when she picked Teja's picture out of the police mug book.

Lisa told him that she was really scared about what happened with Teja. She had been doing business on the Boardwalk for years and nothing like this had ever happened to her. Lisa related Teja's attempt to Kosta's affair with Deidre.

"You can't tell me that Deidre didn't know Teja came to rob me," she said.

Kosta just shrugged.

"You don't think that Teja would try to hurt me, do you?"

Kosta said, "Yeah. I think so."

"Why do you think that?"

"If I was the one to come after you," Kosta said, "I would kill you."

"That doesn't make sense."

"Then you couldn't identify him," Kosta said.

Suddenly Lisa was afraid that Kosta might be trying to have her killed. She remembered the warning that Bill and Barbara passed on to her brother Dino.

Lisa was terribly frightened. She looked at Kosta, who had taken his gun out of the shoulder holster, and was toying with it. The gun made

163

metallic clicks as Kosta played with it.

"Kosta, if you're behind this," she begged, "please don't kill me."

"Why would I do that?"

"To get my life insurance."

"Oh, I could get more out of you if I stayed with you."

"Yes, but I'm not staying with you. I'm going to leave you."

"Yeah, but if you were dead, I'd get everything."

Kosta made a sudden movement with the gun, and Lisa jumped in terror.

"What are you going to do?" she asked.

"I'm adjusting the mirror. What do you think, that I was going to shoot you?"

"I don't know. I'm scared."

"I wouldn't shoot you here," Kosta said. "It would dirty my car. You ought to know me better than that."

Kosta got back in touch with Deidre.

"Tell him he's got to come back to the house and finish the job while Lisa's asleep," he told her. "I'll leave a light on in the basement. Tell him to break in down there."

Deidre said that she would pass the information on to Bryan.

When Deidre found Bryan, he looked scared.

"Do you still have that little gun I gave you?"

Bryan said yes.

"Kosta's going to leave a light on for you," she said, then went on to explain what he was supposed to do. She told him once more how the house was laid out and where Lisa's bedroom was.

"Be sure to shoot her in the back of the head," she

told him. "That part of the brain controls everything. That way, you can be sure she's dead."

That night Peter Kouracos went to Joyland to see Kosta and Lisa. Kouracos no longer liked going to Top Shots because of the clientele. Kouracos had been to Jacksonville all day taking tests which related to law school entrance exams. He had stopped to eat on the way home but when he arrived in Daytona Beach he was still "strung out."

Kosta wasn't at Joyland, but Lisa was. She told him that Sheila Calderone had told him that Kosta was having an affair with Deidre. Then Lisa talked about the robbery attempt and that she suspected that Kosta was behind it.

"She told me that she said, 'If you're behind this, Kosta, please don't kill me.' "

Kouracos told her he didn't believe that Kosta was trying to have her killed. Kouracos recalled his past dates with Deidre and how he thought of her as a gold digger.

"I had a sneaking suspicion that Deidre was interested in Kosta," he said. "I thought that if she's a gold digger thinking she can hang in there, I've got to help Lisa get rid of her.

"I told her, 'There's no way, if anything happens to the marriage, there's no way that Kosta's going to come out owning Joyland and all the assets.' "

They talked a little about the Greek Festival that started that day and lasted for a week. It was a bittersweet time for Lisa: her father had died during the festival several years before, and now she had problems with her marriage.

Lisa invited Kouracos to come to the house and

watch a video. They left Joyland and arrived at Lisa's house about ten-thirty p.m., and Kosta arrived a few minutes later. It was Friday, November 3. Lisa cooked for them.

Kouracos had a large library of videotape movies, but they had seen most of them and decided to rent one at the video store. Kosta volunteered to go. Kouracos said he would go, too.

"I don't want him going to pick out the movie," he told Lisa, "because we'll both hate it."

Kouracos and Kosta drove to the video store and looked around for about half an hour, but they couldn't find a movie that Kouracos liked. They went home, ate, and watched cable television.

The evening wore on, and Kouracos fell asleep in a reclining chair. Both he and Kosta were carrying handguns. It was about two-thirty a.m. on Saturday, November 4, when Kouracos woke up.

"Hey, guys, I got to go," he said.

It was unusual for Kouracos to be the first one to leave the room. Ordinarily, Kosta went upstairs to bed first while he and Lisa sat up for a while and talked.

Lisa and Kosta went upstairs to bed. The bedroom was dimly lit from the light of the aquarium. Lisa fell asleep, but Kosta waited for Bryan Chase.

Chase went back to the house that night and still couldn't get in. The Exacto knife didn't work, and he heard a neighbor shouting. Chase left and drove back to Krystal's where Deidre and Lori waited. Deidre was so angry she seemed close to apoplexy.

They went into the parking lot where she screamed at Chase.

Lori said Deidre was angry for two reasons: she was

166

afraid Kosta would be mad at her and afraid that he might tell her she had to do the job herself.

"Deidre really didn't want to kill Lisa," Lori said. "She was afraid to kill Lisa. At that point, I think she wanted to back out, but it was too late."

"You have to go back," Deidre told Chase.

Chase protested that it was already four a.m.

"It has to be done today," Deidre said.

Chase agreed to go back, but Deidre didn't trust him. She and Lori got in a car and followed him just to make sure. Chase parked his car on a street a block east of Lisa's house, and Deidre drove around to make sure that he did what he was supposed to. When Chase disappeared behind the house, Deidre drove to a side street where she could keep an eye on Chase's car and parked.

19

Dino Paspalakis arrived home about one-thirty a.m. on Saturday. Lisa, Kosta, and Kouracos were in the living room watching television when he went to his upstairs bedroom to see a movie on HBO before he fell asleep.

Dino was suffering from a bad cold and woke up around four a.m. with a sore throat. He went to the second floor to get a glass of milk from the refrigerator and noticed that the stairway light was on in the basement. At first, Dino thought Kosta was up making bullets, but when he checked, the room was empty. Dino turned the light off, took two aspirins with his milk, and went back to bed.

About fifteen or twenty minutes later he heard a series of explosions that sounded like a string of ladyfinger firecrackers going off. Dino went to the hallway and called out, "What's going on?"

"Call 911," Kosta said.

Kosta spoke in a normal tone of voice and didn't act as if anything out of the ordinary had happened. From Kosta's demeanor, Dino didn't think it was a serious situation, and it occurred to him that somebody might be shooting at the house from outside.

He started to dial Emergency Rescue and asked Kosta, "How's Lisa?"

"She's been shot."

Dino dropped the telephone and ran into the bedroom. He saw Lisa on the bed, and it looked as if she was trying to say something. Dino realized that he had not completed the 911 call and reported the shooting. At first he didn't notice the body of a young man on the floor.

Mary Paspalakis ran into the room and saw that her daughter had been shot. She panicked. She kept thinking that she had lost her husband during the Festival, and now she was losing her daughter. Mary was almost hysterical, weeping, and saying, "No, no, no."

Just a few minutes earlier, Bryan Chase had broken into a first-floor window and entered the basement. A stairway light was on. Following the instructions he had been given, Chase crept up the basement steps, then went to the third floor. He walked softly down the hallway and entered Kosta and Lisa's bedroom, which was eerily lighted by a dim bulb in an aquarium. Chase stood over Lisa and pointed the .22 caliber pistol at Lisa's head and fired.

Kosta lay still as Chase slipped into the room and watched him point the gun at Lisa's head and pull the trigger. The .22 made a loud pop. Kosta waited a few seconds for Chase to fire two more shots, but the gun had apparently jammed. Chase tried to clear the weapon to shoot again, but said "Fuck it," and started toward the door.

At that point, Kosta got up and rapidly fired six or seven shots at Chase. Chase went down, and Kosta went to him and fired a bullet into his head to make sure he was dead.

* * *

Lisa was sleeping when she heard a noise that woke her up. Her head hurt. The first thought that went through her mind was dreamlike, and she thought of a judge banging a gavel. *Boom. Boom. Boom.* She didn't know how many *Booms* there were, but she thought, *I wish he'd stop because my head is hurting,* and then she opened her eyes.

Kosta was beside her in a crouched position, and he had his arm around her and was crying his eyes out. Lisa heard her mother in the background screaming, "Oh my god! My child! My child!"

Kosta was sobbing and saying over and over, "I'm going to kill him. I'm going to kill him."

Lisa's mother saw someone lying on the floor and asked, "What's — who's this?"

Kosta said, "That's the guy that shot Lisa."

Lisa realized then that she had been shot and went into shock. She could feel herself going into shock and thought, "What do I do? Do I just lay here or do I come out of shock and tell these people who love me, and who I love, that I'm okay?"

Lisa willed herself to keep from slipping away and said, "I'm all right."

She looked at Kosta and asked, "Is that Teja?"

"No, it's not Teja. It's Teja's friend from Ohio. He must have hired him. I'm going to kill him."

Lisa heard Kosta begin his litany again, repeating over and over, "I love you, I love you. I'm going to kill him. I'm going to kill him."

Lisa tried to reassure Kosta: "I'm going to be all right. Don't worry, I'm going to be all right."

Mary left the room but she was still screaming.

Kosta said, "She's going to drive me crazy."

Kosta continued to sob, with tears streaming from his eyes, and it was the first time Lisa had ever seen him cry. She thought, *He's crying. Maybe he really does love me.*

Several police cars arrived with their sirens whooping and blue lights flashing, and an Emergency Rescue vehicle with paramedics drove up. Dino ran outside in his underwear and told them what had happened. In his haste he didn't turn off the security system and set off the alarm when he opened the front door.

The police said they wouldn't go inside with Kosta and Mary in the house.

Dino got on the bullhorn and spoke in Greek. "Kosta, Mom. You've got to come out because the paramedics won't go in unless you come out."

Kosta took Mary outside. Mary and Kosta were both dressed. Kosta was even wearing his jewelry.

Lisa was wide awake the whole time.

The paramedics took Lisa's vital signs and transmitted them to the Halifax Medical Center Emergency Room. A team of doctors and nurses experienced in treating gunshot wounds went on alert.

On the dark side street where they waited in a parked car, Deidre and Lori heard the sirens.

"I think he did it," Deidre said.

To make sure, she started the car and drove by the house several times. There were several police cars there with their blue lights flashing.

"The deed has been done," Deidre said.

They drove back to Lori's apartment where Teja was still asleep. Deidre and Lori went into the house and woke him up with the news. Deidre was delirious.

"The bitch is dead!" Deidre said happily. "The bitch is dead!"

"What are you talking about?" Teja asked.

171

"Lisa's dead," Deidre said.

"Did you kill her?"

"No."

Deidre and Lori told him about Bryan and the attempts that he had made to kill Lisa that failed, but that he had apparently succeeded that night. If so, they said, Bryan was dead, too.

"What gun did he use?" Teja asked.

"That gun you gave me," Deidre replied.

Teja knew it was the .22 caliber semiautomatic that jammed after the first shot, and he thought, *You can't shoot someone once with a .22 and expect them to die. You've got to shoot them five or six times.* And he knew the gun only fired once.

Teja thought, *The kid's dead and the woman's not.*

He was disappointed because he had hoped Lisa would be killed because then she couldn't identify him. Teja didn't want to be charged with attempted armed robbery.

Deidre seemed to read his mind. "Yeah," she said. "That's good for you because now she can't identify you."

Immediately after the shooting, Dino told a police officer that he had found a light on in the basement, which was unusual.

"Can I make a request?" he asked. "I'd like to have the light switch to the basement stairs checked for fingerprints."

Kosta spoke up. "That's not necessary, Dino. I left them on by accident."

Dino dressed and went to the hospital while doctors worked to stabilize Lisa and determine a course of action. Dino thought of the attempted robbery at Joyland, Kosta's affair with Deidre Hunt, and of the warning he had received from Bill Markantonakis. Dino thought that Kosta was behind the attempt on his sister's life, and he was determined to do what he could to protect her.

He approached a police officer and said, "I want twenty-four hour protection for my sister."

"That's not necessary," he was told.

"I don't care whether you think so or not," Dino said. "I'll pay for it myself."

However, as further evidence made it clear that the attack was not a simple burglary the Daytona Beach Police changed their position and established a schedule to have Lisa guarded around the clock while she was in the hospital.

In the meantime, the medical team in the Trauma Center stabilized Lisa's condition. The bullet had struck her forehead at an angle and entered her brain. They believed that it was better to leave the bullet where it was rather than risk surgery to remove it, which would put her in greater jeopardy, Lisa would survive without complications unless the bullet moved—something that could happen at any time.

Kosta arrived at the hospital later, but Dino had nothing to say to him then. Kosta saw Lisa for fifteen or twenty minutes and left.

He telephoned Deidre that morning and disregarded his paranoia about her telephone being bugged. He told her that Chase had come into the bedroom and shot Lisa.

"What happened to Bryan?" Deidre asked.

Kosta laughed. "He's meatloaf."

That was the only thing that amused Kosta because, although Chase was dead, Lisa was still alive. Deidre was also alarmed when she heard this.

173

"Teja knows how to make a bomb," she said.

"Then get him to do it," Kosta said. "Have him make a bomb and have it taken to her room in some flowers. A vase. Anything."

Deidre said she would tell Teja. When she did, Teja said, "I wanted to make a bomb. I wanted her dead."

Deidre was thrown into a state of panic and started thinking of all sorts of ways to kill Lisa, none of which had any tactical intelligence attached to them. She had plummeted from euphoria at thinking that Lisa was finally dead into panic and desperation.

20

About midmorning on Saturday, Tony Calderone received a telephone call at his car dealership from Holly telling him that Kosta had not shown up at Top Shots. Calderone told her that he would see if he could locate Kosta. He telephoned around but was unsuccessful. Since he had a stake in Top Shots, Calderone decided to open up the poolroom.

Lisa's shooting occurred too early on Saturday morning for the story to be reported in any of the newspapers, and Calderone was unaware of what had happened. He went to Top Shots and started to work behind the bar. Not long after that, he heard the news on radio and television broadcasts.

The story reported that a burglar had entered the house and that something had gone wrong. The burglar, the news reports said, shot Lisa in the head while she was asleep, but she was still alive, thanks to the quick action of her husband, who had killed the intruder.

Calderone had heard Kosta talk about having Lisa killed, but he hadn't taken it seriously.

Matthew Chumbley, who had also heard the news, ran into the pool hall. Chumbley was flushed, wide-eyed, and nervous. Calderone thought he was on speed.

"That could have been me!" Chumbley said.

Calderone was perplexed. "Who could have been you?"

"The kid that Kosta killed!"

"What?"

"Kosta offered me ten thousand dollars to kill Lisa."

"Jesus Christ!"

Calderone was struck for the first time that Kosta had been serious in his murderous schemes.

"You better keep your mouth shut, or your life won't be worth fifty dollars," Calderone told him.

He shooed him out of Top Shots and telephoned Kosta's home. A police detective answered.

"There's been an accident," the detective said. "Lisa's at the hospital. Who is this?"

Calderone hung up, closed Top Shots, and drove to the hospital to see if he could find Kosta. He didn't know what he was going to do. His thoughts reeled. He drove to the hospital and circled the area several times and didn't see Kosta's car, so he went back to Top Shots and stayed for two hours before he became too nervous to function. He closed the place and drove home.

Kosta's black BMW was parked in his driveway. Calderone was surprised and nervous. It was about four p.m. The windows of the BMW were tinted black, and Calderone couldn't see whether or not Kosta was inside the car. He unlocked the front door of his house, went inside, and found Kosta sleeping on the couch.

Kosta was unshaven and wore rumpled clothing. Calderone woke him up, and Kosta's eyes were bloodshot; he looked very tired. Kosta lifted his head from the couch and sat up. Calderone collapsed in a chair.

"You son of a bitch," he said. "You did it, didn't you?"

176

Kosta gave him what he later called a "cat who ate the canary grin," and said, "I told you Greek men never divorce their wives."

Kosta then gave Calderone a stony look, rose from the couch, and started patting him down. This scared Calderone. He was afraid he was going to be killed.

"What are you doing?" he asked.

"I've got to make sure you aren't wired," Kosta said. "I can't be too careful."

Calderone said that Kosta whispered something to him that he couldn't quite understand.

"What did you say about the kid?" he asked.

"The kid fucked up. I had to eliminate him."

Calderone almost trembled in fear but settled down somewhat when Kosta was satisfied that he wasn't wired or armed.

"I have to kill Matt and Teja," Kosta said. "They're the last links in the chain."

"My God, you just can't go around killing everybody," Calderone said. "What are you going to do, kill the whole Boardwalk?"

Kosta gave him a cold look. "If I have to."

Kosta told Calderone to meet him for the buffet later on at the Casa Del Mar. Calderone collapsed in relief when Kosta left. He was glad to be alive, but he was too scared to go to the police. He followed Kosta's instructions and met him at the Casa Del Mar. When they were eating, Calderone asked, "Why did you kill the kid?"

Kosta answered, "Dead men tell no tales."

Calderone was glad when they parted company. He knew that Kosta had planned to kill Lisa. He remembered that Kosta planned to kill Chumbley and Teja to keep them from talking. Was he on Kosta's list, too?

Kosta's words resounded in his mind: *Dead men tell no tales.*

Dino had gone to see lawyers to get advice about hiring a private investigator to look into Kosta's activities after the attempted robbery at Joyland. Dino thought Kosta was behind it and that Deidre was involved. He was very much concerned about Lisa's life being in danger.

The lawyers told him to forget about it. "Kosta wouldn't be stupid enough to try to kill her twice in the same week."

Dino was almost completely certain that Kosta had done it, but considered that there was a slim possibility that Deidre was responsible. He told the police about his suspicions.

As Dino drove Kosta to the hospital the day Lisa was shot, he said, "Kosta, I went to the police and I told them everything I know about the Lori Henderson and the Teja-Cherri [Deidre] connection.

"You know more about these people than I do," Dino continued. "Why don't you talk to the police?"

Kosta didn't reply, and Dino approached him again on Sunday.

"Now, listen, Kosta," he said, "this lies somewhere between the Teja-Lori-Deidre connection. Why don't you go to the police?"

"I'm going to take care of it myself," Kosta said.

"No, you don't take care of it yourself," Dino said. "You go to the police and you tell them everything you know, and you let them take care of it."

Kosta refused. Dino went back to the police. "I think it's my brother-in-law," he said, "but if I'm wrong, I don't want this conversation repeated."

178

Dino thought that by talking to Kosta and voicing his suspicions he had put his own life in danger.

Peter Kouracos went to the hospital on Saturday when he heard that Lisa had been shot. He not only wanted to keep Kosta company but said he was "a loyal and trusted friend of the whole family" and wanted to show his support.

About seven p.m., Kouracos and Kosta left the hospital and went to the house on Halifax Avenue where they heated up some leftover pizza. After they finished eating, Kosta said, "I want to go to the Boardwalk."

Both men were carrying handguns when Kouracos drove to the Boardwalk. Kouracos parked on the Main Street side of the Boardwalk, and both he and Kosta talked for about twenty minutes with some police officers they recognized. They walked to an arcade and sat down on a bench.

After a few minutes, Kosta said, "I'm going to look around the place."

Kosta was gone for about an hour and Kouracos talked with a businessman he knew until Kosta returned. It was about ten p.m. when they left to go back to the house. Kosta said that he had been looking for a black guy named Teja.

Kouracos knew the name because Lisa had telephoned him after the attempted robbery at Joyland and told him Teja's name. She had told him, he said, that Teja had once worked for her.

"I heard from the street people that Teja was around," Kosta said.

Kosta didn't say what he wanted with Teja, just that he wanted to find him. Kouracos thought that Kosta had one of two things in mind: either capture Teja

179

and turn him over to the police or to deal out his own brand of justice.

Before they had gone far, Kouracos pulled into a spot between the Desert Inn and the Carousel and parked. He waited for ten minutes in the car while Kosta made a call from a pay telephone. Then Kosta went to another pay telephone, farther away, and made another call.

Afterwards, Kouracos suggested that they drive by Deidre's apartment and Kosta agreed.

"The lights are on," Kosta said as they drove by.

"Well, I certainly don't want to stop," Kouracos said. "Let's call the police."

Neither man called the police. Kouracos dropped Kosta off and went home.

The first police on the scene after the shooting had filed a report saying that it had occurred during an attempted burglary. Dino didn't buy it and neither did the police after their initial report. There were just too many things that didn't fit in with a burglary.

Officers Ted Riegel and Vicki Miles of the Daytona Beach Police Department thought everything was too pat. Chase had known exactly which window he could break into without setting off the security alarm, and he had walked past expensive items that a burglar would have taken and ran. And he walked directly to the third floor and into Lisa's bedroom, bypassing Mary's bedroom on the second floor and Dino's bedroom on the third floor.

All of that was odd enough, but there were other suspicious things. If it had been a burglary, and Lisa had awakened, why did the burglar shoot her instead of Kosta. "The man poses the greatest threat," Riegel said. "A burglar would have limited the greatest threat first."

Chase has also been wide awake, and his eyes had probably become accustomed to the dark. How could Kosta wake up from a sound sleep and react fast enough to reach under the bed, get a gun, and shoot Chase before Chase shot him? How could Kosta see well enough? There were a lot of suspicious circumstances that pointed to something far more sinister than burglary.

Michael Palatis, a young assistant state attorney who was Lisa's cousin, went to the house at Halifax on Saturday. He listened to the police officers express their doubts. He questioned whether or not Lisa had been shot in an attempted burglary or whether it was a deliberate attempt on her life.

There were enough questions that Paul Crow, Daytona Beach's chief of police, was notified while he was on vacation. Crow cut his vacation short and immediately returned to Daytona Beach.

Officer Mike Mittleman of the Ormond Beach Police Department was called to the Intensive Care Unit waiting room at the Halifax Hospital on Saturday because of a suspicious person report. Mittleman met the security guard at the hospital.

"There's a black guy wandering around the hallways," the guard told him, "and he keeps saying he's looking for Lisa."

Mittleman, who knew about the shooting, walked over to the man who was still in the ICU waiting room.

"What are you doing here?" he asked.

"I'm here to find out how Lisa is doing."

Mittleman asked the man for his name and was told it was John Polk, which later proved to be fictitious. The policeman asked Polk if he would be willing to answer some questions, and Polk said he would. Mittleman read Polk his rights and listened to a story that he didn't believe.

"He said he was on the Boardwalk and met up with a subject by the name of John Smith," Mittleman reported. "He said that he had never met the person before and that this John Smith out of the blue asked him to go to the Halifax Hospital and inquire about her [Lisa's] medical condition. He was supposed to report back to Smith once he obtained the information."

Mittleman didn't believe Polk, and although he didn't think there was much to be concerned about, he wasn't taking any chances. He called in detectives who questioned Polk further and released him.

"Polk" was described as being in his mid-twenties, about five feet-ten inches tall with a medium build.

J.R. had checked into a room at the Side O Sea Hotel and was there on Saturday when Robin Bergdorff knocked on his door and woke him up.

"Did you know Lisa got killed?" she asked.

"What?"

J.R.'s mind flashed back over the plots that Kosta and Deidre had made to kill Lisa, and remembered that he had been offered the contract himself. Obviously they had found someone to do the job.

J.R. telephoned 911 and asked, "Do you know anything about a woman being killed?"

A detective got on the line, and J.R. hung up.

Robin said she thought that Bryan Chase had been killed.

J.R. wasn't sure what to do next. He knew he had to do something because Kosta and Deidre had tried to set him up. J.R. believed that Kosta would try to kill him because he knew too much. He was also mad because Bryan had been his best friend.

Matthew Chumbley rushed around the Boardwalk looking for Deidre.

"I'm going to beat her ass for trying to set me up," he said.

Chumbley had no luck finding Deidre, but he met J.R., who had spoken with a friend who talked with Deidre on the Boardwalk. J.R.'s friend said Deidre told him that Kosta was going to kill everyone who knew he had put a murder contract on his wife. At the time, J.R. didn't know that Chumbley had been involved in the same scheme.

Chumbley and J.R. discussed the various offers to kill Lisa and how they were supposed to have done it. Both of them were scared.

"Man, I'm not stupid," Matt said. "I knew that I was going to be dead and I knew that I was already supposed to be dead."

J.R. and Chumbley were walking together near the Civic Auditorium, then headed toward the Holiday Inn, when Kosta's black BMW started coming toward them slowly. The window came down, and Chumbley said he saw Kosta holding a gun. J.R. was scared to death and tried to use Chumbley as a shield.

"Man, he's going to kill me," J.R. said. "He's going to kill me."

"Don't hide behind me, man," Chumbley said. "I ain't nobody's target."

183

Both Chumbley and J.R. were relieved when a police cruiser showed up and the BMW took off. That was the last time J.R. and Chumbley saw one another.

J.R. returned to the Side O Sea Hotel more worried about being killed than he had ever been. He dialed 911. This time, when a detective came on the line, he didn't hang up.

J.R. said the shooting was a setup and that Kosta had tried to hire him and others to kill Lisa. J.R. was picked up for questioning by Daytona Beach police and taken to headquarters to be interviewed. J.R. told the police that Deidre Hunt had offered him ten thousand dollars to kill Lisa Fotopoulos and that Kosta was behind it to collect insurance money from his wife's death. J.R. said that Teja Mzimmia had attempted to kill Lisa at Joyland during what was reported as an attempted armed robbery and again at a Halloween party at Razzles.

J.R.'s statement reinforced the police's hypothesis that Kosta's story about the shootings at the house on Halifax Avenue was a lie. Lt. Charles William Evens, who was assigned to the Criminal Investigation Division, of the Daytona Beach Police Department, was called to the house on Halifax not long after the shooting. At first, Evens thought it was a burglary, but he changed his mind after talking with other police officers and looking at the evidence. Evens called for Corp. Greg Smith, a black police officer considered one of the best detectives in the department, to come over and help with the investigation. Smith agreed that something in Kosta's story was odd.

While Smith, who took charge of the Fotopoulos-Chase case, conducted his investigation, a policeman in the patrol division who was assigned to the Board-walk, developed suspicions on his own. Officer

184

Thomas O'Neal, who knew about the attempted armed robbery at Joyland, thought too many suspicious events had occurred to Lisa Fotopoulos.

In the meantime, Dino was engaged in his own brand of detective work. But he contacted James L. Wells of Port Orange, just south of Daytona Beach, who was friendly with the Paspalakis family and with Lisa.

Dino asked Wells to meet him for lunch and the two men talked about the attempted armed robbery and the shootings at the house.

"We were talking it over," Wells said, "and we both thought that what happened was kind of a funny situation, that Lisa got shot instead of Kosta. And between the conversation and everything, we came to the conclusion that something was very wrong here."

Dino asked Wells to visit Top Shots for several hours over the next few days and keep an eye on anything suspicious that happened.

21

The Sunday morning editions of the *News-Journal* of Daytona Beach and the *Orlando Sentinel* gave front-page coverage to the attempt on Lisa's life. Kosta was portrayed as a hero. Radio and television affiliates of NBC, ABC, and NBC carried additional stories with the same theme.

While the media sounded the trumpet for Kosta's heroism, Dino and the Daytona Beach Police thought otherwise. The police had placed a twenty-four armed guard on Lisa at the Halifax ICU because Dino had insisted on it. After hearing J.R.'s story and having their own doubts about Kosta's version of events at Lisa's house, no one doubted that this was the right thing to do.

The Daytona Beach Police were now involved in what appeared to be shaping up as murder, attempted murder, and conspiracy to commit murder.

Officer O'Neal, a policeman who patrolled the Boardwalk, became increasingly suspicious about Lisa's shooting and the attempted armed robbery at Joyland. He had been briefed, as all the police were, that a subject had implicated Deidre Hunt, Kosta, Teja, and Lori Henderson in a plot to kill Lisa. From Kosta's report of the events, O'Neal knew that Kosta said that the man who shot Lisa was "Teja's friend from Ohio."

O'Neal remembered Deidre from Top Shots and "had a negative opinion of her from the start." Toward the end of summer he had investigated a report where Deidre had "battered" other employees at Top Shots and had "threatened them with physical harm."

O'Neal knew that Teja had been in trouble before, regarding a shooting with a .44 Magnum pistol at the Ormond Beach Octoberfest. At that time, O'Neal had investigated the alleged shooting, found no basis for it, and concluded that Teja "was a personable, outgoing young man."

He fumbled to find words to describe how he felt about Teja's girlfriend, Lori. "She struck me as a non-personality type, nothing," he said. "She struck me . . . she didn't strike me, let me put it that way."

The police officer compared notes with two other patrolmen about the attempted armed robbery at Joyland and concluded that Lisa might still be in danger. The three patrolmen agreed that they should find Deidre Hunt and talk with her.

Officer Dennis Maurey, a tall policeman with a shock of red hair, was with O'Neal when they found Deidre and Lori Sunday evening on Ocean Avenue across the street from Krystal's. The two police officers read them their rights, but Lori and Deidre waived them, including the right to have an attorney present.

The two police officers questioned Deidre and Lori about the shooting involving Chase. Deidre said they knew nothing about it. Then the officers said they were looking for Teja in connection with the attempted armed robbery at Joyland. Deidre and Lori said they didn't know anything about the attempted armed robbery, where Teja was, or the shootings at Lisa's house.

O'Neal said, "If either of you have knowledge about

what we have talked about it can be used against you."

Maurey and O'Neal allowed Deidre and Lori to leave. O'Neal didn't believe the two women but had no grounds on which to arrest them. In his own mind he was sure that Deidre and Lori were involved and that they were hiding Teja. Nevertheless, he had to let them go.

"I knew that Teja was Lori's boyfriend, and I just reasoned that she knew where he was," he said. "And I thought she probably had some knowledge about the incident at the game room [at Joyland] that Teja was involved in."

By Sunday, Dino was almost certain that Kosta was behind the attempt to kill his sister. He discussed his fears with his cousin, Michael Palatis, and found they both had the same suspicions. Palatis didn't have much experience as a prosecutor, but he saw that Kosta's account of the shooting was riddled with holes.

Dino decided that it wasn't safe for his mother or himself to stay at the house. When he was sure Mary was in a safe place, he camped out in Lisa's room behind the armed guard.

"I figured if anybody [was] in danger, it would be either my sister or I," Dino told the police.

On Monday, Dino met with Harvey Altez, a private detective, and told him he suspected that Kosta was behind the attempted murder.

Altez listened, then told him, "Listen, this case is so hot that there are probably a dozen police officers on it. I could ask you for a couple of thousand dollars and get on this case, but I'm not going to do that. Chances are the police are really looking into it, so you'd be wasting your money."

A while later, Dino went to the house and confronted Kosta.

"I want you to take your things and get out," Dino said, then he went back to the hospital.

Kosta didn't follow Dino's orders.

On Sunday night, Peter Kouracos had planned to go to Razzles but went to the hospital instead and stayed there until about five a.m. Monday. Kosta had given Kouracos a key to the house Saturday when Kouracos had stayed overnight, because his family didn't think Kosta should be alone. This was after they had made the trip to the Boardwalk so Kosta could look for Teja.

Kouracos said that Lisa was being cared for and had family around her, but that Kosta needed all the support he could get.

Chumbley was back to square one. He didn't have the ten thousand dollars he hoped to get from killing Lisa Fotopoulos, but he was still alive. He couldn't shake the image of himself lying dead instead of Bryan Chase. Chumbley, after all, had one of the first choices to commit the murder.

In the meantime, Chumbley had to eat and get money to buy crack cocaine. Just after midnight on Tuesday, November 7, Chumbley hooked up with a black gay man and headed toward Fag Hill, hoping to make a score by pimping for him.

Chumbley saw a car creep by and saw two men in it. The car came by again, just as slowly, and Chumbley figured that the men were potential johns. He motioned to the driver, who parked the car, and

189

called over to see if they might be interested. He got the idea that they were and walked toward the car, talking about what the young black would do for them, then telling them how much it would cost.

Chumbley got closer and saw that the driver was wearing what appeared to be an expensive gold necklace. Having been on the streets for a while, Chumbley figured he could snatch the necklace and run. He knew he could get more for the necklace than he could from pimping, and it was a sure thing. After all, he wasn't even sure that he could strike a deal with the two johns for his boy.

When Chumbley was close enough, he reached inside, grabbed the necklace, yanked it from the driver's neck, and started to run. So did the male prostitute, who managed to get away. Chumbley wasn't so lucky. He had only ran a few feet when he heard the familiar words:

"Freeze! Police!"

Chumbley stopped and was taken into custody by officers Dan Overby and Rob Taylor of the Daytona Beach Police Department, who were working as decoys to catch prostitutes and pimps.

Chumbley was scared. He had been arrested dozens of times on misdemeanors and had served time in jail but had never been in prison. Now he was afraid he would be charged with robbery, which was a felony, and that the felony would be compounded by the fact that the necklace he had yanked off the policeman's neck was valuable enough to warrant a charge of grand larceny. He envisioned himself going to prison.

He started talking up a storm, trying to save himself. "That shooting at the Fotopoulos place," he said. "I can hand you that case on a silver platter."

Sure, the detectives said.

"It was a setup by Kosta Fotopoulos and Deidre Hunt. She offered me ten thousand dollars to kill Lisa."

The detectives looked at each other. They didn't know if Chumbley was on the level or if he was merely trying to get himself off the hook. But he kept on talking about a murder-for-hire plot and said he wanted to make a deal with the state attorney. Chumbley was put in jail, where he continued to say he wanted to see a state attorney.

Chumbley thought he was safer in jail than he was on the streets with Kosta roaming the Boardwalk with a gun, trying to "tie up loose ends." But a long stay in prison scared him almost as much.

22

The Criminal Investigation Division (CID) of the Daytona Beach Police Department had been working almost around the clock since the shootings at Lisa's house. Almost everyone in the CID had been involved until Police Chief Paul Crow and Captain B.F. Neall assigned Lieutenant Charles William Evens to be the chief investigator.

Evens began paring down the number of people working on the case to keep them from getting in each other's way. When the fine-tuning had been done, those who were involved in the investigation included Evens, Smith, and Detectives Adamy and Allison Ebel.

After talking with J.R. on Sunday, Evens decided he should have a talk with Deidre Hunt. Evens, Ebel and Smith found Deidre at her new apartment on Lennox Street. J.R. had implicated Deidre, but the police didn't have enough evidence to arrest her. Deidre volunteered to talk with them. At the time, Chumbley had not been arrested.

When the detectives started to talk with Deidre, they didn't know that Lori Henderson was in the apartment. But not long after the conversation began, Evens asked,

"Is anyone else here?"

"Just my girlfriend," Deidre said. "She's asleep in the bedroom."

A short time afterward Lori came out and tried to join in the conversation. Evens thought that the two women had a strange relationship.

"Deidre did all of the talking for Lori," Evens said. "She wouldn't allow Lori to answer any of the questions on her own. We were still looking for Teja, so I asked Deidre if there was anyone else in the apartment."

Evens asked Deidre if he could look around the apartment. She said that was fine, but she had to accompany him. That was exactly what Evens wanted: he wanted to get Deidre away from Lori so that Lori could talk to Smith and Ebel. The ploy worked. Lori said to Smith and Ebel.

"I could tell you a whole lot more if I could talk to you alone."

The two detectives told Lori to come to the police department on Monday.

Lori Henderson didn't show up for her meeting with Evens, Smith, and Ebel on Monday. The three detectives realized Deidre was keeping Lori from talking to them. They decided to wait the rest of the day and if Lori didn't show up, they would go look for her.

Teja was hiding out at Lori's apartment and making a bomb with three people he knew. He had made bombs before, and he was making this bomb out of Tide and gasoline. When they were mixed together and set to go off by a detonator, the mixture created a powerful fire bomb, similar to napalm.

Kosta had told him to make a bomb powerful

193

enough to "blow up the whole hospital" but that was clearly impossible. The best Teja could do with the material he had on hand was to blow up a hospital room.

But Teja had no intention of delivering the bomb to the hospital when the police were looking for him. He made the bomb and gave it to Deidre. It would be her job to see that the bomb was delivered to Lisa's room.

Kouracos and Kosta were tired when they arrived at Lisa's house on Monday after having been at the hospital. They slept for a few hours, then Kosta told Kouracos to stay at the house.

"I'm going out," he said. "I will be back in about half an hour."

Kouracos stayed at the house for several hours and started to get worried. He wondered if something had happened to Kosta. Kouracos went to the front of the house and saw that Kosta's car was still there, and was afraid that Kosta had been arrested when he had stepped out of the house.

The telephone rang and Angelo was on the line. "I'm worried about Kosta," Kouracos said.

Angelo told him to sit tight. Kouracos waited two more hours and started to worry about his own situation. Perhaps he was being set up by the police, maybe even Kosta. He was concerned that he might be a target for murder. Kouracos telephoned Angelo.

"Look, I'm worried," he said. "I don't know what's going on here. I'm afraid I might be getting set up."

Angelo arrived, and Kouracos gave him the Smith

& Wesson handgun he was carrying. He wanted more protection.

"Angelo, take me home right now so I can get a rifle," he said.

Angelo drove Kouracos home where he got a rifle and two magazines, and they returned to the Halifax house together. Angelo stayed with him until about six a.m. and left when Kouracos went upstairs to sleep in the guest bedroom. He thought he would be safe, and when he awakened, he intended to go home.

Early Tuesday morning, the Daytona Beach detectives assigned to the Chase-Fotopoulos case had an opportunity to talk with Chumbley, who corroborated the story that J.R. had told them earlier. The detectives had waited more than a full day for Lori Henderson to keep her appointment Monday, but she hadn't appeared.

An interview with Lori had assumed greater urgency now that she had been mentioned by both J.R. and Chumbley.

"We needed to talk with her," Evens said. "It became apparent on November seventh that Deidre Hunt was trying to keep her away from us."

The detectives determined that the two women were together on November 7 and that they would be returning a rental car to Cheaper Rent-A-Car on Volusia Avenue. Evans, Smith, and Ebel were waiting when Deidre and Lori arrived to turn the car in. The situation became somewhat bizarre.

"We asked Miss Henderson to come to the police department for the interview she had promised,"

Smith said. "She didn't have any objections to coming, but Miss Hunt became irate about it. In fact, she got physical and tried to pull Miss Henderson away from Detective Ebel."

Evens's description was similar: "Deidre pitched a fit. She did not want us to be alone with Lori Henderson. I really didn't want Deidre Hunt to come to the police department that night, but she insisted."

Deidre said she didn't know where the police station was and wanted to ride in the same car with Lori. Evens wanted to separate them. Deidre kept her rental car and followed them to the police station, where she said she would wait for Lori.

Tuesday morning Michael Palatis stopped by David Damore's office and asked if they could talk. It had been less than three days since Damore and his wife Nona had read the first newspaper accounts of the shooting at Halifax Avenue.

Palatis told Damore that he was worried about his cousin, Lisa Fotopoulos, based on his talks with Kosta, other family members, and the police. Palatis said he thought the incident was more than a burglary that turned violent.

"The stories just didn't jive with the physical evidence," Palatis said.

Damore told Palatis that he had been suspicious since he read the first newspaper article.

"What should we do?" Michael asked. "Who should we contact?

"Let me call Homicide and find out who's working the case."

196

Damore didn't think it was a good idea for Palatis to be involved if there were to be an investigation, because he was related to Lisa Fotopoulos. Damore telephoned to speak to Chief Crow. At the time, Damore didn't know anything about the case except what he had read in the newspaper. Crow told him that the police had serious questions about the story Kosta had given them.

Moments after he got off of the telephone, Damore called Robert Wheeler, the chief investigator for the state attorney's office, and passed on the questions that Palatis had raised. Crow's comments had given them added weight. Wheeler knew Lisa. He had been one of her teachers at Seabreeze High School before he had become the principal, then retired to join the investigative staff for the state attorney. Wheeler obviously had a personal interest in the case.

Damore arranged for himself and Wheeler to meet with Crow at Daytona Beach Police headquarters. Damore discovered that Crow didn't believe Kosta's story made sense.

"The house has a sophisticated burglar alarm system," Crow said. "The burglar came in through a window he had broken that wasn't connected to the alarm system."

Crow said the police had received a telephone call from J.R. Taylor the evening of the shooting, J.R. claiming he had been offered money to kill Lisa by Kosta Fotopoulos by way of Deidre Hunt. Crow said J.R. believed that the man Kosta killed in Kosta's bedroom was Bryan Chase, one of J.R.'s best friends.

Crow briefly outlined the police suspicions con-

197

cerning Kosta's story, namely, why would a burglar shoot someone who was asleep? Why Lisa before Kosta?

How could Kosta wake up, retrieve a gun from under the bed, and react faster than a wide-awake intruder whose eyes were accustomed to the dark and who already had a gun in his hand?

Evens had a lot of questions, and an officer at the scene of the crime noted that the intruder's gun, a .22 caliber semiautomatic pistol, was jammed in the "open" position underneath his body. Why had Kosta found it necessary to fire almost an entire magazine of 9-millimeter bullets into Chase and then shoot him in the head at close range?

While the three men talked, a detective came in and said, "We've got an individual in custody who wants to see a state attorney. He says he has information about the shootings of Bryan Chase and Lisa Fotopoulos."

The meeting broke up. Damore inquired about the man. Matthew Chumbley, known on the street as Mike Cox, was in custody but had not been charged. The police intended to charge him with two misdemeanors: petty theft and solicitation for the purposes of prostitution. Chumbley believed he was going to be charged with robbery and was talking up a storm about cutting a deal because he had information about the shooting at the Fotopoulos house.

Damore decided to meet with Chumbley. The only information he had was what he had seen in the newspaper story, plus what he had learned from Crow. He approached Chumbley with no pre-conceived opinions. In spite of his emaciated, scruffy appearance, Chumbley was lucid and articulate.

"I want to cut a deal," Chumbley said. "I got something to give you, but I want the charges against me reduced."

"I can't offer you a deal without knowing what you have to offer," Damore said. "I'm not going to buy a pig in a poke. You tell me what you know, and then I'll decide what it's worth."

Chumbley told him that Deidre Hunt had offered him ten thousand dollars to kill Lisa Fotopoulos. He said that Deidre had also offered Teja James the same amount to kill Lisa. Chumbley said that Teja's "attempted armed robbery" at Joyland was actually a murder attempt that failed.

Damore listened, but said, "I took everything he said with a grain of salt. I really didn't have enough information to believe or disbelieve. I didn't want to approach the investigation with the attitude that I had already made a determination. I wanted to assemble all the information I could and let the chips fall where they may."

Damore remained objective but had assembled enough information in the past hour to reinforce the feeling he experienced when he first read about the shootings in the newspaper.

Chumbley's attitude was persuasive: "Matt thought he was going to prison and wanted to do what was in his own interest. You don't usually meet someone who will look you in the eye and say, 'Yes, I would have murdered, no doubt about it. I wanted to do it. I wanted to be sure about getting the money. If I was sure about getting my money, I would have killed her,'" Damore said. "They usually make all sorts of excuses for themselves."

Damore had some luck on his side when it came to getting information from Chumbley. Chumbley was afraid that he was going to be charged with robbery and grand larceny and was eager to cooperate to keep from going to prison. He was wrong, but his fear played into Damore's hands. Snatching a necklace didn't constitute enough force to be considered robbery, and the necklace was fake, not worth enough to merit a charge of attempted grand larceny.

"I didn't really have to cut a deal with him," Damore said. "He gave us the information, and I told him that we wouldn't press for felony charges against him. We weren't going to anyhow, but he didn't know that."

Damore finished talking with Chumbley and the Daytona Beach police and went back to his office. Not long afterward, Captain Evens and the other detectives arrived at the Daytona Beach Police Department with Deidre and Lori. The police separated the two women and, although Lori was there voluntarily, she was reluctant to talk.

Lori's interview corroborated what the police had heard from J.R. and Chumbley. The tall blond tried to remain tightlipped when it came to talking about Teja, but she let it slip that he was at her apartment. She said that Teja was making a bomb.

Damore pondered the facts that he had about the shootings, but he actually had very little hard evidence. The Daytona Beach police knew that Deidre Hunt was a sometime prostitute and petty thief, and that she had worked at Top Shots, where she was well-known as a troublemaker. Damore had far more questions than answers.

Why, he wondered, would a street girl hatch a plot to murder Lisa Fotopoulos? Where would she get ten thousand dollars to pay someone to kill Lisa? Why were so many street people, who were generally petty thieves, being implicated in a murder plot?

Damore studied police reports, then went home at seven p.m. He was there about two and a half hours when the telephone rang. All hell was breaking loose at Daytona Beach Police headquarters.

23

Sergeant Leonard Lewis was on the line.

"We've got Teja James in custody," Lewis said. "We need you back down here. He's made a bomb, and it's going to go off at midnight. We need somebody down here who's in a position to make some deals, if necessary. We've got to find that bomb."

Damore telephoned Joe Gallagher, assistant chief investigator for the state attorney's office, and told him to come to his house. Damore needed him to go with him to police headquarters.

Gallagher was five feet, eleven inches tall and was slender and fit. He had dark blond hair and was fifty years old, although he looked closer to thirty-five. Gallagher had an unusual wealth of experience as a law enforcement officer. He had served twenty-five years with the Daytona Beach Police Department and had reached the rank of Lieutenant. Gallagher was deputy commander of the CID when he retired in March 1989. The day following his retirement, Gallagher went to work for the state attorney.

The trip to police headquarters was hectic, with Damore getting additional information from the police on his car telephone. The case was coming together from all sorts of angles. The most urgent problem was Teja

The luxurious house where Lisa lived with Kosta, her mother, and her brother. (*Courtesy of the News-Journal*)

Lisa Fotopoulos and her brother, Dino, at Joyland in March, 1991. (*Courtesy of the News-Journal*)

Kosta Fotopoulos hears the jury recommend that he be sentenced to death in the electric chair for the murders of Mark Kevin Ramsey and Bryan Chase. (*Courtesy of the News-Journal*)

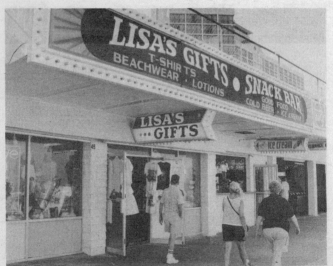

Lisa's gift shop on the Boardwalk was only part of her family's multimillion dollar dynasty. (*Courtesy of the News-Journal*)

Deidre Hunt before her arrest. (*Courtesy of the News-Journal*)

Yvonne Lori Henderson, Deidre's lover, knew about the plans to murder Ramsey, Lisa Fotopoulos and Bryan Chase. (*Courtesy of the News-Journal*)

Carol Ann Hunt testifying at her daughter's sentence hearing. (*Courtesy of the News-Journal*)

Despine and Charalampas Fotopoulos, Kosta's parents. (*Courtesy of the News-Journal*)

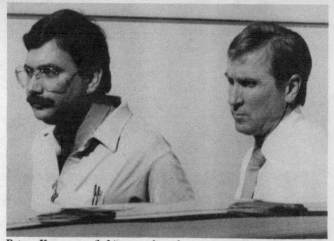

Peter Kouracos (left) was found innocent of counterfeiting charges in a U.S. District Court. Lt. Joe Gallagher of the 7th District State Attorney's office escorts him to court. (*Courtesy of the News-Journal*)

Bryan L. Chase, who contracted with Kosta to kill his wife Lisa, shot her in the head as she lay sleeping and was killed at the scene by Fotopoulos. (*Courtesy of the News-Journal*)

Mark Kevin Ramsey was murdered by Deidre Hunt while Kosta recorded it on videotape. (*Courtesy of the News-Journal*)

Pamphlets on silencers, survival, a plastic human head, spent bullets, and other evidence found in Kosta's workshop. (*Courtesy of the State Attorney's office*)

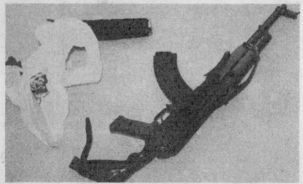
The AK-47, silencer for an automatic weapon, and (inside plastic bag) the .22 caliber Ruger with silencer that Deidre used to kill Ramsey. Police found them buried in a barbecue pit at Lisa's home. (*Courtesy of the State Attorney's office*)

Judge S. James Foxman presided over the trials and sentencing of Kosta Fotopoulos and Deidre Hunt. (*Courtesy of the News-Journal*)

David Damore, the assistant state attorney who spearheaded the investigation that led to the conviction of all the defendants in the murders of Bryan Chase, and Kevin Ramsey. (*Courtesy of the News-Journal*)

Carmen Corrente, Kosta's court-appointed defense attorney. (*Courtesy of the News-Journal*)

Matthew Chumbley accepted an offer of ten thousand dollars to kill Lisa Fotopoulos, but was arrested on burglary charges before he could commit the murder. He testified against Fotopoulos and Hunt. (*Courtesy of the News-Journal*)

Lisa Fotopoulos testified against her husband. After her ordeal, she continued to live with a bullet lodged in her head. (*Courtesy of the News-Journal*)

Police found two hand grenades that Kosta had buried in the woods. (*Courtesy of the State Attorney's office*)

Evidence found at Kosta's home. At bottom right is the video
tape showing the Ramsey murder. Also shown is a metal container Kosta used to bury things in, an Uzi automatic, ammunition pouches, and a gray vinyl bag containing the AK-47 and
.22 Ruger used by Deidre in the murder. (*Courtesy of the State
Attorney's office*)

J.R. Taylor accepted a contract to kill Lisa Fotopoulos. He identifies Kosta in court. (*Courtesy of the News-Journal*)

Teja James attempted to kill Lisa on two separate occasions, but failed. (*Courtesy of the News-Journal*)

Deidre Hunt winces as she receives the first of two death sentences for her crimes. (*Courtesy of the News-Journal*)

James. According to Teja, the bomb to go off at midnight was to kill four people who had information concerning the attempt to kill Lisa Fotopoulos. Teja said Deidre Hunt relayed instructions from Kosta Fotopoulos about the bomb.

Evens was successfully keeping Deidre, Lori, Teja, and Chumbley separated. Once Teja had been arrested at Lori's apartment on a warrant for attempted armed robbery, he began to talk about the Fotopoulos case.

"They've given us enough information so that we can arrest her [Deidre] on probable cause," Evens told Damore. "I think it's imperative that we have an interview with her."

Information was coming rapidly, and Damore was getting corroboration from different players. There was little doubt now that Lisa's shooting had been an attempted murder and that Kosta Fotopoulos could be responsible. It appeared that there was probable cause to arrest Kosta for the murder of Bryan Chase.

Damore and Gallagher arrived at the CID at 11:20 p.m. and met Sergeant Lewis.

"Teja James said he was offered ten thousand dollars to kill Lisa Fotopoulos," Lewis said. "He said he tried twice. Deidre Hunt offered him the money from Kosta Fotopoulos. She's here and has been for quite a while. She wants to talk to a state attorney."

"Where is she?" Damore asked.

"In Captain Neall's office." Lewis was tense. "The bomb's set to go off at midnight," he said. "We've got to make some decisions."

Captain B.F. Neall was interviewing Deidre in the Detective Sergeant's office. Neall said Deidre was cooperating and giving additional information concerning her relationship with Kosta and Bryan Chase.

Damore was introduced to Deidre, who looked as if she had been crying. Damore asked her if she wanted a tissue or water, but Deidre said she was okay.

Damore felt the pressure. Four people could die in an hour and a half if the bomb couldn't be found. Gallagher went with Damore into Neall's office. Damore and Gallagher saw Deidre for the first time. The small woman's long dark hair was permed and pulled back, fasted with a metal beret. She wore a long-sleeved red pullover and dark pants. A heavy bangle bracelet that looked like gold was on her left wrist. She sipped a diet Coke and munched potato chips.

"I'm Dave Damore," he said. "They tell me you've been wanting to talk to a state attorney."

Deidre said yes, she had.

"I'm a prosecutor. Do you know what a prosecutor is?"

"Yes."

"I just want to make sure that you understand," Damore said. "I'm not here as a defense attorney. I'm not your attorney. I put people in jail."

"Yeah, I understand."

"I just want to make sure that you do."

Damore told Deidre that he had been told that she had information about what had happened at Lisa's house. But he added, "I don't want to talk about that right now. Right now, I'm more concerned about a bomb."

"There isn't any bomb," Deidre said.

"We've been told that you've planted one and that it's set to explode in a couple of hours," Damore said. "Whatever trouble you're already in, it'll only get worse if the bomb goes off tonight and people are killed."

Deidre, who had been looking down, lifted her eyes. "I swear to you that there's no bomb," she said. "I don't know anything about it."

From his experience in criminal law, Damore knew that people frequently denied things they had done or twisted them. Teja said he had planted a bomb for Deidre in behalf of Kosta Fotopoulos. Now Deidre was denying it. Damore decided to apply some pressure in an attempt to find the truth.

"I want you to understand something," he said. "If it happens, it's going to be on your shoulders. You can tell me about it right now, and there'll be no problem because we can stop it. You're talking about much less severe effects than if a murder occurs."

"I'm telling you, there was no bomb," Deidre said.

Damore threw up his hands. "Okay, if that's what you say. I can't disprove it one way or the other. I understand you wanted to talk with me."

Deidre lit a cigarette, then exhaled a cloud of smoke. "Well, I don't know what to do."

Damore looked at her for a moment. He knew that she had been involved in a murder-for-hire plot to kill Lisa Fotopoulos and Bryan Chase. He had also been told that Chumbley, Teja, and J.R. had been offered money to kill Lisa. Kosta may have been the catalyst, but Deidre Hunt was a suspect for first-degree murder, solicitation to commit murder, and attempted first-degree murder.

Damore looked at Deidre. "What are you holding in your lap?" he asked.

"Potato chips," Deidre answered.

Damore shook his head. "No, you're holding the bag," he said. "Right now, you're holding the bag for Kosta Fotopoulos. You need to make up your mind

205

what you want to do. It's getting late and I'm about to leave."

"I want immunity," Deidre said.

Damore shook his head. "Miss Hunt, there are no deals, no immunity," he said. "If you want to talk to me, you'll be advised of your rights, and anything you tell me can be used against you in a court of law. It's your decision whether you want to talk to me or whether you want to hold the bag for Mr. Fotopoulos. It's up to you."

Deidre turned her head aside and spoke under her breath, but Damore and Gallagher both thought she intended for them to hear what she said.

"I have to make a decision which way to go, whether to take a chance with Kosta or tell you what happened," she whispered. "I'm afraid of Kosta. He will kill me. I have to tell you what happened."

Deidre turned around to look back at Damore. "Okay, I'll tell you. What do you want to know?"

"Why don't you start from the beginning?" Damore said. "Why don't you tell me about the shooting of Lisa Fotopoulos?"

It was as if a dam had burst. Deidre talked about Kosta using her as a front to hire someone from the streets to kill Lisa. She talked about an assassination club, money laundering, CIA assassinations, Kosta's automatic weapons, hand guns, silencers, counterfeit, and a Secret Service investigation.

Deidre made a big point of telling Damore and Gallagher how Kosta could manipulate her and force her to do things she didn't want to do.

Damore and Gallagher had arrived at police headquarters thinking that they were going to be investigating the murder of Bryan Chase and the attempted murder of Lisa Fotopoulos. But almost as an after-thought, Deidre said:

"Oh, and by the way, there's a boy out in the woods that we shot."

Damore, unable to keep up with the flood of information, almost fell out of his chair. Gallagher and Neall were surprised. Damore thought, *Maybe this woman isn't all there. Maybe she's just rowing with one oar.* But he noticed that when talking about the boy in the woods, she used the pronoun "we," meaning that she was involved.

Damore didn't have a tape recorder with him. He had no idea that so much information would come so quickly.

"You're just going too fast for me," he said. "I can't write it down accurately. For your protection and mine, would you mind if we stopped and went into another room? We'll put a tape recorder on, and you'll be readvised of your rights, and you can tell us what's going on, and we can ask some questions. I just can't get all the information down. You're jumping into too many areas."

Deidre shrugged and said, "No problem."

Damore, Gallagher, and the CID detectives thought that Deidre's behavior was remarkable. She talked animatedly, smoking cigarettes, eating potato chips, and sipping from her Coke. She seemed to be enjoying herself. Damore and Joe Gallagher both thought that she enjoyed being on center stage.

Damore felt that Deidre was a manipulator who was doing her best to present herself as a victim. She maintained that Kosta had forced her to do everything. She was so convincing that Damore felt himself responding sympathetically to her.

207

"There's a Christian part of me that wants to see the good in everybody," he said later. "No matter what she had done, I knew that at some point in her life, Deidre Hunt had been an innocent babe in someone's arms. That part of me wanted to reach out and respond to her presentation of herself as a victim."

But the image that Deidre tried to portray shattered when Damore asked her, "If you were afraid of Mr. Fotopoulos, why didn't you just go to the police?"

She looked up at him with sorrowful eyes. "But, Dave, he had the videotape."

That put Deidre Hunt in perspective for Damore.

By the time everything was ready to go in the main interview room it was midnight. The next two hours were among the most memorable that Damore, Gallagher, and Smith had ever experienced.

24

It was 11:58 p.m. on November 7, 1989, when the official interview began. Deidre was advised of her rights, and Corporal Greg Smith mentioned that she had talked about an "incident."

She started to answer that she had met Kosta through Tony Calderone at Top Shots. "Oh shit," she said. "He's gonna kill Tony, too. I'm just saying because I forgot about it." She gave a little laugh.

Deidre said that Kosta bought her clothes and had an affair with her. She said he made plans with J.R. and Chumbley to rob a bank and an armored car. Kosta, she said, wanted her to pass some of his counterfeit one hundred dollar bills. "He said it was really easy." But Deidre said she never did it.

She said that Kosta had a lot of guns, including an Uzi, an AK-47, which she called a "Russian rifle," handguns, and silencers. Kosta took her shooting in the woods several times, she said. Deidre held a hand about a foot in front of her face. "He shot an AK-47 in front of my face one time," she said. "He shot it right out of the window into the woods and demolished a tree. I was sitting in the passenger seat."

Deidre talked about how she and Kosta had killed Mark Kevin Ramsey, but claimed that she didn't really think they were going to kill him. But once they had Kevin tied to the tree, she said Kosta handed her a .22 caliber pistol, pointed the "Russian rifle" at her, and turned on a video camera. She said Kosta ordered her to shoot Ramsey.

"I didn't know what to do," she said. "I was scared. He could easily have shot him, shot me, and just left. So the video camera was on. I didn't know it was a video camera until after I shot him three times in the chest and once in the head." Deidre pointed a finger at her temple. "After I shot Kevin, he shot him again with the Russian rifle. He made me catch the shell."

Deidre astonished the interviewers with the information she gave.

Deidre said that too much had been going on for three months: killing Kevin, the Hunter-Killer Club, counterfeiting, and "other shit."

"Did he ever plan that you have his wife killed?" Smith asked.

Deidre said yes. First he wanted her to kill Lisa, she said, but she wouldn't do it. Kosta said she should find someone who was "expendable" to do the job.

"He wanted her dead because she had a three hundred and fifty thousand dollar life insurance policy that would pay double if she was murdered," Deidre said.

Deidre said that ever since Lisa found out that she and Kosta were having an affair, Lisa kept Kosta on a tight leash. "He couldn't stand her

210

anymore because all she kept doing was saying, 'Where are you going? What are you doing?' She stuck like glue to him and he couldn't stand that. He wanted her dead. He wanted her dead then." Deidre slapped the table for emphasis.

Deidre gave details of how she and Kosta had plotted to have Lisa killed. Deidre was to offer the hit man ten thousand dollars for the job, but the killer would never collect. Plans called for the assassin to make Lisa's murder look like it had occurred during a robbery. Kosta would hold money out to the killer, who would lower his gun, and Kosta would kill him. Kosta, Deidre said, wanted to come out looking like a hero.

According to Deidre, there had been six bungled attempts to kill Lisa before she was shot on the seventh attempt. She said that Chumbley, J.R., Teja, and Bryan Chase had agreed to kill Lisa, but only Teja and Bryan Chase actually tried. Chumbley wanted to kill Lisa, but he had been arrested. J.R. didn't show up when he was supposed to, but Deidre didn't know why.

Deidre said that she was afraid of Kosta and was especially frightened during the times he took her into the woods to talk. "I never knew where he was taking me or when he was taking me," she said. "He would just call and I'd go. It was just unreal. He could have shot me any time he wanted to. I'd go with him because of that goddamned videotape."

Kosta kept her on a tightrope, she said, and she did exactly what he told her to do because she was afraid to make him angry. "When he said jump, I jumped," she said.

211

The law enforcement officers at the interview had to ask very few questions. Damore interrupted her occasionally to clarify a point, to put things in order, or to get her to slow down. Deidre seemed to enjoy it. She pulled her feet up under her, waved her arms, smoked, and described murder and attempted murder as if making small talk at a cocktail party.

Deidre said Kosta was so frustrated that he was about to come unglued. Too many people knew about the murder plot. "This shit is fucked up," Deidre said. "It's really fucked up. Now he wants to kill them in the middle of the day, in the middle of the street, on the Boardwalk. He doesn't care, it doesn't matter. He just wants to take his AK-47 and kill them all."

Although Kosta was ready to throw caution to the wind, Deidre said, "We did have a plan. To take Matt and a friend named Rick—"

"Is this the bomb?" Smith asked.

"Wait, wait," Deidre said excitedly. "Let's come to that later."

Deidre said she knew nothing about a bomb, then remembered differently. Teja, who didn't know he was on Kosta's hit list, came up with a plan to eliminate Chumbley, J.R., and two of their friends who knew about the murder scheme.

"Teja said we should throw a party and get [those people] to come," Deidre said. "They were expendable. Teja was supposed to make a napalm bomb out of Tide and gasoline and blow them up. I never planted a bomb."

Smith changed the tape on his audio recorder,

and Deidre lit a cigarette, then wrinkled her brow in thought.

"He blew up them cars at City Hall," she said. "Do you remember them cars at City Hall? Three or four. Does anybody remember? They got blown up."

No one answered her; they were all astounded at how freely Deidre was talking. Damore asked if anyone had additional questions.

"No, I think she's doing a fine job," Smith said.

Deidre continued talking, describing Kosta's plans to rob banks and armored cars, his stash of hand grenades, guns, and how he had hid his counterfeit when the Secret Service started to investigate him. She said Kosta gave her money every day, but it was never more than fifty dollars.

Damore asked, "What did you expect to get out of this [Lisa's murder]?"

"Don't ask me," Deidre said. "He didn't offer me no money. I just expected to stay out of jail. That's all I expected to do. I didn't expect no money."

Damore asked, "You've voluntarily said you would take someone to Kevin Ramsey's body in the woods. Do you think you can find the spot?"

Deidre puffed on a cigarette and nodded. "I'm sure I can."

Damore asked Deidre to confirm that she had talked willingly, that no coercion was used, and that there were no deals. She did so.

The interview ended at 2:01 a.m. Damore said later, "Her demeanor was really remarkable. She was an actress taking center stage. She basically gave us the facts, but she presented them in a way that portrayed herself as a victim."

The police were going to look for the body, but even before that, Captain Neall ordered that Kosta be arrested on probable cause.

When police arrived at the house to arrest Kosta, they found Peter Kouracos in Kosta's bed alone. Kouracos explained that he had "crashed on the couch" and was completely "burned out."

He said he had gone into Lisa's bedroom. "Bro," he told Kosta, "I've got to get some sleep."

Kouracos said he lay down on the bed and thought that Kosta had gotten up.

"It must have looked pretty strange to the arresting officers," Kouracos said.

Kosta offered no resistance when he was arrested. At police headquarters Kosta and Deidre were charged with solicitation to commit first-degree murder. Just hours later Deidre would be hit with an additional charge of first-degree murder.

Teja was charged with attempted armed robbery and Chumbley was charged with solicitation for prostitution. Lori was released from custody, and there were no charges against J.R. All of them would soon face various charges, including solicitation to commit first-degree murder, attempted murder, and conspiracy to commit murder.

For Damore and Gallagher, it was the beginning of a sweeping investigation that would occupy them for just over a year, including courtroom proceedings. Besides the Daytona Beach police and state attorney, the U.S. Secret Service and Volusia County Sheriff's Department would be involved.

Following Deidre's interview, Sgt. Jacob F. Ehrhart of the Volusia County Sheriff's Department was summoned to accompany Deidre and Lewis to look for Kevin Ramsey's body. Although Deidre had described the murder in detail, it was so bizarre than no one was sure whether or not she was telling the truth.

They left Daytona Beach police headquarters at 4:40 a.m. Deidre had no trouble finding the spot, even in the darkness. In the lonely scrub woods, the badly decomposed body of Kevin Ramsey sagged from a palm tree.

25

Ehrhart called for support teams to begin an investigation of the crime scene. Deidre was taken back to jail but wasn't charged with murder, pending the initial investigation. It was clear to Ehrhart that she had at least been present when the murder occurred.

"The area was wooded and isolated," he said. "Only those involved in the victim's death would know of its location."

Investigators combed the area and examined the body for evidence while others took photographs. Mike Rafferty, a crime technician, found a spent .22 caliber casing by using a metal detector. The other three casings weren't located. It looked as if there were three holes in the victim's shirt where it covered his chest.

The remains were transported to Halifax Medical Center where Dr. Arthur Botting, Medical Examiner for the 7th Judicial Circuit, conducted a hasty autopsy. Since the hospital was meant to serve live patients, the body had to be removed within four hours. An x-ray showed three .22 caliber bullets in the chest and another in the head. This confirmed what Deidre had said about the type of weapon she used and how she had shot Ramsey.

The body was transported to the morgue until positive identification was made.

The process of gathering evidence is difficult, frustrating, tedious, and exacting. For three days following their initial marathon session with Deidre, Lori, J.R., Teja and Chumbley, neither Damore or Gallagher saw much of their families and became strangers to sleep. They were dog tired, but they were fueled by adrenalin and a sense of urgency.

"A lot of the people we were dealing with were transients," Damore said. "If we didn't get the evidence quickly, it might slip away."

On the morning that Deidre had made her remarkable statement to the police, Damore and Gallagher had wanted to put a wire on her and have her meet with Kosta and ask him something that might cause him to implicate himself. Deidre would have been under heavy guard for her own protection. The Daytona Beach police refused.

Gallagher tried a compromise. How about having Deidre telephone Kosta and record the conversation?

"That posed no danger to her and at least we might have had something incriminating," Gallagher said. "They wouldn't let us do that, either. There's always some tension when police departments are protecting their own areas of jurisdiction."

Damore and Gallagher weren't the only ones who were following up leads and gathering information. Detectives from the Daytona Beach Police Department were also burning the midnight oil and getting dark pouches under their eyes.

The arrest of Kosta and Deidre on attempted murder and conspiracy to commit murder made headlines on November 9, four days after the shooting at Lisa's house. Reporters had done a remarkable job of gathering evidence quickly and getting it into print. The area television stations were also giving the story big play.

The *News-Journal* of Daytona Beach managed to assemble a front-page story written by Kathy Kelly that showed remarkable journalistic ability to gather information. The story even reported Deidre's background in the attempted murder of Veronica Rudzinski in New Hampshire. The story was accompanied by a graphic illustration showing the sequence of events that lead to the shootout in Lisa's bedroom. There was an accompanying story that quoted family friends under the headline: "Friends say couple seemed happily married."

The newspaper and television reports were the first salvo of a media blitz that was unprecedented in Volusia County. It eventually caused trouble for the investigators and the people of the county.

While the media blitzed the public, the police investigation continued at a brisk but thorough pace. Deidre, Teja, J.R., Chumbley, and Lori had given authorities the names of people to whom to talk. There were scores of people to interview and a great deal of physical evidence to uncover.

The police had Ramsey's body, four .22 caliber bullets, and a spent .22 caliber casing, but they had no murder weapon. Deidre had said that Kosta shot Ramsey in the head with an AK-47, but that had not been substantiated by the autopsy. The video-tape recording of which Deidre spoke was not available, and the police questioned whether or not it existed.

Damore and Gallagher spearheaded the investigation and were helped by the Daytona Beach police. The Volusia County Sheriff's Department realized that the state attorney's office could handle the investigation into Ramsey's death and quietly bowed out of the picture.

On November 9 at eleven-thirty a.m., Gallagher, Damore, and Evens went to the Boardwalk to execute a search warrant at Top Shots. While they were searching Top Shots, Darrell Hunter, who owned a restaurant called Captain Darrell's, told them that Marjeanne Powell, who had been Ramsey's girlfriend, wanted to talk to them.

Marjeanne said she was engaged to Ramsey and that at one time had carried his child. On the night Ramsey disappeared, Marjeanne said she saw him talking with Deidre and Kosta on the Boardwalk at eight p.m. Ramsey was supposed to meet her at nine p.m. in a hotel where she had just registered, and she got worried because he didn't show up.

"He was never late," Marjeanne said.

Marjeanne she thought Ramsey was blackmailing Kosta and that he was afraid of him. She said Ramsey was wearing a black T-shirt with some type of insignia on it and dungarees when she saw him talking with Kosta and Deidre. Marjeanne had described the clothes that covered Ramsey's remains. Marjeanne said she had not seen Ramsey since he was with Kosta and Deidre on the Boardwalk.

Marjeanne knew Chase by sight but had never

seen him with Kosta, but she told the investigators that she had seen him in a car with Deidre the same day that Teja tried to kill Lisa at Joyland.

Marjeanne left, but before they went to Top Shots, Damore, Gallagher, and Evens were stopped by Hunter.

He said he had just had a brief conversation with Tony Calderone. "He told me that he had found Kosta at his home Saturday afternoon," Hunter said. "Kosta told him that 'it was botched, that he [Chase] was supposed to shoot Lisa three times in the head, but the gun jammed.' "

It was about one-thirty p.m. when the investigators contacted Calderone at Top Shots. Damore asked Calderone if he could cooperate in the investigation of the attempted homicide of Lisa, the homicide of Bryan Chase and Kevin Ramsey. Calderone said he would.

Damore started to advised him of his rights, but Calderone interrupted.

"That's all right. I'm willing to answer any questions."

"Have you had any conversations regarding Kosta shooting Chase?" Damore asked.

"I don't understand the question."

Damore asked the question again.

"All I know is what I read in the newspaper, heard on the news, and what Kosta told me," Calderone said.

"What did Kosta tell you?"

"Nothing."

Calderone said the only thing he could remember was that Holly had called him on Saturday to tell him that Kosta had not shown up for work.

220

Calderone said he called Kosta's house and was told there had been a tragedy. Calderone said he didn't see Kosta until Saturday afternoon at about four p.m. when he found him sleeping on his couch.

"I don't know how he got in," he said. "The door was locked. Kosta had never been to my house before."

Calderone described how Kosta had patted him down, looking for a wire. Calderone said he asked Kosta some questions, then Kosta whispered something he didn't understand.

"What?" he asked.

"Forget it."

Calderone said he asked Kosta some more questions.

Kosta said, "What happened happens."

Calderone asked him to clarify that.

"You talk too much," Kosta told him.

The interview progressed and Calderone said, "I know that Kosta shot his wife."

"How do you know that?" Damore asked.

"Two plus two equals four," Calderone said.

The investigators didn't think that Calderone was being completely honest with them. He revealed some things and held back on others. He said Kosta had never said anything about Lisa's shooting, but told them that he told Lisa that her husband was having an affair with Deidre. Calderone said he knew that Ramsey had been fired for stealing, but that was as far as it went. Calderone was vague about his own salary and painted a confusing word picture about it. He didn't receive the same amount each week.

221

Calderone said that he and Kosta were together at Deidre's house one time, and Kosta suggested that they take out life insurance policies on one another. Calderone said he told Kosta to forget it.

The investigators had already heard from others that Kosta had automatic weapons and that he sometimes carried them in the trunk of his car. Calderone said he had seen guns in Kosta's car but noted that he wasn't an expert. Pressed further, he said, "They looked like automatic weapons." Then he admitted that Kosta had machine guns buried in the woods near Atlantic Avenue and said they would need a metal detector to find them. Calderone refused a request to help find them.

The investigators weren't surprised when Calderone asked to go off the record, headed into the men's restroom and motioned for Damore to follow him. Damore did so. They were inside for about ten minutes. When they returned, Damore asked Calderone if he would repeat what he had said privately. Calderone refused.

When Calderone left, Damore told his two associates that Calderone had confirmed the conversation that Hunter had reported to them. Calderone also asked for remuneration. When Damore asked what he meant, Calderone said, "If I tell you, I'll have problems with other Greeks. I got to do business with them."

Damore said, "If these people find out you're protecting Kosta, and he tried to kill his wife, then you'll have problems."

Calderone said he wanted immunity.

"If you're involved, there's no immunity," Damore told him. "But if all you have is information after it happened, you're not breaking any laws if you co-operate and tell the truth."

Calderone told Damore that Kosta had said "the kid fucked it up, the gun jammed, and the kid said, 'Now what do I do?' and started to walk away; that's when I shot him."

Calderone said Kosta told him that Chase tried to get up, so he shot him in the head, and added, "Dead men don't tell tales."

The three law officers started to leave but Calderone stopped them.

"Kosta told me Ramsey was going to frame him and that he was going to get him," Calderone said.

"What do you mean 'get him'?" Damore asked, wanting to have more specific information.

"He had a hit on him," Calderone said.

That wasn't specific enough for Damore. "Hit him physically?" he asked.

"No, kill him," Calderone answered.

During their investigation, Gallagher and other investigators had found a number of inconsistencies with the story Deidre had told them. There were too many people who knew at least something about Ramsey's murder and the murder contract on Lisa.

Based on information from other sources, Gallagher thought he needed to interview Deidre again. He and Investigator Meyers of the Volusia County Sheriff's Department went to the Volusia County Branch Jail, a forbidding complex with high hurricane fences topped with barbed wire, to talk with Deidre. Gallagher read Deidre her rights again, and

Deidre waived them, but said she wanted an attorney present.

"Would you clarify that?" he asked.

"Dave told me an attorney would be present, and I just want one," Deidre said.

"Then I guess we have to leave."

Gallagher and Meyers started toward the door.

"No, no, no," Deidre said. "I want you people here."

Gallagher told her there were inconsistencies between what she had told them and the facts they had uncovered.

"I asked her to be completely truthful in her statements," he said, "particularly how and under what circumstances Kevin Ramsey ended up in the woods."

Gallagher wanted to know the precise date that Ramsey was killed, but Deidre was uncertain. "It was the same day that Teja went to work for his father," she said. She thought the company Teja worked for was Ottis Construction Company.

Deidre had another version of what she had been doing before being involved in Ramsey's death. She said she was at Top Shots when Kosta called her from Joyland. Deidre said that Kosta told her to go behind Popeye's and that before Kosta's call she had seen Ramsey and asked him if he had talked with Kosta. Ramsey told her that he had.

From that point on, Deidre was inconsistent about the time and whether or not Ramsey went with her to Popeye's. She claimed that Ramsey suggested that they go to Lori's old house to get away from the crowds and that Kosta picked them up there. When Kosta showed up in his BMW, she said Ramsey got in willingly, thinking that they were going shooting. This was at least around nine p.m., according to Deidre, which Gallagher thought was a little late for target practice.

When they arrived at the shooting scene, Deidre said Kosta took an AK-47 from his trunk and said he would shoot at Ramsey's feet. "He said, 'The enemy will shoot at you and you need to get used to it.'" Deidre said Ramsey never questioned what was happening or why.

Deidre said she remembered taking the .22 pistol with the silencer and putting it in her waistband. Kosta and Ramsey walked ahead of her, chatting. Kosta told Ramsey he was going to tie him up, and Deidre said Ramsey never questioned why. She said that Kosta had a video camera and a rechargeable flashlight that he kept in the trunk of his car.

Deidre claimed that Ramsey was laughing and thought it was all a joke. "He really trusted Kosta," she said.

Deidre said Kosta pointed the rifle at her and told her to shoot. She said Ramsey was still smiling when she shot him. She told the two investigators that Kosta was about seven to ten feet to her left. Deidre said that at some point Ramsey moved, but she didn't remember if it was before or after he was shot. She said Kosta told her to shoot Ramsey three times in the chest and once in the head. She said she couldn't remember if that was before or during the shooting. Deidre, who had described the shooting in detail earlier, claimed that she didn't remember shooting Ramsey.

But Deidre told Gallagher that Kosta didn't believe Ramsey was dead after she shot him because he had moved. Deidre said Kosta made her take her jacket off to catch the shell of his automatic weapon which he fired once into Ramsey's head.

At this point, Armando Molina, a public defender, appeared to represent Deidre. The interview was stopped so Deidre could confer with the attorney, then said she would continue.

Meyers asked why she didn't question Kosta's order to shoot Ramsey. Deidre said she had looked at Kosta and realized that he was serious and that he had an AK-47. Although she said she didn't remember the shooting, Deidre said that Kosta untied Ramsey and put the rope in his car.

"Why are you doing that?" she asked.

"Because I have more of the same rope at home."

Very little of what Deidre said made sense to Gallagher and Meyers. She seemed to be altering her story to portray herself as a victim who was forced to commit murder by Kosta, who completely dominated her.

Even at this early stage, the police investigation had uncovered the fact that Ramsey was blackmailing Kosta, that Kosta intended to kill him, and that his intention was widely known.

The two investigators thought Deidre was lying. "We questioned why Ramsey would enter Kosta's vehicle when it was common knowledge that he was trying to blackmail Kosta," Gallagher said. Deidre claimed that she didn't know about the conflict between Kosta and Ramsey until after he was killed. Then, she said, Lori told her.

It was obvious to Gallagher and Meyers that Deidre was refining her story to convince them that she was little more than a puppet who was manipulated by Kosta Fotopoulos. But it was a strange interview. Deidre confirmed that she offered J.R. ten thousand dollars to do a job for her but refused to say what it was for, and she told Gallagher and Meyers that Kosta had asked her to call Lisa's insurance company to see if a homicide would pay double indemnity. Deidre said she never made the call but said that Kosta did.

She said the insurance policies on Lisa's life were for two hundred and fifty thousand dollars and one hundred thousand dollars and that Kosta believed he would get double that amount if Lisa died from other than natural causes, plus the car and part of the businesses. Deidre told the two investigators that she and Kosta had talked about getting married.

At that point, Gallagher lost any feelings of sympathy he had for Deidre. She was a manipulator, and she was changing her story to her best advantage. It was unthinkable that Kevin Ramsey, who was afraid that Kosta was going to kill him, would willingly get into a car with him at night to drive into the woods for an initiation. And Deidre, who had remembered the shooting so vividly just the day before, was suddenly developing a selective memory.

In the meantime, Damore and Gallagher were certain that they had saved additional lives by having Kosta arrested in such a relatively short time. Both of them believed that Kosta fully intended to kill anyone who knew about his plot to have Lisa murdered. In the days following Lisa's shooting, Kosta had very little time to go about his murderous business.

"Kosta had a real problem," Damore said. "Lisa

wasn't dead but was at the hospital in critical condition. That meant he didn't have unlimited time to go looking for Teja and others who knew about the plans to kill Lisa. He had to be available to avoid suspicion."

26

The morning Kosta was arrested, Peter Koura-cos went to Halifax Hospital to visit Lisa. He was surprised to find out that there was a trespass warrant against him being on the hospital grounds.

Kouracos thought that he was above suspicion. According to him, Dino told him, "We know you didn't have anything to do with it. We know that Kosta was just using you."

Uniformed police officers were stationed around the house on Halifax Avenue to keep anyone from tampering with evidence. Early on November 8, Gallagher and Neall got a consent form from the Paspalakis family to search Joyland and acquired search warrants to search Kosta's BMW.

The investigators discovered miscellaneous items at Joyland that belonged to Kosta, includ-ing *Soldier of Fortune, Playboy,* and other maga-zines. There was a magazine on guns and a filing cabinet containing things that belonged to Kosta.

The investigators obtained a search warrant to go through the file, but there was little in it that helped them with the case.

Kosta's BMW was impounded, and one of the investigators read the search warrant to it. Although this seems odd, it's a legal requirement. The investigators found miscellaneous items inside the car, but when they opened the trunk they found ten thousand dollars.

On November 11, Kouracos met with Damore, Gallagher, Ehrhart and Smith for a videotaped interview at Daytona Beach police headquarters. Kouracos, who appeared voluntarily, was accompanied by his attorney, Michael Lambert. Kouracos told the investigators that he considered both Kosta and Lisa as brother and sister.

Kouracos admitted that he knew about Kosta's counterfeiting operation and said, "Lisa knew as much about it as I did." Kouracos told the investigators that he had acted as a lookout when Kosta talked with Barbara and Vasilos Markantonakis after they had been arrested for counterfeiting. Kouracos denied involvement in the counterfeit operation or threatening Barbara and Vasilos.

The four-hour videotaped interview covered a wide range of topics. Damore and Smith both told Kouracos that they felt he was being vague about dates and events. Kouracos retorted that he was angry with the police for not warning him about Kosta's involvement in the deaths of Ramsey and Chase, since he might be a target for assassination.

"How could we have done that when we didn't know about it?" Damore asked.

Kouracos stammered. "I don't know."

"What do you think of Kosta?" Damore asked.

230

"I thought he was a pretty great guy. Now, if what they say is true, I don't think he's so great."

The investigators had heard about torture tapes that Kosta had and also that Kouracos was involved in a videotape recording of a sex orgy involving at least one prominent local politician. Kouracos said that it wasn't true.

He admitted that he had taken Deidre Hunt to two political parties but that he wasn't involved with her. Kouracos said that Deidre had been popular, but she had embarrassed him, and he was worried that she might shatter Kosta and Lisa's marriage, and had tried to get her to go back to New Hampshire.

Kouracos said he had gone with Kosta in the woods to bury things but had not considered this unusual because it reflected Survivalist thinking. Kouracos said he would be happy to show the police where he had taken Kosta to bury things.

Just after the incident at Joyland, Kouracos said that Lisa thought Kosta was trying to have her killed. He was asked why he didn't report it.

"I couldn't believe it, so I dismissed it," Kouracos said.

The prominent politico presented another scenario to the investigators regarding the attempt on Lisa's life. He said they should investigate David McGrath, a developer who wanted to get control of a portion of the Boardwalk held by several small Greek business owners. However police found that Kouracos's theory had no basis in fact.

The same day that Kouracos was interviewed, he took investigators to the areas where Kosta might have buried automatic weapons and counterfeit currency. The police searched the area but didn't find anything.

But Robert Wheeler, chief investigator for the state attorney's office, wasn't about to give up. He rented a metal detector. Wheeler, who looks as powerful as a Mack truck, went with his wife to the woods every weekend to look for whatever Kosta had buried.

Dino accepted a collect call from Kosta, who was locked up in the Volusia County Branch Jail.

"Why don't you take a lie detector test?" Dino asked.

"My attorney advised against it, and it can't be used in court," Kosta said. "Do you think I had anything to do with Lisa being shot?"

"As of today, I'm one hundred percent sure that you did it," Dino said.

"What did they find today?" Kosta asked.

The news media widely reported that Kosta had tried to have Lisa killed on five different occasions. Although Lisa was in serious condition at Halifax Hospital, she accepted a call from her jailed husband.

"I miss you," Kosta said.

"Yeah, you missed me five times," she said, and hung up.

Chief Paul Crow of the Daytona Beach Police

visited Lisa at the hospital and talked with her. Crow didn't divulge the specifics of his conversation, but had this comment for the press when he emerged from his talk with Lisa.

"This is the most bizarre case I've seen in Volusia County in twenty-five years," he said. "It was about money, pure and simple. We've been in a footrace to get the suspects arrested, now we have a long, detailed investigation ahead."

Damore's feelings were even stronger. "It isn't bizarre so much as it is sickening," he said.

Lisa changed her insurance policies, deleting Kosta as a beneficiary, and wrote a will that excluded him. Dino made certain that the news was made public. He said Lisa had taken the action to protect herself. They were still concerned that someone might still have a contract to kill Lisa, even though Kosta was in jail. But if Kosta would not benefit from Lisa's death, they hoped it would discourage anyone Kosta had hired from carrying out the assassination.

By November 14, investigators had gathered enough information to arrest Lori Henderson. She was picked up at her apartment on Kennedy Avenue and charged with conspiracy to commit first-degree murder and solicitation to commit first-degree murder.

Detective Adamy's arrest sheet noted that Lori knew all about the plans to kill Lisa, had gone with Deidre and Teja to buy a gun and a knife to kill her, and knew that the murderer would be killed.

"She knew when Hunt hired Bryan Chase, knew about the murder attempt, and that Chase would be killed by Kosta," Adamy's report noted. "The defendant made no attempt to notify authorities during any of the plans and acts that were attempted/carried out." Adamy noted that Lori had gone with Deidre and waited near Lisa's house "to see that the plan was carried out."

Two new charges were lodged against Teja in addition to attempted armed robbery; he was also charged with attempted murder and conspiracy to commit murder.

The charges against Kosta were two counts of murder, attempted murder, and several charges of conspiracy and solicitation to commit first-degree murder. Two charges of murder were entered against Deidre, along with a charge of attempted murder, and several charges of conspiracy and solicitation to commit first-degree murder.

Lori's arrest caused immediate legal problems. Since she was broke and couldn't afford to hire an attorney, Christopher Quales, an assistant Public Defender, was ordered to represent her. This was an unacceptable situation since Lori's father was employed as a Public Defender, and Teja and Deidre had been appointed legal counsel from the same office.

James B. Gibson filed motions from the Public Defender to have the office released from representing Lori, Teja, and Deidre because of the position Lori's father held. Gibson noted that if the Public Defender represented Lori, it could lead to "the appearance of impropriety and conflict of interest."

The Public Defender's office was released and a private attorney, Gary W. Tinsley, was appointed to represent Lori. His legal fees were to be paid with public money. By this time Ray Cass had been appointed from the Public Defender's office to represent Deidre. He also filed a motion to be released, noting that the Public Defender had "been engaged in confidential communication" with both Deidre, Lori, and Teja and that "conflict exists."

Cass said that "the Public Defender cannot provide meaningful assistance to counsel Deidre Hunt at this time." Cass noted that the Public Defender had been released from representing Lori and said, "the Public Defender cannot provide meaningful assistance . . . to Deidre Hunt at this time."

Cass's plea noted the complications that had arisen because Lori's father was an assistant Public Defender.

"It is unrealistic to expect a father of a criminal defendant to refrain from actively participating in his daughter's defense," Cass wrote. "This is especially true where the father is a lawyer with considerable expertise in criminal law. At the very least, it should be expected that the father would offer solace and advice. It would be impossible to build a 'Chinese Wall' in an attempt to eliminate the existing conflict of interest. Under the worst scenario, the continued representation of Deidre

235

Hunt could result in a member of this office cross-examining Ms. Henderson. . . . That situation must be avoided at all costs as it reeks of conflict of interest and the appearance of impropriety."

Judge Foxman saw the wisdom of the argument and granted the request. Teja had already been assigned a Public Defender and Kosta, who was not yet broke, had hired Theodore Zentner to represent him. Peter Niles, a stout man of medium height with a full head of salt-and-pepper hair and a penchant for expensive jewelry, was hired as a Special Public Defender to represent Deidre.

A hypnotist was engaged by the police to interview Lisa in the hospital. They hoped that in a relaxed state, Lisa would be able to remember more details that would help in the investigation. Lisa couldn't remember anything more than she had already told the police.

"I don't really think I was hypnotized," she said.

The media continued with an uninterrupted barrage of stories about the murder-for-hire plot. Two nationally syndicated television shows, "Hard Copy" and "Inside Edition," televised what they call "reenactments" of Deidre shooting Kevin Ramsey "while the camera rolls." A lot of people who saw the shows thought they were seeing the actual murder. State Attorney John Tanner and

Damore were worried about the jury pool in Volusia County becoming contaminated.

The Constitution stipulates that a defendant is presumed innocent until found guilty by an impartial jury of their peers. Finding an impartial jury in Volusia County seemed almost impossible, even at that early stage of the investigation.

Deidre telephoned Gallagher from the Volusia Branch Jail on November 17 and asked if he would visit her. When Gallagher arrived, Deidre said that she had received a letter from Tony Calderone, who wanted her to telephone so he could "tie up some loose ends." Deidre said she had no idea why Calderone would need to speak to her. Gallagher looked at the unsigned letter but checked the telephone number, and it was for Calderone's home. Deidre tried twice to reach Calderone by phone but was unable to reach him.

At this time, Deidre was altering her original story of Ramsey's murder and the plot to kill Lisa. Each version was increasingly refined to make her the victim and to implicate others to a greater degree.

During this meeting, Deidre remembered that Kosta had told her about a conversation he had with Calderone after Lisa had been shot. "Kosta said Calderone asked, 'Why didn't you come to me?' " Deidre remembered. " 'Because she would be dead and we would both be rich.' "

Deidre recalled that Kosta tortured her to maintain control.

"She stated that Fotopoulos would actually burn

237

her with a clothes iron and then take a razor and scratch it back and forth until it bled," Gallagher wrote in his report. "He would then lick the open wound, which contained blood."

The investigators had a doctor examine Deidre for scars.

"She had a couple of little scars," Gallagher said. "But nothing more than what you would expect to find on anybody."

27

On November 22, just two days after Lisa had been released from the hospital, a small army from the state attorney's office and Daytona Beach Police Department descended on her home. Among those who arrived with search warrants and consent forms from Lisa, Mary, and Dino were a number of heavy hitters. From the state attorney's office were Damore, Wheeler, and Gallagher. The Daytona Beach police were represented by Evens, Adamy, and Brad Crowell, who was a bomb and explosive technician. They were afraid that Kosta had set booby traps. Corporal Jeff Lilly from the Volusia County Sheriff's Department was on hand.

Under police supervision, a contractor cut out a portion of bloodstained carpet and wood in Lisa's bedroom. There was a bullet embedded in that section of the floor, which was where Chase's head had been when Kosta shot him.

The investigators conducted an exhaustive search of the house, grounds, and garage. The garage revealed Kosta's obsession with weapons and guerrilla warfare. Among the things the investigators found were four double-edged knives, a bayonet, several camouflage holsters, several empty boxes for military-class bullets, a gas mask, helmet, bulletproof vest, a detonator and fuse, a camouflaged bow with matching aluminum arrows, full-face ski masks, and various kinds of live ammunition and other military equipment.

The investigators found books on how to make silencers and evidence that Kosta had attempted, if not succeeded, in making such illegal devices. There were also books on how to make semiautomatic assault weapons fully automatic, along with equipment needed to do the job. The investigators found several books on survival and a portable radio scanner with forty active channels. Such scanners allow the user to hear and pinpoint the locations of various police departments, fire departments, armored trucks, ambulances, and other operations that use their own radio frequencies.

The searchers discovered several empty 8-millimeter videotape cartridges and some miscellaneous movies, but they didn't find the murder videotape after almost a full day of searching.

"We were a little doubtful that it existed," Damore said. "The story was almost incredulous."

After an exhaustive search, the murder weapons used to kill Ramsey had not been found. Lisa remembered that Kosta had been digging in the backyard after their trip to Edgewater.

"I saw Kosta digging around the barbecue pit," she told Damore and Adamy. "I think he might have buried a brown briefcase there."

Dino took them to the barbecue pit, and Lisa wanted to come along. The police had to help her because she was wavering on her feet.

Adamy, Wheeler, Damore, Crowell, and Jeff Lilly searched around the pit.

"We checked all the grounds and could not locate anything," Adamy said. "Mr. Wheeler was over by the barbecue pit section himself, and he started removing miscellaneous items, basically garbage that was piled in this one section."

The others joined in the search and found a black vinyl bag that was hidden beneath the garbage. Everyone backed away to the safety of the house and left the bag for Crowell, the bomb technician, to open.

Crowell carefully opened the bag after checking to see if it might be set to explode. He opened it and saw the muzzle of an AK-47. Crowell was still cautious. He needed to see what was inside the bag by moving the objects in it to make sure there was no booby trap set to go off when things were removed. When Crowell was satisfied that the bag was safe to open, it was taken into custody by the Daytona Beach police. The contents weren't removed.

Crowell told the investigators that in addition to the AK-47, he had seen a .22 caliber Ruger semi-automatic with a silencer still attached and what appeared to be a silencer for an automatic weapon, probably an Uzi. He also saw a bayonet and a magazine for an automatic weapon. The investigators were excited about the discovery because the Ruger and the AK-47 were both described by Deidre as the weapons that had been used to kill Ramsey.

Near the end of the day, Damore and Adamy were in the garage discussing the search and were getting ready to leave. As Adamy turned to walk out of the garage, he glanced up on a top shelf

241

on the east wall and saw a brown vinyl bag.

"Has that bag been checked?" he asked.

Damore said they better make sure.

Adamy stepped up and saw that the bag was lying on its side. The left side of the bag was zipped closed, and the top was closed by a belt that locked. But the left side of the bag was opened, and when Adamy got close, he looked inside and his heart skipped a beat.

"There's a tape cassette inside," he said.

Damore hurried to the house, went upstairs, found Lisa, and brought her to the garage so she could see the bag.

"Do you know whose bag that is?" Adamy asked.

"Does Kosta own the bag?" Damore asked.

Lisa answered that the bag belonged to her mother and late father and that Kosta had access to it. She said the bag was used at Joyland. Damore and Adamy received permission to take the bag with them as well as the bag containing the weapons and ammunition.

That evening the investigators watched the videotape they had found inside the bag. It was shot at night, using a poor light source, but it clearly showed Ramsey tied to a tree wearing a black Harley-Davidson shirt and jeans. Deidre was shown shooting Ramsey in the chest three times, just as she had described. Deidre's voice was recorded, as was that of the man who had shot the video.

The tape was fifty-seven seconds long, but it was stunning. None of them had ever seen anything like it.

"Kosta must have watched it a lot of times," Damore said. "He kept that incriminating tape for more than two months."

Finding the videotape of the shooting as Deidre had described it was of major importance. There might be fingerprints on the cassette, and there was a man's voice that could be compared with Kosta's to see if the voice prints matched.

Deidre had told several versions of how the shooting was carried out, growing more imaginative or forgetful, as it benefited her. One thing she had not wavered from was the fact that Kosta had shot Ramsey in the head with an AK-47. The fact that such an assault rifle was found along with the Ruger gave her claim some credence.

But if Ramsey had been shot in the head with an AK-47, why didn't the Medical Examiner's autopsy show the massive wound it would have made? The case had gotten off to a fast start, but there was much to be done. Damore and Gallagher knew they were going to be running a marathon.

The next day, which was Thanksgiving, Adamy obtained a search warrant and read it to the bag found in the barbecue pit while Damore and Gallagher looked on. They opened the bag and carefully removed the contents for forensic tests, then the evidence was taken into custody by the Daytona Beach police.

The videotape cassette was examined and a palm print was found on it. Police laboratory technicians compared the print against Kosta's, and it was a perfect match. There was no doubt that Kosta had handled the tape.

* * *

Robert Wheeler, the chief investigator for the state attorney for the Seventh Judicial Circuit, had sunk his teeth into the case and was hanging on like a pit bull. He reminisced about Lisa and Dino when he worked at Seabreeze High School. "They were both good kids," he said. "Lisa was one of my assistants. She called me early on about the case, because we're good friends."

Like Damore and Gallagher, Wheeler was working on other cases while he plowed ahead with the Fotopoulos investigation. He, therefore, had little time to spend with his wife. So they could be together, Wheeler took her into the woods with him while he searched for Kosta's hidden cache with a metal detector.

On December 3, a Sunday, Wheeler and his wife got a beep. They had found something buried in the ground. Wheeler got on his radio and contacted the Daytona Beach police. Before long, Detectives Lewis and Daniel Overbey joined the Wheelers, along with Crowell, the bomb expert.

Crowell uncovered two canisters. One contained an automatic AK-11 and counterfeit currency, and the other contained two live hand grenades, a .38 caliber pistol, and more counterfeit. Later examinations showed that the canisters, the guns, grenades, and counterfeit were covered with Kosta's fingerprints.

Vicki Andrinopoulos, one of Lisa's cousins, told Gallagher that she had been disturbed at Kosta's behavior at the Halloween party at Razzles and immediately after Lisa had been shot. At Razzles, Vicki said that Kosta met her uncharacteristically with a big hug, then disappeared for three hours while Vicki sat with Lisa. Lisa was disturbed because Deidre was at the party.

While the family waited at the Halifax ICU, Vicki said that Angelo called. He wanted to talk with Kosta, but didn't ask how Lisa was.

"I looked all over for him," Vicki said. "I finally found him about half an hour later lying on a gurney in the hallway which was quite a distance from ICU. I wondered why he didn't stay with the rest of the family nearer to Lisa."

The Sunday after Lisa was shot, Vicki told Gallagher that she had attended a party celebrating the Greek Festival at George Vouvakis's home.

"I heard Peter tell someone that he had joked with Kosta about how hard it would be for Lisa to travel in the future," Vicki said. "He told Kosta that the bullet in her head would set off alarms at the airport."

Vicki said she didn't think it was funny and telephoned Kosta to ask about it, and he told her it was true. Vicki was angry and asked Kouracos to drive her to Lisa's residence. Kosta opened the door, holding a gun.

Vicki went inside the house. Kosta had never pointed a gun at her before, but she wasn't afraid. "I want to see the room where Lisa was shot," she said.

Kosta refused.

"It's my aunt's house," she said and went upstairs, with Kosta following her.

Vicki said Kosta still had the bloodstained com-

245

forter on the bed and said that he was sleeping with it.

"I don't like the way you and Peter are joking around so much," Vicki said. "You don't show any remorse."

Kosta was still holding the gun.

"What's it like to kill a person?" Vicki asked.

"It felt great. I would do it again if I could."

Vicki looked him in the eye. "I know how it feels, because I would like to do it to the person who shot Lisa."

Kosta said, "You're hard like me. You understand what I'm saying. Your husband's too soft, he wouldn't be able to do it."

Vicki told Gallagher that Kosta didn't say he was sorry that Lisa had been shot or feel badly about killing Chase. Instead, it seemed to her that Kosta was bragging.

On December 4, a petty criminal named Sheila Lorch was in a holding cell at the Courthouse Annex, waiting with other inmates to be transported to the Branch Jail.

Kosta introduced himself to her and asked, "Do you know Deidre Hunt."

"Yes, I do," Sheila said.

"How is she doing?"

"Oh, she's getting along fine, watching television, laughing and talking to everybody."

"Will you give her a message from me?"

Sheila said she would.

"Tell the bitch I'm going to kill her ass."

Sheila said Kosta was trying to get out of his

246

handcuffs and was examining the lock on the cell door.

"Has anybody got a bobby pin?" he asked.

One of the women started to give him one, but Sheila and another woman started screaming to get a guard's attention.

"You might as well give up because you can't get out," an inmate told Kosta.

"Oh, I'll get out," Kosta replied. "I've got some people who are coming to get me soon." He spoke again to Sheila, "You tell Deidre that if I don't die soon, I'm coming to get her."

A deputy sheriff reacted to the yelling and asked what was going on. No one said anything, but Kosta made a bizarre request.

"Can I order a pizza?" he asked.

The deputy looked at him as if he were crazy.

"How about at least letting me use the phone. I'll give you a hundred dollars."

The deputy told him to forget it.

Sheila telephoned Gallagher just as soon as she got a chance. He met her at the Branch Jail.

"I'm only telling you this because I'm afraid I might be killed, too," Sheila said.

David Damore wanted to try all of the defendants collectively to save time and expense. Much of the evidence would be unnecessarily redundant if they were tried separately. Damore presented evidence to the fall term of the grand jury on December 6, 1989.

Kosta and Deidre were indicted on two counts of first-degree murder in the deaths of Ramsey and

247

Chase. Kosta, Deidre, Teja, and Lori were indicted for conspiracy to commit first-degree murder. Teja was indicted for attempted armed robbery and attempted first-degree murder. All were ordered held without bond.

28

Judge S. James Foxman had been assigned to preside over the Chase-Ramsey murder cases and the lesser charges stemming from the shooting of Lisa Fotopoulos. Judge Foxman, a tall, handsome man with rimless eyeglasses was no stranger to tough cases.

Foxman had been a trial lawyer for eleven years before he was appointed a circuit court judge in 1979. A week after his appointment he presided over his first case, a man charged with murdering two teenagers. The case, which resulted in a guilty verdict, the jury recommending a death sentence, was a shock to Foxman, but it was only a prelude to what was to come.

Every dirty, nasty case seemed to end up on Foxman's docket. Before being assigned to the Hunt-Fotopoulos case, as it was commonly referred to, he had imposed the death sentence ten times. Only one of the sentences had been overturned on appeal.

A judge has to be concerned with defendants receiving a fair trial, especially in murder cases, where the stakes are literally life and death. Foxman worried that the media blitz about the Hunt-

Fotopoulos case could make it impossible for them to receive a trial by an impartial jury.

Foxman had another problem besides guaranteeing the defendants a fair trial: he had to be concerned about the First Amendment, which guarantees freedom of the press. The judge thought that information reporters were gathering from defendants and attorneys could be used as evidence.

All four defense attorneys were making frequent statements to the press. Damore, who practically ignored the press throughout the case, even succumbed to temptation after the videotape of Ramsey's murder was found. "God must have been looking out for us in this investigation," Damore said.

"Reenactments" of Deidre shooting Ramsey were broadcast on two nationally syndicated television shows, *Hardcover* and *Inside Edition*. Kathy Kelly, an enterprising reporter of the *News-Journal* of Daytona Beach, interviewed Deidre at the Branch Jail by telephone to write an article that upset the judge, defense attorneys, and Damore.

Kelly's story was an excellent piece of investigative journalism, and it was the first article that reported a defendant's point of view. The December 7 issue of the newspaper featured a banner headline that read: "Suspect says she tried to warn Lisa Fotopoulos."

Kelly had written a letter to Deidre at the Branch Jail saying that she might like to tell her side of the story. She gave Deidre her telephone number, and Deidre called.

Kelly's story quoted Deidre as saying she had tried to warn Lisa that Kosta was trying to have her killed. Deidre said she had a telephone number

250

that only rang in Lisa's bedroom, but on the times that she called, she reached Kosta and hung up.

Kelly asked why Deidre didn't tell anyone about the contracts on Lisa's life. "I didn't tell anyone because I didn't want to involve anybody else," Deidre told her. Kelly wrote that Deidre painted Kosta as "a cold-blooded mercenary who liked to watch torture videos" and who claimed to have killed people for the Central Intelligence Agency. Kelly wrote that Deidre said Kosta showed her checks to back up his claim and told her "I don't even know these people. They just call me up and ask me if I wanted [*sic*] the job, then name a price."

Kelly's story reported that Deidre asked Kosta what was the smallest amount of money he would accept to kill someone. According to Kelly, Deidre said that Kosta answered anywhere from two thousand dollars to one hundred thousand dollars, depending on how hard it was. The article said that Kosta told Deidre that he killed for two reasons: profit and revenge.

"The man is filthy rich," Deidre was quoted as saying. The story reported that Kosta told Deidre he had one hundred thousand dollars in counterfeit and good currency, buried.

The article recounted Deidre's version of Ramsey's murder. Deidre said she had been forced to shoot Ramsey and that Kosta would have killed her otherwise. Deidre told Kelly that Kosta shot Ramsey in the head with a rifle. Deidre said the videotape recording of her shooting Ramsey was Kosta's insurance to prevent her from revealing his plans to kill Lisa.

Kelly wrote that Deidre's relationship with Kosta had initially been employee to boss, but that they soon started a sexual affair. "He was a nice guy, he was a friend to me," Deidre told Kelly. "It wasn't love. We had a thing going."

Deidre told Kelly that Kosta sometimes bought her roses and clothing, but that he revealed a dark side that scared her. Part of that dark side, Deidre said, was what she claimed were his contract murders. But she said Kosta's darker nature ran even deeper than that.

"He showed me a [homemade] video once," Deidre told Kelly, and went on to say that it was of a person being tortured. Although Deidre couldn't see the face of the torturer, she recognized it as being Kosta because of his body movements.

Deidre was reported to have said that she tried to break up with Kosta, but was afraid to. She claimed that she wanted to save Lisa's life. "Lisa was already in danger," Deidre told Kelly. "I figured if I told her [Lisa], she would take him out of her will, and he would leave her alone."

Kelly noted that Deidre was considered a co-conspirator in a plan to have Lisa Fotopoulos murdered. Deidre said she was worried about being found guilty of murder and being executed in the electric chair, something she hoped wouldn't happen. On the other hand, Deidre told Kelly, "I'm not totally innocent because I didn't call the police, but this man held a gun on me and ordered me to shoot someone to death."

Deidre claimed that Lori should not be charged with conspiracy to commit murder or anything else. "This thing is getting totally out of hand," Deidre told Kelly. "She was my best friend, she was comforting me. I will do anything to get them to drop the charges on her. She is innocent of everything."

252

Deidre said that she was afraid she would be killed before the trial. Without her testimony, she said, there was no case against Kosta. Deidre said there was a contract on her life. "I don't think I'll make it to court," Kelly's story quoted Deidre as saying.

Court convened three days before Christmas. First Kosta was led into the courtroom with manacles on his wrists and legs, and a chain around his waist which was held firmly by a deputy. Then came Teja, Deidre, and Lori, all manacled and linked together by chains round their waists. Six armed deputies stood guard as Foxman called the court to order.

Concerned about the pretrial publicity, Foxman wrote a restraining order on December 20. The hearing on December 22 was to get advice and hear arguments from the attorneys involved. The *News-Journal* was represented by Lester Kaney, who was associated with the prestigious law firm of Cobb Cole & Bell.

Foxman opened the proceedings by saying that the national and local publicity could make a fair trial impossible if the attorneys and defendants continued to "battle it out" in the media.

"This case has been the subject of great and unusual pretrial publicity," Foxman wrote. "The case is also highly unusual—far from other murder cases." The judge was cautious: "The court is reluctant to articulate why it is so unusual because to do so would cause the same harm the court is trying to avoid."

The judge said the court had concluded that "there is a reasonable likelihood the prejudicial news prior to trial will prevent a fair trial."

253

Foxman said that his order prohibited defendants, attorneys, and police from talking about the case. If they did, they would be found in contempt of court. The order, however, did not apply to journalists, even if they were subpoenaed to testify.

"I am not prepared to address myself to the First Amendment," Foxman said.

Besides the defendants and attorneys on hand, Kathy Kelly had been subpoenaed. Kelly looked far more worried than the four defendants.

Niles noted that Deidre was concerned about the television broadcasts that showed "reenactments" of her shooting Ramsey. Deidre's concern, he said, was that viewers might think they were seeing the actual murder.

He argued that Deidre was in custody and had not been advised of her rights. He said he knew nothing of her interviews with the media. Miles noted that Kathy Kelly deliberately destroyed her notes concerning the interview with Deidre, "thereby preventing the defendant from verifying their authenticity . . . or . . . being able to refresh her recollection by referring to the notes."

The letter from Kathy Kelly to Deidre was in the record and raised some eyebrows concerning Niles's association with the press. Kelly's letter read in part, ". . . I know by now you have met your attorney. He called me here Friday to ask how I had gotten my interview with you. When I asked him why he wanted to know, he said he had been appointed to represent you.

"In the future, he said, he wanted to sit down and talk with me about what you told me."

Kelly's letter said that she had intentionally destroyed her notes because she was under no obligation to tell Niles what they had discussed.

"I really don't know why he would want to talk to me any further since you are his client and free to tell him anything you told me," Kelly wrote. "In the event I am subpoenaed, the *News-Journal* will represent me with an attorney to block any efforts for further questioning."

Kelly's letter raised questions about Niles later on as to whether he was being paid to arrange interviews with Deidre or concerning Deidre. There was never any question that Niles did a competent, professional job of defending Deidre.

Foxman returned to the basic issue, concerning pretrial publicity and allusions to other crimes.

"It's my job to make sure everybody gets a fair trial," Foxman said. "Let's tone down the case and get on with the litigation. In the Christmas spirit, I'm asking you for suggestions on how to proceed." He added, "This is a restrictive order, not a gag order. I'm not telling the media what they can or can't do, but restricting defendants."

Tom Mott, Kosta's new attorney after he'd let Zentner go, said that "the bottom line is that Kosta has been tried and convicted in the media. This man cannot get a fair trial in the community, perhaps not anywhere else." He said the press's reaction was repugnant. Caught up in his own rhetoric, Mott decried this as an age of "yellow journalism" and said that the *News-Journal* had become the *National Enquirer* of the Eighties." Mott made karate chops with his hands to emphasize his points. "The media is surreptitiously giving false evidence. Kosta Fotopoulos doesn't stand a chance of having a fair trial in this city. Everybody's liberty is in jeopardy. This could go on forever."

Foxman interrupted, "There's a good chance that I'm going to put a stop to that."

Mott replied meekly, "I didn't intend to criticize the press. There are competing sides in conflict."

Arguments, or as Judge Foxman called them, "suggestions" from the attorneys went on for several hours. Foxman made it clear that he wanted no prior restraint, which would violate the Constitution. On the other hand, he was steadfast in trying to guarantee a free trial.

The result of Foxman's restrictive order was intended to cut off the flow of information to the media. Attorneys couldn't talk with the media. Police reports were restricted. The judge even took control of the docket so that the press couldn't see official court documents.

Whether it was called that or not, Foxman issued an order that essentially "gagged" the press. It was one of the few times a "gag order" had been issued in Volusia County.

29

On January 9, 1990, Mott asked to be released as Kosta's attorney because his client was broke. A hearing was held to determine if, in fact, Kosta was indigent and was eligible for a lawyer appointed by the court. Kosta was questioned by David Smith, an assistant state attorney.

For a man who had the Boardwalk poor thinking he was rich, Kosta was no better off now than they were, except that he had a home. He was in jail and was either going to spend the rest of his life in prison or die in the electric chair if he was found guilty of first-degree murder.

Kosta said that his income was fifteen thousand six hundred dollars a year.

"From the day I got married I was getting three hundred dollars a week," Kosta said. "When I opened my own business, which was six months ago, I was getting an additional two hundred. That's it."

"What properties do you own?" Smith asked.

"By myself, nothing."

Kosta explained that he and Lisa owned a duplex in New Smyrna Beach with a mortgage of sixty thousand dollars, but it had been bought with Lisa's money. They built a house for one hundred eighty-five thousand dollars and had used the fifty thousand dollars they had paid for the lot as a down payment.

Of the fifty thousand dollars for the lot, Lisa paid twenty-five thousand dollars, and Kosta borrowed twenty-five thousand dollars for his share. "I paid back ten thousand dollars, and I still owe fifteen thousand dollars, which the Sun Bank is suing me for because I could not make payments. Everything was owned by an estate which my wife had. . . . I could not go in and get five hundred dollars if I wanted it. I had to ask for it."

Kosta's BMW was repossessed and his jewelry was confiscated by the state. He said that Lisa did all of the accounting. "I just sign what she gives me," he said.

Besides being broke, Kosta was deeply in debt. He owed ten thousand dollars on a student loan, twenty-seven thousand dollars on two separate credit cards, ten thousand dollars to a savings & loan and fifteen thousand to the Sun Bank.

Mott had been paid twenty thousand dollars for the few weeks that he had represented Kosta. The attorney said that it all went for expenses and had received "not one penny."

Kosta said he had borrowed the twenty thousand dollars from his uncles in Chicago and added, "I have to pay that back when I get out."

Foxman declared that Kosta was indigent and appointed Carmen Corrente, a sharp criminal lawyer with experience in capital cases, to be Kosta's special public defender. Corrente, in his early forties, is small and wiry, with wavy dark hair and a quick

258

mind. It would have been hard to find anyone better qualified to represent Kosta than Corrente.

Deidre had entered a plea of Not Guilty when she was arraigned on December 12, even though she had confessed to the police. On January 23, 1990, Deidre wrote to Judge Foxman:

Thank you for listening to me. I seem to have a growing problem with my lawyer. I do not feel that Peter is doing anything in my behalf. Since he was appointed I have been surprised four times by the papers and totally taken in by the National shows. He has admitted to have [sic] previous knowledge of these incidents. His interest in this case is relatively none. . . . I have not known what is going on and still seem to be in the dark.

I have been requesting to be released from Protective custody since the day I was incarcerated.

I would like to have my say. If you do not grant me a new lawyer, I'd like to represent myself in this matter. No one but I could explain better the behind [sic] Mr. Fotopolos [sic] will not be silly in this matter. This is quite trivial but I would like to be released.

At a court hearing, Foxman denied Deidre's request to be let out on bail. Deidre claimed that Niles wasn't preparing a proper defense. Niles responded that Deidre didn't cooperate with him.

Deidre, who apparently saw evidence stacking up against her, broke down and sobbed. It was the first time she had shown any real emotion in court.

After the tears, Deidre agreed to continue with Niles as her lawyer, but the two of them would battle for months.

The only thing Niles would say about his relationship was that, "It was interesting. There was never a dull moment."

Deidre seemed to think that her testimony was essential to getting Kosta convicted. "She was the center of attention, and she liked it," Damore said. "But she thought her testimony was essential in convicting Kosta Fotopoulos. In many ways, our case against him was stronger without her cooperation."

The police investigation continued at an exhausting pace. It was taking a heavy toll on Damore, who not only had to help with the investigations but be present for depositions and court hearings.

"It took me away from my family," he said. "I knew I was in for a long haul, and I just kept telling myself to hang on until I got my second wind. But at that point, I couldn't see any light at the end of the tunnel."

The investigators had to watch every step they took to avoid any possibility of impropriety or tampering with evidence. On December 20, when they needed to reproduce a duplicate of the video recording of Ramsey's shooting for the Secret Service Crime Lab in Washington, a team of law officers and prosecutors accompanied Gallagher to Beach Photo in Daytona Beach. Those who went with Gallagher were Damore, Captain Neall, Lieutenant Evens, Sergeant Lewis, Detective Adamy, Gary Tinsley, who represented Lori, and Niles.

The equipment at Beach Photo couldn't produce the first three or four seconds on the original tape. The representatives of the state attorney's office and the Daytona Beach police talked about the problem, but the defense attorneys weren't included because it wasn't sure that those few seconds were actually missing on the duplicate. It wasn't until they compared the duplicate with the original at the state attorney's office that they were certain.

Gallagher told the Secret Service Crime Lab that the first three or four seconds were missing because the playback heads were different. Damore passed this information on to Tinsley and Niles.

There were several reasons to take a duplicate of the tape—and the original—to the Secret Service Crime Lab. Damore and Gallagher wanted an absolute guarantee that the tape had not been edited, spliced, or tampered with in any way. The Secret Service Crime Lab would also use the tape to prepare audio voice exemplars recorded by Gallagher to verify that they were the voices on the original videotape.

Gallagher prepared short exemplars because there was little talking on the tape. The exemplars were designated with an F for female and M for male: (F) *You got it (?)* (F) *Don't shine that shit in my eyes.* (F) *Don't shine it on my eyes. Shine it down. Low.* (F) *Where is it (?)* (F) *Got it (?)* (M) *Come closer. I can see you (or) come closer I can't see you.* (M) *Hold the light (?)* (F) *Like that (?)* (M) *Hey.* (F) *Right.* (M) *Okay.*

On January 25, Gallagher, Damore, Smith, and Corrente met at the Volusia County Branch Jail inmate library to conduct a voice exemplar on Kosta that had been ordered by Judge Foxman.

261

Gallagher used an 8-millimeter Sony video camera, like the one used to make the original tape, and also recorded it on an audio cassette as backup.

On January 31, Gallagher checked out the video-tape of Ramsey's murder to hand deliver it to the Secret Service Crime Lab in Washington. Ed Ross, of the Secret Service Crime Lab, coordinated the testing. The original tape was duplicated by Ed Ross and Ken Pfarr to a professional 3/4 tape.

The tests were done to prove that the tape had not been edited, to use for voice identification, for computer enhancement of certain portions of the tape, and to check the case for fingerprints. The last test was conducted after the tape had been removed from the original cassette and placed into another.

Besides the tape, Gallagher gave Kosta's voice exemplars to the Secret Service for testing, plus Smith's recorded interview with Kosta. Gallagher never let the evidence out of his sight at the crime lab.

The tests bore fruit before Gallagher returned to Daytona Beach. Ratliff verified that the latent print lifted from the video cassette was Kosta's. The next day, Gallagher gave the Daytona Beach police the original Secret Service report and the video cassette to be placed into evidences.

Every human voice has certain qualities that can be translated by a spectrograph into lines to make a "voice print." This spectrographic comparison isn't considered a positive means of identification, such as a fingerprint. It is accurate enough to be a useful tool to guide an investigation.

Experts at the crime lab compared Kosta's voice

prints on the tape with the exemplars that had been recorded at the Branch Jail. The conclusion was that there weren't enough words in the exemplar to be "absolutely positive" that both voice prints were Kosta's, but that "there were similarities in the words uttered."

Gallagher wanted more evidence about the identity of Kosta's voice, plus having people listen to various voices saying the same words to determine which one was Kosta's. Gallagher also wanted all of the voice exemplars to be matched against Kosta's voice to see if the prints matched.

He took the tapes to Robert Averill, an audio specialist for NASA at the Kennedy space center, for a spectrographic comparison. The NASA official matched several words from the original tape to Kosta's voice: *"Come closer. I can't see you. Hold the light. Hey. Okay."*

Gallagher found eight volunteers, all with Greek accents, who agreed to read the same exemplars that Kosta had. This presented some social problems.

"I didn't want to get people who knew Kosta and Lisa," he said. "They might start pointing fingers at each other, or they might not want to be involved. So I went to Embry-Riddle and found eight men with Greek accents."

Averill put all eight exemplars, plus Kosta's, on a single cassette. Two days later, Lisa visited Gallagher at his office and had her read the text of the exemplars, then listen to the tape that contained all nine voices.

Lisa said that Number Six was Kosta's voice, but to be sure, she had Gallagher play it again. This

263

time she said she was even more positive that Number Six was Kosta's voice.

Gallagher followed the same procedure with Dino, who also identified the sixth voice as Kosta's. A few days later, Gallagher went to Calderone's car dealership on Nova Road and had him read the script, then listen to the voices. Calderone said Kosta was the sixth voice. Holly Ayscue also identified the sixth voice as Kosta's.

30

Besides helping with the investigation, Damore was busily engaged in legal work that was necessary to prepare for trial. The more that Damore, Gallagher, and Wheeler looked, the more widespread the case became.

"There were so many leads, so many things to uncover, that it was hard to stay focused," Wheeler said. "The guy who really kept everything in perspective and had us concentrate on things was State Attorney John Tanner. He's the kind of guy who gives all the credit to his staff, but no one should underestimate the powerful influence he had on this case."

As the investigators worked, there were leads that splintered off in all directions. Sometimes the leads were good, and at other times, the authorities were sent on wild goose chases or had obstacles thrown in their path. Nevertheless, the scope that the investigation covered mushroomed.

At one point, the prosecution placed more than two hundred names on the list of witnesses it would call during the trial. No one in the state attorney's office seriously expected that many people would testify, but potential witnesses had to be provided to the defense.

"We wouldn't have been able to keep the jurors interested if we called all of those witnesses and presented all of the evidence that we had," Gallagher said. "They'd get bored and lose interest in the case."

Damore worked out plea bargains with Lori and Teja. In exchange for Teja's testimony for the state, Damore dropped the charge of attempted armed robbery against him, and Teja pleaded guilty to attempted murder and conspiracy to commit murder. Judge Foxman agreed to consider sentencing Teja as a youthful offender, which would result in a lighter sentence.

Lori pleaded guilty to conspiracy to commit first-degree murder if the state would not file more serious charges against her. In exchange for the plea bargains with Teja and Lori, Damore had secured the testimony of two witnesses who had been intimately involved with the plots to kill Lisa, Chase, and Ramsey.

J.R., who was in jail on unrelated charges, complained that the state wasn't treating him as well as he expected. Unless the state agreed to reduce the charges pending against him, J.R. said he would not testify. Damore eventually resolved this problem and secured J.R.'s cooperation.

Chumbley was held in protective custody as a material witness and wanted to go home. The trouble was, he didn't have a home. The *News-Journal* of Daytona Beach published a long letter by Chumbley under the headline: 'This is a letter of desperation . . . do I have rights'? Chumbley

266

said his grandfather in Tennessee was sick and needed him, and he promised to return to testify if he were freed on bail. A few days later, an attorney posted bail, and Chumbley was on his way to Tennessee, promising to return to give testimony for the state.

In the meantime, Gallagher followed up leads and sometimes chased his tail because the people he talked with led him far astray.

"Some of them didn't want to get involved at all," Gallagher said. "They had read the newspaper stories and watched television, and thought that Kosta was some kind of powerful figure tied to the Mafia who could hurt them."

Others stretched the truth simply to protect themselves from being implicated in any way. Some people who were in jail embellished stories in the hope of getting a reduced sentence by plea bargaining with the state. Finding the truth was challenging, and the investigators had to follow every lead.

On December 18, 1989, Donald Stillwell Miller was in the Volusia County Correctional Facility for auto theft. He told Gallagher that he often saw Deidre give J.R. one hundred dollar bills, which he now believed were counterfeit.

Miller said that shortly after Ramsey disappeared, Deidre began spending more time with Kosta. He told Gallagher: "Her whole attitude was different, more positive, and she was wearing a lot of new clothing. She would also fool around with Kosta in the shop and brag about her ability to buy a new BMW with cash."

Miller claimed he was on the Boardwalk with

J.R. when Deidre told her former boyfriend that Kosta would pay him ten thousand dollars to kill his wife. "We were both afraid that Kosta had put a price on our heads because we knew too much," Miller told Gallagher.

Robert Holm, who had been a cellmate with J.R., wanted to talk to Gallagher about things J.R. had told him. Holm said J.R. knew where burgled items were stored, that he had stolen cars and committed burglary for Kosta, and that he had burgled an Ormond Beach home and taken about thirty thousand dollars worth of jewelry that was wrapped in aluminum foil and hidden in the refrigerator. According to Holm, the jewelry was buried across Atlantic Avenue from the Side O Sea Hotel by a house that was scheduled to be torn down.

Gallagher was also told that Kosta buried one hundred fifty thousand dollars worth of counterfeit in Hollyland Park and that there was money buried in Kosta's yard not far from the barbecue pit.

Gallagher contacted Manny Lawrence, a painting contractor, at the Desert Inn Motel on Atlantic Avenue on March 12, 1990. Lawrence recounted how Chase had hidden from a brunette and a tall blond girl who came to see him. Lawrence told Gallagher that he had to lay Chase off but that the youth volunteered to work for nothing.

The leads continued to spread and the investigators widened the scope of their research. Gallagher found Michael Peck, who had been one of Ramsey's close friends, working at a Pic 'n' Save store. Peck said he had been with Ramsey on the Boardwalk when Kosta and Deidre approached.

"Kosta said, 'I want to talk to you,'" Peck said. "Kevin was really afraid of Kosta. He was visibly shaking and didn't know whether or not to talk with Kosta or not."

Peck said he asked Ramsey why he was afraid of Kosta, and Ramsey answered, "He carries a weapon and he's into things."

Peck said Ramsey was also afraid of Kosta because he knew about some videotapes that Kosta had showing important politicians having sex. The sexual activity was taken without their knowledge, Ramsey said, and Kosta wanted to blackmail the politicians.

Peck said that Ramsey was robbing people, targeting homosexuals and drug dealers.

The entire force of investigators had heard about the sex videotapes but couldn't find them. Wheeler, for one, was sure they existed.

"There was too much talk about them for it to be a lie," Wheeler said. "I think Kosta set up a camera, got the politicians in bed with some of his girls, and let the camera roll. I don't think he could have done much damage if he made the tapes public, except that they probably wouldn't be reelected."

Gallagher followed a lead to Dan Garcia, who worked at the Marriott Hotel on Atlantic Avenue. According to Garcia, he had been at Razzles the night of the Halloween party and tried to get into the men's restroom.

"I tried to open the door, but it seemed like someone was holding it closed," Garcia said. "I pushed on the door for a few seconds, then the door opened and I saw Kosta with two men."

One was a light-skinned black man about five ten and of medium build, and the other was a white man about twenty of medium height and build, with straight blond hair to his shoulders.

Garcia said, "Hi," but got no response. He said Kosta seemed to be in shock when he saw him.

Teja told Gallagher that Tim Hopson had seen him at Razzles the night he was supposed to stab Lisa. Gallagher located Hopson's father, but his son was in a Louisiana jail on a DUI charge. The investigator interviewed Hopson by telephone.

"He wanted to talk to me about doing something," Hopson said, "but he never told me what it was."

Hopson said that later on that, Deidre explained that Kosta wanted someone to kill his wife.

"That's the reason he wants to talk to you," Deidre told him. Deidre added, "Don't get involved."

"Why?"

"Just don't get involved."

Hopson said he took Deidre's advice.

Two weeks before Kosta was arrested, Hopson said Teja and Holly Ayscue were present when Kosta talked to him again. They agreed to meet at the Great Barrier Reef, but Kosta didn't show up. Later on, Hopson asked Holly if she knew what Kosta wanted, but she didn't know any more than he did. Two or three days later, Hopson saw Deidre and Lori on the pedestrian over-

270

pass of the Main Street approach to the beach.

"What does Kosta want?" he asked Deidre.

Dee looked at Lori and asked, "Do you think he could do it?"

Lori shrugged her shoulders.

"Never mind," Deidre said. "I like him too much."

Thinking back to Halloween night, Hopson said Teja told him, "Feel my arm." Hopson did and clearly felt the outline of a long knife.

"Kosta's going to pay me one hundred thousand dollars to kill his wife," Teja said. "He told me to stab her three ribs up, twist the knife, and push up before she could scream."

"You're crazy to get involved with something like that," Hopson said, then left Razzles.

Judge Foxman released the November 11 videotaped interview with Peter Kouracos to the public in late January. The media picked it up, creating sensational news in Volusia County. It was the stuff of which scandals are made: a pretty young woman charged with two murders and attempted murder is wined and dined by a prominent political worker and wows two city commissioners.

The city commissioners and other dignitaries who were taken in by Deidre's charm had no idea about her seamy past or present. The stories also concentrated on the fact that Kouracos and Lisa both knew about Kosta's counterfeit operation.

The articles touched only the highlights of the four-hour interview, during which Kouracos had admitted to committing at least three felonies.

271

In mid-January, Kouracos had been "invited" by the U.S. Attorney's Office in Orlando to testify before a grand jury investigating counterfeiting charges. Kouracos was advised that he was "a subject of the investigation." On the advice of his lawyer, Michael Lambert, Kouracos refused the invitation.

"I didn't want him to appear without a subpoena," Lambert said "He's angry that he's been associated with a crime. He's extremely nervous, but I think that's his personality."

This was the first salvo of a small skirmish that occurred within the larger scope of the investigation. Both Kosta and Kouracos were indicted by a federal grand jury on counterfeiting charges and witness tampering. Kosta was already in custody, but Kouracos's arrest could have been featured as a comedy in a Keystone Cops film.

Counterfeiting isn't a dangerous crime, but police officers knew that Kosta was a firearms dealer who owned automatic weapons. A small army of police, including a SWAT team, stormed his house at night to make the arrest. A few of them were nervous and fired their weapons.

The police were very sheepish about their actions after the arrest had been made. "I guess a couple of guys got nervous and thought they were Rambo," one of the officials said. "They're pretty embarrassed about it."

Kouracos posted bail of twenty-five thousand dollars and was released from the Seminole County Jail. Commissioner Bud Asher turned on his political beneficiary by calling for the City Council to kick Kouracos off the city's Drug Related Nuisance Abatement Board.

"I subscribe to the American system of justice under which someone is innocent until proven guilty," Asher said. "It's obvious in his present predicament that Kouracos is unable to fulfill his duties. Being under indictment, it raises a cloud."

Asher was quick to try and put additional distance between himself and Kouracos, and to deny that he had liked Deidre Hunt and had asked Kouracos to bring her to a party. He admitted that his wife, Dawn, got along well with Deidre, but pointed out: "Nobody connected with the city of Daytona Beach has ever been connected with this girl."

Kosta pleaded guilty to the counterfeiting charges, saying it was "a stupid thing to do." He received a sentence of three years in federal prison. Kouracos pleaded not guilty and was acquitted in U.S. District Court of all charges by a jury that deliberated three hours.

Kouracos, relieved and happy, was also angry that the charges had been brought against him. He blamed it on politics. "Volusia County politics are as cutthroat as they come," he said.

Having been acquitted, Kouracos went before the City Council and said that the charges against him had been lies. He said the commission should take no action to remove him from his appointed post. Asher sheepishly withdrew his motion to drop Kouracos from the Drug Related Nuisance Abatement Board.

Kouracos faded into the background of the Hunt-Fotopoulos murder case, but Wheeler wasn't satisfied that justice had been done. "We had plenty of evidence against him," Wheeler said, "but the U.S. Attorney didn't meet with us until about twenty minutes before the trial."

For Kouracos's part, his lawyers said they were "hot" and intended to have Damore and Wheeler investigated for mispropriety.

31

While the police continued to gather evidence, Deidre frustrated the court. She changed her plea several times from Not Guilty to Guilty, and back again. She agreed to testify for the state during Kosta's trial, then reversed herself, and reversed herself again.

On April 24, Judge Foxman held court and granted Deidre's most recent request to have Niles replaced. Deidre promptly changed her mind again.

For his part, Niles had asked to be removed from the case on three different occasions. He said that Deidre paid absolutely no attention to him and demanded that he do things which were contrary to the strategy he was developing for her trial. Niles once more asked to be replaced, claiming that Deidre demanded that he use temporary insanity as a defense, seek a delay, and have the confession she had made to the police thrown out.

"Against my recommendation, Miss Hunt in the last few days has demanded a one hundred-eighty degree reversal in tactics at the trial," Niles told the court. "Miss Hunt has made both a personal and professional attack upon her attorney."

Foxman was becoming exasperated with Deidre's disruption of the orderly proceedings of the court.

He called Deidre before him and explained exactly what was going on so that even a child could understand it. The judge asked her to specify the lies Niles had told her and what errors he had made in her defense strategy.

"I don't know our defense," Deidre replied. "I never knew it."

"What's happening here now is you're on trial for your life," Foxman reminded Deidre. "I saw Mr. Niles represent a defendant in a similar situation successfully, and I thought the best I could do for you was to get an attorney who has faced this situation before."

Foxman gave Deidre and Niles half an hour to discuss things before he released Niles and appointed a new attorney. When the thirty minutes had passed, both agreed that they were satisfied with one another.

There was a truce, but the war between Niles and Deidre wasn't over, and Deidre was not through changing her mind. Foxman set April 30 as the day Deidre's trial would begin.

Gallagher was joined by Damore and Neall at police headquarters on February 13 for another interview with Tony Calderone. The police had found that the story Calderone had previously told them was full of holes. Their investigation had also turned up allegations that Calderone was involved in counterfeiting, prostitution, and dope dealing.

They had one question to ask Calderone: was he going to be honest and cooperate or was he going to lie?

"Is there any reason for your lack of cooperation?" Damore asked. "Have you been involved in criminal activities?"

Calderone's nerves were on edge. "I didn't cooperate because I was worried about my marriage," he said. "I'm sorry I lied. I just didn't want my wife to find out that I had an affair with Deidre."

"Is that the only reason?" Damore asked.

"I don't have anything else to hide."

Calderone said he had been truthful but that he had withheld information. This time he told the investigators about finding Kosta sleeping on his couch the day that Lisa was shot, and how Kosta had laughed when he asked, "How's Lisa doing?" Then, he said, Kosta patted him down, looking for a wire. Calderone continued, "You son of a bitch, you did it, didn't you?" and that Kosta grinned and said, "I told you Greek men don't divorce their wives."

Calderone said Kosta told him that "the kid fucked up" and that Lisa was still alive. Calderone said Kosta claimed to have videotape recordings of himself killing someone, torturing someone, of Deidre killing someone, and that he held the rank of Commander in the Greek Army.

The investigators learned from Calderone that Kosta had wanted him to go on the road with him to help pass counterfeit one hundred dollar bills, a deal Calderone said he refused. He said that Kosta was "extremely jealous" concerning Deidre and told him not to "mess around" with her.

Calderone said that he had told Daytona Beach police about a car theft ring and had even given them the names of suspects. Neall checked the records and found out that Calderone was telling the truth.

"There were a lot of allegations about Calderone being involved in drug dealing, prostitution, and other things," Damore said. "We investigated every allegation and didn't find anything to substantiate them. We didn't have to make a deal with him to testify, because we didn't have anything to charge him with."

"He was more afraid of his wife than the law," Gallagher added. "He didn't want her to find out about his affair with Deidre."

Damore and Gallagher had the Secret Service Crime Laboratory make a photograph from the videotape of the man that Deidre had shot. Gallagher beat the bushes to find people who could independently identify the photograph. He found Holly Ayscue living with her sister behind a laundromat in Holly Hill, a Daytona Beach suburb.

"She was pretty decent and attractive," Gallagher said. "Not like some of the people we came across."

Gallagher showed Holly the photograph.

"Can you identify this man?" he asked.

"It's Mark Kevin Ramsey," she said.

Gallagher, who was also trying to find Marjeanne Powell, asked Holly if she knew where the girl was. Holly said no, but volunteered some interesting information. Holly said she was at Top Shots the day after Lisa was shot, and when Kosta came in about eleven a.m., she told him: "You made the front page."

Holly said Kosta read the newspaper article, then laughed and started to ridicule the story. "How many times do they know he got shot?" he asked. "How do you know how many rounds were fired?"

"What do you mean?" Holly asked.

"There were more shots fired than were mentioned in the article," he said, and added that some parts of the article weren't completely true.

Still doing some hard legwork, Gallagher tracked down Robin Berghdorff. She identified a photograph of Ramsey and said that he used to live with her. Robin said the last time she had seen him was just before she had gone to Halifax Hospital Emergency Room with a kidney infection.

"I'm living with Chris Sharpardon," Robin said. "You should talk to him."

Sharpardon, an eighteen year old, said he met Deidre at Top Shots, and she asked if she could stay at his place. He said yes, and Deidre stayed there about two weeks. Deidre visited Top Shots regularly, then got a job at Checkers Lounge on Broadway and Atlantic Avenue. Sharpardon remembered that Deidre worked at Checkers for two weeks before she got a job at Top Shots. Ramsey was already working at the poolroom.

Sharpardon said that he had worked with Ramsey, under Kosta's direction, to ripoff drug dealers for both money and drugs. Kosta picked the targets. Sharpardon said the last time he saw Ramsey he was wearing a black T-shirt with a Harley-Davidson insignia.

Sharpardon became uneasy, and he wouldn't reveal anything else unless he was granted immunity. What he had to say was considered important enough to grant it. Once Sharpardon was assured that he wouldn't be prosecuted, he began to talk in earnest. He recalled that Kosta had given him and Ramsey 9-millimeter pistols in late July or early August. Ramsey's gun had a silencer attached. Sharpardon said he and Ramsey kept the guns for awhile but gave them back when Kosta started talking about killing his wife.

According to Sharpardon, Ramsey worked for Kosta by ripping off drug dealers of both money and drugs because they were "on his turf." Once Sharpardon said he was in Kosta's office at Top Shots when Kosta gave Ramsey a photograph, a name, and two thousand dollars and said, "Take care of him tonight, I'll take care of the rest. You know what you have to do."

Sharpardon said he heard no other instructions, but said he acted as a lookout on at least two other "hits" that Ramsey made for Kosta. He said Ramsey made at least eleven hits and was paid two thousand dollars for each one.

Sharpardon told Gallagher that Ramsey started to keep some of the money and drugs from the hits and that Kosta found out. Ramsey apparently didn't use much discretion, Sharpardon said, and sold drugs on the Boardwalk. Sharpardon said Kosta was selling acid and cocoa snow (counterfeit cocaine).

According to Sharpardon, Ramsey started to worry about his own life when Kosta started talking about killing Lisa. Ramsey warned Sharpardon that "something was going to happen," and it scared Sharpardon enough to make him flee to Michigan for two weeks. When Sharpardon returned, he saw Ramsey on the Boardwalk and Ramsey told him to "stay off the east side," which is the oceanside of Daytona Beach.

"There were some drug hits," Gallagher said, "but nothing like Sharpardon said. They probably ripped off a few small-time dope dealers, but Ramsey didn't go around killing people. There's no evidence to support the allegations of major drug deals or gunrunning."

Gallagher dug around some more and found Marjeanne Powell, who had been one of Ramsey's girlfriends. Marjeanne had fallen on hard times. She was living with two gay men and was out of work. What's more, she had invented the story about Ramsey moving to Orlando because she was too embarrassed to want people thinking she had been dumped.

Marjeanne answered a subpoena to come to the state attorney's office on April 10. Marjeanne admitted that she was unemployed but hoped to be dancing soon at the Red Garter, Shark's Lounge, or another club.

She didn't want to testify against Kosta, that her nerves were bad, and that she was pregnant. She was also afraid of Kosta, even though he was in jail. Marjeanne admitted that she had lied about seeing Ramsey in his father's truck after he had been killed.

She defended herself: "I'm not going to court and you can't make me."

Damore asked her if she had told people that Ramsey had gone to Orlando to work for her father "to save face." She nodded yes. When Damore asked if her father was in Orlando, Marjeanne said she didn't know where he was.

Marjeanne verified that about two weeks before he disappeared Kevin told her he was planning to blackmail Kosta. She said Ramsey told her he was going to see a private detective at Krystal's Restaurant.

When asked why, Marjeanne said Ramsey told her that he was afraid of Kosta, that Kosta wanted him kicked off the Boardwalk. Damore and Gallagher spent a long time reassuring her that she wouldn't be in danger if she testified truthfully. Reassured, Marjeanne said she would cooperate and appear in court.

Damore and Gallagher wanted to know more about Deidre's activities in New Hampshire, particularly concerning the shooting of Veronica Rudzinski. They left Daytona Beach's temperate climate and arrived on a cool, blustery day in Manchester, New Hampshire, where they met with Detectives Richard Gillman and Mark Putney of the Manchester Police Department. It was March 29, just a couple of weeks before Deidre's trial was scheduled to begin.

The Manchester detectives guided the state attorney officials to Chris Margoritis, who had lived with Deidre in the spring of 1989. Margoritis had an interesting story to tell. While he had no special relationship with Deidre, Margoritis said he had received an anonymous letter telling him to teach Deidre how to shoot. He said the letter came with one thousand dollars in cash.

Damore and Gallagher found Margoritis's story hard to swallow. At the time, Margoritis said, Deidre's boyfriend was John Beauvier but, while he was teaching her to shoot, Deidre told Margoritis that she knew Kosta Fotopoulos, a man who owned Top Shots in Daytona Beach. Deidre claimed that she was once a pool hustler and that Kosta was going to buy her a ticket to go back to Florida.

(Deidre and her mother had previously lived for a short time with Deidre's aunt in Maitland, Florida.)

Margoritis told Damore and Gallagher that Deidre left Manchester around September 1989 and flew to Florida. It was Deidre's second trip to Florida, not counting the time she had lived with her aunt. Shortly after her birthday Margoritis said he received a telephone call from Deidre.

Gallagher reported: "Dee told him that she was 'getting involved in things, war shit, scary things, that two guys just got shot by the guy she was dealing with.' Margoritis said that she should return to New Hampshire and offered to pay for her ticket. According to Margoritis, Dee declined, advising things were 'getting too serious' and that she couldn't leave. She then went on and talked about the *Soldier of Fortune* magazine. That she was meeting with 'fucking mercenaries.' According to Margoritis, Dee talked about getting her picture in the magazine, but didn't realize you had to kill someone first."

When Gallagher and Damore asked if Margoritis had ever talked with Deidre about shooting Veronica Rudzinski, he said she admitted doing it. Deidre told him, "I was shaky at first, then I looked the lady in the eye and popped her."

The next day Damore and Gallagher talked with Bridgette Riccio, who had been with Deidre when Rudzinski was shot. Bridgette, who professed to be a born-again Christian, was residing at the New Hampshire State Prison for Women. Her spiritual rebirth notwithstanding, Bridgette had blown her chances for a parole in three months by running away from a halfway house.

Bridgette said that Deidre shot Veronica at Deer-

283

field Park and offered to take a lie detector test to prove it. Just before they left the apartment on the day of the shooting, Bridgette told Damore and Gallagher, Deidre said she needed money.

"She said she had a gun and was talking about 'ripping people off.' Deidre told our neighbors that she was 'tripping out on acid,' but she wasn't."

Bridgette said Deidre told her that "she had shot people before and it gets easier." A man named Tod was cleaning his gun in the room when Deidre made the comment. Bridgette said she knew Deidre had a gun when they left the apartment but hoped she could talk Deidre out of committing a robbery.

They walked around with no particular place in mind and ended up an hour later at Deerfield Park. They saw a car parked. They approached and asked the driver, Veronica Rudzinski, for a light. Hunt pulled her gun out and fired four shots in sequence.

Bridgette said that she got into an argument with Deidre over the shooting the next day. Deidre was proud of what she had done, saying, "I shot the bitch." Bridgette said that several people were present when Deidre made the statement.

Damore and Gallagher were able to talk with Veronica Rudzinski that same day about the shooting. Rudzinski said that it was Deidre who shot her, and that she herself was unable to identify Bridgette.

Back in Florida, Gallagher had Kosta's voice exemplars analyzed again by Dr. Tony Halbrook at Florida State University's College of Communication in Tallahassee.

Halbrook said that the lack of words on the tape and exemplars "created a hardship," but out of the ten words he identified, he matched nine of them to Kosta's voice prints. Halbrook wrote, "I have a pretty good picture which will identify Fotopoulos as the person behind the video camera."

Dino contacted Gallagher to show him a Polaroid photograph of Deidre and Kosta sitting together before background props of a boat and tunnel. Over the top of the tunnel the inscription read "Tunnel of Love."

Dino found the photograph at Joyland, wedged between some of Kosta's magazines. Along with the photograph, Dino discovered a receipt for a Western Union currency transmittal for five hundred dollars to Kristen Staske of 1146 S. Salina, Syracuse, New York. The sender was identified as Scott Allen of 1103 North Ridgewood Avenue, Daytona Beach. Gallagher checked and there was no such address. The date the money was sent was July 28, 1989.

A few days after he received the photograph, Gallagher was able to find the location where Kosta and Deidre had been photographed in the "Tunnel of Love." It was at the Bubble Room Restaurant in Maitland, just a few miles from Daytona Beach.

The police would have conducted a thorough investigation under any circumstance, but checking Deidre's background was of even greater importance than usual. The state believed that Niles intended to use a "domination" defense: that Deidre committed crimes only because she was totally controlled by Kosta.

The information that Damore and Gallagher received from Bridgette and Rudzinski showed that Deidre had a history of violence before she met Kosta. There was no one in New Hampshire forcing Deidre to shoot Veronica, either; she did it because she wanted to shoot someone.

Depositions from others in Daytona Beach were important in disproving the "domination" defense beyond a reasonable doubt. Several people who had been involved had given statements that Deidre wasn't controlled by Kosta or afraid of him. Gallagher reinforced this position when he talked with Holly again.

Holly was subpoenaed to the state attorney's office to go over information from previous interviews. Holly verified that Deidre had once beat her up and that they never got along. Once they were arguing at Top Shots, Holly said, and Kosta tried to get Deidre to cool off.

According to Holly, Deidre snapped at Kosta: "Shut up!"

32

In spite of Deidre Hunt's on-again, off-again relationship with her lawyer as she threw sand in the gears of the legal apparatus, her trial was scheduled to begin on May 7. It was a clear morning and unusually warm, even by Florida standards. People went to work, set sail in their boats, or basked in the sun on the Atlantic beach.

The prospective jurors had been drawn from every walk of life. They sat in an empty courtroom without even a bailiff to tell them if they were at the right place. They had to ask one another why they were there before they realized they had reported as ordered. After an hour of confusion and uncertainty, the prospective jurors became restless. They buzzed impatiently among themselves, wondering what was happening.

Some ninety minutes after jury selection was to begin, Judge Foxman, wearing a plaid shirt, a tie, and a jacket, came into the courtroom. He thanked the men and women for their patience.

"If what I think is going to happen happens, it will be advantageous to you and to me," he said. "I can't say that it will happen, but it could. Just bear with me a little while longer."

The judge disappeared, having been sufficiently

vague to confuse the prospective jurors. The author, sitting among the prospective jurors, was thunderstruck. It appeared that Niles was trying to work out a plea bargain with the state so that Hunt would testify against Kosta in return for her life. Her most recent plea was Not Guilty.

At ten-thirty a.m., the prospective jurors were dismissed, and the media came scrambling into the courtroom. Television cameras were set up in the jury box and began to roll when Deidre was led in accompanied by several armed deputies. This was the first public appearance Deidre had made since her arrest wearing something besides her orange jail jumpsuit. It was also the first time she wasn't wearing handcuffs and ankle chains.

Deidre walked into the courtroom like an actress who had given a stellar performance and was ready to receive accolades. She wore a white dress with a pleated waist, black piping, and an embroidered black flower just above her heart. She wore matching black and white shoes with spike heels, and her dark hair was neatly brushed, parted on the right. In spite of her clothing and bearing, the strain of her situation was beginning to show. Deidre didn't radiate the energy she had in previous appearances, and there were dark half circles under her eyes from lack of sleep and from weeping.

Deidre sat down while two armed deputies kept an eye on her. She laughed and flirted with them while the press waited to see what kind of plea bargain would be struck.

Niles and Deidre had finally agreed that the evidence against her was incontrovertible. There was, after all, a videotape showing her shooting Kevin Ramsey. Niles hoped he could save Deidre from the death sentence in return for Deidre agreeing to testify against Kosta. The smallest sentence she would receive under such an arrangement was life in prison, but at least she would not be electrocuted.

Deidre seemed hopeful, although she crossed her legs and shook a foot nervously. A black woman outside the courtroom looked through a glass panel in the courtroom door and caught Deidre's attention. They smiled at one another, and Deidre crossed her fingers for good luck and waved. Another thirty minutes passed before Niles, looking harassed, sat beside Deidre and whispered in her ear.

Deidre listened for a few moments, then screwed her face into an expression of utter disgust, and threw a pencil on the table. She sat with slumped shoulders, looking sour while Niles left and returned minutes later with Damore. Both men looked strained and angry. Damore told the court that the state was ready to proceed on all charges, including those of first-degree murder.

Niles said that Deidre had decided to withdraw her Not Guilty plea and plead guilty to all charges.

"In view of the videotape and depositions from other witnesses, Miss Hunt wishes to throw herself on the mercy of the court and to testify truthfully in the Kosta Fotopoulos trial," Niles said.

Damore stood up quickly. "Your Honor, I want it to be clearly understood that there have been no negotiations, no back-room deals," he said. "The state is in no way waiving the right to seek the death penalty. The state *does* intend to seek the death penalty."

Niles agreed that no deals had been arranged.

"We're hoping the state will relent when Miss Hunt testifies truthfully and that the court will also take her testimony into consideration."

Damore wanted to make the state's position perfectly clear. He said the only thing the state would agree to would be to defer Deidre's sentencing until after Kosta's trial, where she might be called as a state witness.

If Deidre, who had plea bargained successfully in New Hampshire, had hoped to do the same in Daytona Beach, she failed.

Judge Foxman wanted to make certain that Deidre knew the consequences of her decision to plead guilty.

"She does, Your Honor," Niles said. "In view of the prima facie evidence, it seems to be the only logical thing to do. We're hoping that the court will take Miss Hunt's cooperation and testimony into consideration."

Judge Foxman said, "I'm bound by law to do what I think is necessary. However, I will consider her cooperation."

Deidre stood throughout the exchange with tears streaming from bloodshot eyes. Occasionally she shot a pleading look at Damore. She shifted her weight from one foot to the other and tapped her fingers on the podium. Foxman asked her a series of questions to have it recorded that she was competent, understood the consequence of her actions, and that she was making the Guilty plea on her own volition. Deidre answered yes to each of his questions.

"When you plead guilty," Foxman said, "you limit your Constitutional rights. You can appeal, but there is little chance that an appeal will be successful. Under the state guidelines, I can sentence you to life in prison on all of the felonies, disregarding murder, attempted murder, and conspiracy. The death penalty is still a possibility. Do you understand that?"

"Yes," Deidre said, as tears streamed.

"I've sentenced people to life in prison, and I've ordered the death penalty," Foxman continued. He wanted to make certain Deidre understood the consequences of pleading guilty. "Do you understand that there are no deals, no back-room agreements, and that the state still intends to ask for the death penalty?"

Deidre looked up at Damore again, weeping. "Yes."

The judge said that there would be no presentencing investigation but that he would consider the evidence that the state and Deidre would present at Kosta's trial. There would also be time for the state and the defense to present arguments before sentencing.

Foxman spoke directly to Deidre once again: "I do not know what the ultimate decision of this court will be."

Damore said, "Your Honor, the state wants to make it clear that this is a Guilty plea, not one of No Contest. The state will accept nothing less than a Guilty plea."

"Miss Hunt pleads guilty," Niles said. "It's the only logical thing to do."

Foxman reviewed some of the complaints that Deidre had made about Niles. Deidre said that they had been resolved and that she was satisfied with him. The judge recessed the court about thirty minutes after proceedings began, and Deidre was taken back to jail. In spite of what was said in court, Niles said later that he was certain the state would withdraw its recommendation for the death sentence if Deidre testified against Fotopoulos.

Deidre kept her part about helping with the investigation for a while. She gave part of a deposition in which she continued to portray herself as a victim. Even though Deidre had lived a tough, hard life, with attempted murder in her background, she said she was totally unprepared for Daytona Beach.

Deidre said, "I was amazed, because, like you know, I was brought up in a neighborhood where there was street kids and everything, but I never saw anything, anything like Daytona Beach in my entire life. I mean, everybody was doing all of this mean stuff to people."

Although the investigation had cleared Calderone of the allegations of wrongdoing against him, Deidre said that Calderone seemed to like the fact that Kosta was dangerous.

"He was always saying, 'Don't fuck with Kosta. Kosta will kill. Don't mess with Kosta.' Tony was always just like that, he always boasted about Kosta. He bragged so much about Kosta to everybody. Every kid that walked in there, Tony would tell them, 'Don't fuck with Kosta, he will kill you,' and he used to brag about how Kosta had all kinds of stuff, machine guns, hand grenades, everything all buried and such like that."

Deidre said that Kosta needed to see blood or cause pain before he could have sex. She said it didn't start out that way, but Kosta eventually would scrape her back with a razor blade until it bled, then he would lick the blood. The small wound never got a chance to heal, she said, because he would lick it open to get more blood.

"It was the only way he could get a hard on," Deidre said.

The State Attorney's Office received official permission from authorities and from Ramsey's family to exhume the youth's body for a second autopsy. Damore wanted to have the skull examined again. The family gave permission for the exhumation with the stipulation that Gallagher personally return the skull and see that it was placed back into the casket and properly buried.

The Seventh District Medical Examiner, who had done the first autopsy at Halifax Hospital, argued against the autopsy. The ME didn't like to be second-guessed, but there was little he could do to stop it.

Ramsey's casket was exhumed in Wilmington, N.C., on July 27 under Gallagher's supervision and taken to the Quinn McGowen Funeral Home where it was opened for inspection. Dr. Bob Maples, of the University of Florida, examined the remains while Gallagher took photographs. The skull and a paper bag with soft tissue and bone fragments were removed from the casket to be taken to the University of Florida for examination. Then the casket was returned to the grave.

Three days later, Damore, Gallagher, and Drs. Maples and Lipkovic met at the Medical Examiners office in Jacksonville. Dr. Maples had found a large exit wound in the back of Ramsey's head that had not been detected during the first autopsy because it was covered with soft tissue and debris.

"What Dr. Maples did was absolutely amazing," Gallagher said. "He took all of those tiny bone fragments from the bag and pieced them together to reconstruct the skull. This evidence proved that Ramsey really had been shot in the head with a high-powered weapon similar to an AK-47."

Ramsey returned the skull to North Carolina on August 3 and watched as it was placed in the casket and back into Ramsey's grave.

Somehow, Deidre had learned that the state concluded that Ramsey had been shot with a high-powered weapon three days before his body had been exhumed. On July 24, Damore, Gallagher, and Niles went to the Branch Jail to wait for Deidre to enter the interview room. She had pleaded guilty to first-degree murder in the deaths of Ramsey and Chase and had agreed to be a state's witness in Kosta's trial.

Deidre entered the room with a yellow legal pad on which she had listed complaints and demands. She said she had been denied legal counsel for two months after she had been arrested and said that if the state expected her to testify in Kosta's trial, Damore would have to lower the charge against her, give her a new identity, relocate her, provide her with a new social security number, and place her in the witness protection program.

Deidre told them she had watched "Oprah Winfrey" on television where women who had been charged with homicide used domination and coercion as a legitimate defense and were found innocent. Deidre had written to get transcripts of the show.

294

Furthermore, Deidre said she had talked with the wife of an investigator for the Medical Examiner who told her that a second autopsy revealed that the back of Ramsey's skull had been blown off by a high-powered weapon. Deidre said that Kosta, not her, had fired the fatal shot.

"The autopsy showed that any one of the shots you fired would have been fatal if unattended," Damore said.

"If there's no deal I will go to the newspaper and talk show," Deidre said.

"Even at this point, she still thought her evidence was crucial to getting a conviction against Kosta," Gallagher said.

Deidre attempted to change her plea again, this time to Not Guilty. Judge Foxman's patience had finally worn thin. He refused to let Deidre change her plea again. Deidre, in a huff, reneged on her promise to testify against Fotopoulos or give depositions. To some observers, it looked as if she, in a fit of temper, had strapped herself into the electric chair.

33

Deidre Hunt's sentence hearing began on September 5, 1990. When she entered the courtroom, the change in her appearance was shocking. In previous appearances, Deidre had made attempts to look attractive. She had fluffed her hair, applied makeup, and somehow made her orange jail jumpsuits accent her shapely figure.

On this day Deidre wore her hair pulled into an unkempt ponytail that was fastened with a rubber band. The jumpsuit was so big that she had to roll the bottoms of the legs up several times to keep from tripping over them. Deidre had dark purple half-moons under her eyes, which were bloodshot from weeping and lack of sleep.

Deidre had pleaded guilty to the murders of Kevin Ramsey and Bryan Chase, and to several charges of solicitation for murder, attempted murder, and conspiracy to commit murder. The sentence procedure was to determine whether she would spend the rest of her life in prison or die in the electric chair.

A sentence hearing in Florida is actually a minitrial where witnesses are called by both the prosecution and defense. The purpose is to present mitigating and aggravating factors for a judge or jury to use as guidelines in determining a sentence. A mitigating factor is something that weighs in favor of the defendant while an aggravating factor does the opposite.

There was no jury present because Deidre had already pleaded guilty. Circuit Court Judge James Foxman alone would decide whether Deidre would live or die.

Niles hoped to show that Deidre was totally dominated by Kosta, had a history of domination by men, and that she had been completely under Kosta's control. Deidre had a history of abuse as a child, abandonment, sexual abuse, a mother with mental problems, and had been addicted to drugs and alcohol since she was a child. Deidre had been born out of wedlock and was completely rejected by her father. Niles hoped these mitigating factors would persuade the judge to sentence Deidre to life in prison instead of death in the electric chair.

Niles insisted that Deidre had fallen under Kosta's domination and was terrified of him. He contended that Deidre was so dominated by Kosta that she had lost her own will. Domination and fear of being killed herself, Niles said, were two reasons why Deidre killed Ramsey and participated in the plans to murder Kosta's wife.

Damore argued that Deidre wasn't afraid of Kosta or dominated by him. In fact, he said, she often defied him. Damore said Deidre killed Ramsey for money and that she relished it. He noted that there was no evidence that Deidre was dominated by Kosta and said he would prove that Deidre had a history of violence before she met Kosta.

The videotape of Deidre killing Ramsey was crucial evidence for both Niles and Damore. Niles's only hope of overcoming this damning evidence was to convince the judge that Deidre shot Ramsey only because Kosta was threatening her with an AK-47 or that Ramsey was still alive and died only after Kosta shot the youth in the head.

The video had not been viewed previously by news-hungry reporters, because it had been sealed by Judge Foxman. Deidre had given several versions of its contents and why it had been made. She had admitted shooting Ramsey in the chest but only because she was afraid Kosta would kill her if she didn't. "He was pointing this Russian-looking rifle at me," she had told Kathy Kelly.

In the version Deidre gave to Kelly, she said that Ramsey just stood there, smiling, not knowing what was going to happen. "That was the worst part of it," Deidre said. "He just smiled. I shot him in the chest, and he still kept smiling." Deidre told Kelly that Ramsey still wasn't dead and that Kosta was enraged.

"He looked at Kevin on the ground and said, 'Goddamn it! I knew this would happen!' and told me to shoot him in the head," Deidre said. "I just walked away and Kosta shot him in the head."

Since the actual tape of the shooting was expected to be shown at the hearing, Judge Foxman's courtroom was jammed with reporters, judges, lawyers, and the merely curious. There was standing room only in the courtroom.

Damore played the tape simultaneously on two television screens. It was only fifty-seven seconds long, but it seemed like an eternity. The first scene showed Deidre holding a pistol with a silencer. It was obviously taped at night in a wooded area. Deidre wore jeans and a T-shirt. She held up a hand to protect her eyes from the light and squinted into the camera.

"Don't shine that shit in my eyes!" she commanded. "Shine it down."

Deidre sounded angry and defiant.

The light moved independently of the camera, indicating that the two weren't composed of a single unit. This would be a crucial point. A man's voice said, "Move over there." It was a voice with a heavy Greek accent.

Deidre moved and asked, "Is this all right?"

"Yes."

Deidre fired three quick shots into Ramsey's chest while he screamed and slumped against the ropes that held him to a scrub palm growing almost parallel with the ground. Deidre walked to Ramsey without hesitation, grabbed a handful of hair to pull his head up, and fired a shot into his temple.

Everyone in the courtroom was stunned. Deidre didn't watch: she placed her head on the table and held her ears. Judge Foxman, who tried to maintain a cool judicial posture, couldn't conceal his shock and horror. When Deidre shot Ramsey in the head, the judge jerked back a foot, as if he had been hit with a club.

The scene was over so fast that the judge didn't think he saw it well enough to examine all of the details. He ordered the scene played back in slow motion. It was even worse on slow speed; it was a nightmare.

"You wanted it to be over," said Robert Nolan, a veteran court reporter for the *News-Journal*. "It was horrible and eerie. Ramsey's screams just went on forever. They sounded like recordings you hear of whales, only worse. You just prayed for it to be over with."

Everyone in the courtroom, including journalists, judges, and lawyers seemed to be in a state of shock. Judge Foxman was ashen.

Damore called several witnesses to discuss the videotape, which had been examined by the Florida Department of Law Enforcement and the U.S. Secret Service to make certain that it hadn't been spliced or tampered with. Joe Gallagher testified that if Deidre had been afraid of Kosta, she wouldn't have ordered, "Don't shine that shit in my eyes!" There were no instructions on the tape telling Deidre what to do, Gallagher testified, and noted that she didn't pause an instant before walking to Ramsey and shooting him in the head.

Damore had already established that the videotape was shot with a Sony F-35 millimeter video camera that is made to be operated by right-handed people. Gallagher, who viewed the tape thirty-five times, said the lighting was of two different intensities and showed concentric circles. He testified that the light was consistent with that of a Mag-Lite, a type of flashlight favored by police because its beam of light can be focused.

"It was very clear that he [Kosta] was using a Mag-Lite," Gallagher testified. "You could clearly see the lens coming in and out, like a vortex of light."

This testimony was important. If Kosta was operating the Sony with his right hand, he had to use his left arm to hold the Mag-Lite against his body and focus it with his left hand. With both hands occupied, there was no way Kosta could have been pointing an AK-47 or any other gun at Deidre.

300

Furthermore, Gallagher testified, if a gun was pointed at her, Deidre would have looked at it or at least seemed scared. Instead, he testified, her eyes were riveted on Ramsey once the light wasn't shining in her eyes. He also testified that Deidre's fingerprint had been found on the video cassette, indicating that it had been in her possession at some point when it wasn't in the camera.

Niles got Gallagher to agree that Kosta would have been a "menacing factor" even if the AK-47 was just slung over his shoulder. Niles asked if the Mag-Lite itself was often used by police as a billy club.

"Well, not as a matter of official policy," Gallagher answered.

Niles portrayed Kosta as an "arch criminal" who used his power, money and experience to draw indigents to him, including Deidre Hunt. Niles said that Kosta befriended people who were in their teens, uneducated, poor, impressionable, and who were both impressed and terrified of him.

"Didn't they know that he had money and power?" Niles asked. "Didn't they think he was a hired assassin for the CIA who had been trained by the Israeli Mosaad? Didn't they know that he had explosives, hand grenades, and automatic weapons and a cache of counterfeit? This man might not have frightened you or me, but wouldn't he have been a menacing figure to these poor, homeless, uneducated waifs?"

Niles paced, holding a sheaf of papers, reading glasses perched on his nose, while Deidre alternately scowled, grimaced, or wept. Deidre, Niles said, had followed a boyfriend to Daytona Beach who beat her up and left her penniless, homeless,

301

and with no way to earn a living.

"Wouldn't Deidre . . . with a history of being attracted to dominating men be easily dominated by Kosta Fotopoulos, with all of his power and money?" Niles asked.

Niles said Deidre was faced with two choices regarding Ramsey: to kill or be killed. Niles told the court that Deidre knew that Kosta had an AK-47 with him and that she was terrified for her life.

Damore called Gallagher, who had been present when Deidre initially talked with the police just before her arrest, as a rebuttal witness. Deidre's initial version of what happened in the woods was made before police found the videotape. Gallagher testified that he, other police officers, and members of the Florida Department of Law Enforcement had viewed that tape and that it didn't support Deidre's original story.

Gallagher said that, because of this, he visited Deidre at the Volusia County Jail and told her that she should tell the truth. Deidre, Gallagher testified, then admitted that Kosta had not threatened her with a gun or in any way. He told the court that Deidre claimed the AK-47 was in the trunk of Kosta's car when she shot Ramsey.

Gallagher testified that Deidre told him she had lied about being threatened by Kosta because it would prove premeditation on his part and make her look like an unwilling victim.

Niles asked, "Weren't some of the people you talked with in fear and terror of Kosta?"

Damore objected, claiming that the question was too broad, but Judge Foxman overruled.

"Some witnesses claimed they were afraid of Kosta," Gallagher replied.

302

Damore tried to show a Deidre Hunt who was not a victim but a willing participant. Under questioning, Gallagher testified that Deidre, Teja, Lori, and Bryan Chase were all involved with Kosta because they wanted power and money. Damore wanted to show that it was Deidre's duplicity that lured Ramsey to his death. He asked Gallagher if his investigation showed whether or not Ramsey was afraid of Deidre.

"Deidre had a good relationship with Kevin Ramsey," Gallagher testified. "He thought of her as a friend. They hugged each time they met. He had no reason to be afraid of Kosta with his friend there. Deidre lured him to his death. Ramsey thought he was going to an initiation. I think the gun [that Deidre had] was pointed down or else he would have been looking at it. He wasn't afraid. He didn't know what was happening until Deidre shot him."

Gallagher said he believed that Ramsey was shot in the head with an AK-47 after Deidre had shot him with the pistol.

Niles, who had an uphill battle with both his client and the evidence, asked that the fifty-seven seconds that it took for Ramsey to be killed be taken into consideration. He argued that Ramsey did not suffer long and, therefore, his death was not particularly heinous or cruel. Niles was grasping at straws and knew it.

"They had the videotape of Deidre shooting Kevin Ramsey," he said later. "That was devastating. I had nothing to work with. What could I say in her behalf that would be more powerful than an actual murder shown on the videotape?"

Although it looked grim for Deidre, the truth was

303

that a small window had opened for her. If Judge Foxman sentenced her to death, she might be able to win an appeal that could result in her receiving a life sentence in prison. The first autopsy on Ramsey's body was complicated because it was badly decomposed and because it was conducted at the Halifax Medical Center. Because it is a hospital rather than a morgue, the body had to be removed within hours. The first autopsy showed two bullets in the chest and one in the brain, all of which had been fired from a .22 Ruger semiautomatic pistol. A large exit wound at the back of the skull was overlooked because it was covered with decomposing flesh and debris.

Edward Ross Jr., supervisor of the video operations forensic division for the U.S. Secret Service, testified that six or seven fragments of Ramsey's skull were pieced together after the body was exhumed for a second autopsy. "The damage was much too extensive to be from a .22 caliber bullet," Ross told the court.

Niles pounced on this testimony. If Ramsey had been shot by an AK-47, which shot killed the victim? Wasn't it possible that Ramsey would have survived if he hadn't been shot in the head with a high-powered rifle? Which bullet had been fired first, the one from the AK-47 or the .22 Ruger? The videotape clearly showed Deidre shooting Ramsey, but Niles wanted to cast reasonable doubt on the state's charge that Deidre killed Ramsey. He asked if it wasn't possible that Ramsey was still alive after Deidre shot him and that she had not killed him.

Ross testified that there was no way to determine which shots had been fired first except by looking at the videotape. That clearly showed, Ross said, that Deidre shot Ramsey four times before the victim had been shot by the high-powered rifle.

Niles asked how Ross could be so certain.

"The head would not have been as complete as shown in the videotape," Ross replied.

Niles asked if the head wound made by the .22 caliber bullet would have been fatal.

"A .22 caliber going from one side of the brain to the other would not be considered a healthy situation," Ross observed.

Damore objected that the Secret Service agent wasn't qualified to give such expert testimony. Judge Foxman upheld the objection.

Dr. Arthur Botting, medical examiner for the Seventh Judicial Circuit, was called by Damore to destroy any doubt that Deidre had killed Ramsey. The medical examiner was a respected pathologist and practitioner of forensic medicine.

Dr. Botting testified that the first bullet which struck Ramsey could have been fatal because it penetrated his left lung and caused massive internal bleeding. The second and third bullets caused severe bleeding, he testified, but didn't hit any vital organs.

The bullet that was fired into Ramsey's head, Dr. Botting testified, was a fatal wound. His testimony on that point was disturbingly graphic.

"When a bullet enters the brain it causes massive expansion of the tissue," he testified. "The skull is a solid structure, and isn't made for expansion. A bullet causes the head to swell to the size of a basketball, causing severe damage to the brain and fractures in the skull."

Dr. Botting said he had seen similar .22 caliber

305

bullet wounds on people who had committed suicide. "The bullet in Ramsey's head would have caused hemorrhaging, tear brain tissue, fractures in the skull, and interfere with vital functions," he said. "People with such wounds usually die within five or ten minutes."

Niles noted that Lisa Fotopoulos had been shot in the head at close range with a .22 caliber pistol and had survived, apparently with no complications. Might not the same be true for Kevin Ramsey, he asked?

Dr. Botting testified that he had not examined Lisa, but that Ramsey's body wounds were potentially lethal. The bullet that Deidre fired into Ramsey's head, Dr. Botting said, was "definitely" lethal.

"When the bullet was fired into his [Ramsey's] head, he just dropped," Dr. Botting said. "At that point, I think that he was brain dead."

Niles attacked from another angle, drawing on Dr. Botting's testimony that suicide victims often lived from five to ten minutes after shooting themselves in the head with .22 caliber handguns. If a hospital and medical care had been available to Ramsey within five or ten minutes, Niles asked, couldn't his life have been saved?

"It was a combination of the gunshot wounds that caused the death," Dr. Botting replied. "I don't think anything could have been done to save his life."

Niles tried a flanking move. A .22 caliber wound in the head was not always fatal, he said, but could a wound from an AK-47 "definitely have been fatal?"

"The situation was so severe when the .22 caliber bullet was fired into the man's skull that it didn't

306

matter what kind of weapon was fired later," Dr. Botting said. "The situation was preordained."

Niles tried again to cast doubt on which bullet was fired into Ramsey's head first, the .22 caliber or the AK-47. It was a losing battle since the videotape clearly showed that Deidre shot Ramsey in the head just a few seconds after she shot him in the chest.

Things looked badly for Deidre when court was adjourned for the day, but she didn't seem to realize it. She told deputies she would not get the death penalty and, if she did, she would be granted a new trial on appeal. Niles, however, saw the evidence building against his client.

34

David Damore told the judge that Deidre Hunt was Kosta Fotopoulos's "Messenger of Death" and, in one instance, his "Deliverer of Death."

To prove his point, he trotted out three witnesses who had been involved in one way or another in the attempts on Lisa's life. One of them, Lori Henderson, even knew of Kosta's plans to kill whomever murdered Lisa. The other two witnesses were J.R. and Teja. All of the witnesses had been charged with first-degree murder but had pleaded guilty to less serious charges in return for their testimony against Deidre and Kosta. Matthew Chumbley, who had agreed to kill Lisa for ten thousand dollars, was not called as a witness.

J.R. was the first witness called. J.R. strutted to the witness stand. He had long brown hair and a tattoo on his left forearm. He bragged that Kosta hated him "because he knew I could take Dee back anytime I wanted to."

J.R. testified about his run-in with Kosta when Kosta fired a gun and put it at his throat. He said he had received death threats from Kosta in jail, but maintained that he wasn't afraid. "I'm not afraid of anyone or anything," J.R. said. "If I die, I die."

J.R. testified about the offers Deidre had made to have him kill Lisa for one hundred thousand dollars, then ten thousand dollars. He said he had agreed to take the contract but never had any intention of carrying it out.

"I could never take a human life," J.R. said. "I'm a thief, not a killer."

He testified that he knew of four different plans to have Lisa killed. Deidre made all of the arrangements, he said, but Kosta was the kingpin behind it.

"He used Deidre as a top sergeant, because he didn't have the street contacts," J.R. said, adding that Deidre told him that Kosta would kill whomever killed Lisa.

J.R. told the court that the motive to kill Lisa was for her life insurance money. Deidre told him about Kosta's Hunter-Killer Club. J.R. testified, "She said, 'I love money. It's the best part of life. I'm going to kill people because I love power and I love money.'"

He testified that Deidre defied Kosta by having sex with him. He told the court he could have her anytime he wanted to. "I used her for sex and money," he testified.

Niles saw an opening on his cross-examination and asked if J.R. manipulated Deidre. "I was using her and manipulating her," J.R. said. "It was easy."

"You were using this woman and it was easy," Niles said. "You bragged to friends that you could have her anytime and get money anytime."

"Kosta threatened to kill both of us if he caught us together," J.R. said. "She wasn't afraid of Kosta then. She allowed me to come anyway."

"But you were able to manipulate her," Niles insisted.

"You can't manipulate people unless they want you to manipulate them," J.R. told the court.

Damore called Lori to testify against Deidre. The two young women locked eyes briefly, then Lori looked away. Deidre put her head on the table and fingered prayer beads. Lori's father sat unobtrusively in the back of the courtroom, occasionally making notes as Lori testified.

Lori said that she had been with Kosta and Deidre when they made plans to kill Lisa, Bryan Chase, and Ramsey, and that she knew ahead of time that Ramsey would be killed. She said Deidre was under no threat or pressure to kill Ramsey, but had done it to prove to Kosta that she could kill. If so, Lori said, Kosta would give Deidre the responsibility of having Lisa killed.

"She told me that they had taken Kevin out and tied him to a tree," Lori testified. "She told me she shot him three times and that Kosta shot him once."

Under questioning, Lori admitted that she had gone with Deidre and Teja to buy a kitchen knife with which Teja was supposed to kill Lisa at Razzles on Halloween. Lori said she didn't think Teja would be killed after he murdered Lisa.

"I felt safe because we were friends," Lori testified. She said Deidre told her that Lisa's insurance policy was like "Double Jeopardy," a television game show.

Lori said Kosta made the big plans to kill Lisa but that Deidre fine-tuned them. She went on to describe how both Deidre and Kosta became increasingly frustrated and angry with each botched attempt on Lisa's life.

310

When Teja was arrested, Lisa testified that Lori accompanied Deidre on a search to find another assassin. Deidre, she said, finally talked to Bryan Chase about it.

"Deidre came back to the car and told me that it was okay, that Brian was going to do it," Lori testified. Shortly afterward, Lori described a meeting with Deidre, Kosta, herself, and Chase: "Kosta gave Brian the gun Deidre had bought for Teja and told him to shoot her [Lisa] in the head and keep shooting until she's dead."

Lori said Kosta and Deidre were furious when Chase botched several attempts to kill Lisa. "Kosta told him that he was going to give him one more chance," Lori said.

Lori denied that Kosta abused or dominated Deidre. "Deidre was in charge," she testified. "That's why she killed Kevin, to take over the responsibility. Kosta was behind it. Deidre wasn't afraid of him."

Niles cross-examined Lori and noted that she had known for two weeks that "somebody was going to be killed" and that Ramsey had already been killed. Three people agreed to kill Lisa, he told Lori, "and you helped."

Lori looked shocked. "I didn't plan anything. I was *there*."

Niles said she hadn't notified the police and had participated in murder and attempted murder. "Isn't that what you were doing?" he asked. "Planning a murder?"

Lori looked as if she had been slapped. She jerked back and her eyes widened in surprise.

"Of course not!" she replied.

Lori said that Kosta and Deidre planned to kill at least eight people, including everyone in Lisa's family. She told the court that she didn't really think Deidre and Kosta were going to kill Kevin Ramsey. But even if she had believed it, Lori said, "I wouldn't have reported it because I was afraid of Kosta. He always had a gun. I thought he was a little crazy or wacko. He was a scary, dangerous person. I wouldn't go around him [unless Deidre was there]."

Although Lori testified that she was afraid of Kosta, Deidre was not and couldn't be easily dominated. "Deidre chose to do the videotaped murder," Lori said. "She knew what he [Kosta] was like before she got involved with him."

Deidre's problem, Lori said, was that she became too deeply involved with Kosta: "Deidre wanted to get out," she said, "but then it was too late because of the videotape."

Niles tried to portray Kosta as a kind of evil Pied Piper who gathered impressionable young people around him to do his bidding. It was a point that Niles brought up with every witness.

"Isn't it unusual that all of these young people from different walks of life, who never thought about murder, suddenly got involved in murder after meeting Kosta Fotopoulos?" he asked. "Didn't they know that he was educated, that he had guns, explosives, money, and was dangerous . . . a person to be feared?" he asked. "And wasn't he a man who manipulated everyone?"

"He was behind her, but she was behind everyone else," Lori said. "After she and Kosta killed Kevin, she [Deidre] felt there was no way she could get out."

"The Hunter-Killer Club was Kosta's creation," Niles said. "He wanted his wife dead. You young

312

people were to be his tools. He used you and manipulated you."

"Looking back, Deidre's ultimate goal was to get into the Hunter-Killer Club," Lori said. "That's what she was doing. She was killing people to get in."

Niles made a point to continually bring up Kosta's large arsenal, money, power, and his convincing arguments about being a terrorist and assassin for the Central Intelligence Agency. He quoted from Lori's earlier deposition: "I kind of thought they would do it [referring to Ramsey's death] but I didn't think Deidre was capable of it."

"Why did Lori consider Deidre incapable of murder?" Niles asked.

Lori answered, "I guess I was a poor judge of character."

"Did you think Kosta could kill?"

Lori answered without hesitation. "Yes."

Damore put Teja James on the witness stand. Teja corroborated previous testimony concerning the deaths of Ramsey and Chase, and the plans to kill Lisa, but he disagreed with testimony that Kosta used the videotape of Ramsey's death to force Deidre to participate in the murder schemes.

"She wanted to join the Hunter-Killer Club," Teja said. "The videotape was to show that she was a potential assassin. She [Deidre] said that Kosta would know that she could kill and let her arrange Lisa's death. Then she would get all that power and wealth by marrying Kosta."

Teja remembered that Kosta said, "I'm going to have my wife killed."

"I said 'Yeah, sure.'"

Teja testified that he thought nothing more about

it until later that day, when Deidre saw him. "She said, 'He wants you to kill his wife. He wants to talk to you 'bout it.'" Teja said.

He recounted buying a kitchen knife to stab Lisa and the failed attempts to kill her. He said when he tried to kill Lisa at Joyland with a pistol, she ran outside and he was too afraid to go after her. He claimed that it was "just dumb luck" that he had not committed murder.

Teja testified that Deidre had offered him ten thousand dollars to kill Lisa. Once, he said, she showed him a check for ten thousand dollars and another time Kosta showed him stacks of one hundred dollars bills in the trunk of Kosta's car. Kosta was angry that he botched the attempts, Teja said, and warned him, "'If you don't do something soon, I'm going to kill you.' He was a scary, frightening person. I was afraid of him."

Teja testified how ecstatic Deidre was when she thought that Lisa had finally been killed, then told him that it would be good for him because now Lisa wouldn't be able to identify him. Then, he said, Kosta telephoned Deidre to say that Lisa was still alive.

"She and Kosta were really pissed off about it," Teja said.

Kosta and Deidre wanted him to make a bomb, Teja testified, and blow up Lisa's hospital room. He said he made a bomb but never planted it.

"I found out that Kosta intended to kill me and four of my friends after we blew up Lisa's room," Teja testified. "We knew too much about all of the plans. . . . They were going to invite us all to a party and kill us there. They called to invite us while Lisa was still in the hospital, but nobody

314

went."

Damore's questions elicited responses from Teja that Kosta was behind the murder plots even though Deidre offered the contract murder. "He [Kosta] didn't have the contacts with the street people," Teja said. "Deidre hired people, but Kosta was the one who was behind it. Whenever Kosta wasn't there to tell us what to do, then Deidre did."

So far, Damore had tried to show that Deidre killed without remorse or hesitation, that her motive was greed, and that she had not committed murder or solicited for murder because she was dominated by, or afraid, of Kosta.

Niles tried to show that Deidre only played her role because she was dominated by Kosta. Teja said it was the other way around. "He gave her money and paid her rent," Teja testified. "I listened to what Deidre said because I knew she would go back and report to Kosta. She had power over him. Deidre did what she wanted."

Niles attempted to paint a scenario where all of the young people around Kosta were so much in awe of him, or terrified, or both, that they would do anything he demanded. Teja admitted again that he was afraid of Kosta but that he made his own decisions.

"If he said to jump, I didn't ask how high," Teja said. "If he said for me to go kill that man, I didn't say, 'Yes, master,' and go do it."

Teja testified that his motive was the same as Deidre's: greed. He said that Kosta, Deidre, Lori, and he intended to live together when Lisa was dead and Kosta had collected on the life insurance policies. Deidre, Teja told the court, would do anything to get money and power.

315

"The plans were made by Kosta and fine-tuned by Deidre," Teja testified. "She wasn't the brains, but if Kosta left something out, she would refine it."

Damore had called all of his witnesses except those who might be needed for rebuttal testimony. The assistant state attorney had worked on this case just short of a year. The stress of the investigation, the long hours of tagging evidence, attending deposition hearings, plus preparing to try both Kosta and Deidre had worn him down.

There was also an intensely personal trauma that came with asking that Deidre Hunt be executed. He believed it was the right thing to do under the law, but it was a heavy responsibility, and he didn't take it lightly.

"I believe in the sanctity of all life," he said. "I believe that it's precious. I know that at some point in their lives Deidre Hunt and Kosta Fotopoulos were loved and cherished. They were babes in somebody's arms. But there comes a point when you have to answer for your actions here on earth. They had both gone so far over the line that it wasn't possible for them to be rehabilitated.

In the courtroom, there was the clanking of metallic tripods as the television crews closed down for the day. The spectators had left, murmuring to themselves. The courtroom suddenly felt empty, like a storm that had abated for a moment even though the horizon warned that it was not over yet.

A reporter cornered Damore on his way out of the courtroom. The attorney had been careful not to talk to the press. But he was tired. The reporter said that the witnesses gave similar testimony and asked if they had talked with one another.

Damore bristled at the accusation. "They've been

kept in separate jail facilities," he said. "There's no way they could have communicated. Their testimony is the same because that's the way it happened."

The reporter persisted that all of the accused, except for Kosta, were young and gullible.

"Have you ever taken a ride in a police cruiser at four o'clock in the morning?" he asked. "Daytona Beach is an entirely different town then than it is during the day. These kids are criminals. They're streetwise and tough."

35

Deidre's defense got off to a rocky start the afternoon of September 7, 1990. Niles called Dr. Clifford Levin, a Gainesville psychologist who had tested Deidre on May 13 and again on August 26, as his first witness.

Dr. Levin was sworn in and took the witness stand, but before Niles could begin his questions, Deidre poked him in the ribs and whispered in his ear. She looked angry.

Niles seemed befuddled and asked for a recess so that Dr. Levin could review a deposition Deidre had made.

Foxman almost lost his cool judicial demeanor. He gave Deidre a stern look and said, "I'm not going to let you disrupt the orderly proceedings of this court."

Deidre nodded meekly and said, "Yes, sir."

Foxman announced a ten-minute recess and told Niles that he must proceed when court resumed. Niles left the courtroom to confer with Deidre. Damore shook his head and sighed. Dr. Levin inconspicuously took a seat in the back of the courtroom and began to read Deidre's deposition.

Court reconvened and Niles began his opening argument. He talked eloquently of her emotional and mental problems from childhood that left her an emotional cripple. Niles said she couldn't think rationally and that her judgment was impaired.

"She has been beset by a multitude of problems all her life," Niles said. "She was rejected by her father, who never talked to her, and once had a fight with him when she tried to get him to acknowledge her."

Niles said that Deidre's mother had been abused and carried on a history of abuse to Deidre. Carol Ann Hunt, Niles said, completely controlled her daughter and could make her do anything.

"Deidre was virtually a slave," Niles said. "That's why she left home."

At this time, Foxman noticed that Dr. Levin was still seated in the courtroom. The judge wagged a finger and halted the proceedings just as Niles's tone was taking on an evangelical quality.

The judge asked, "Isn't that Dr. Levin?" Niles peered over his reading glasses and glanced back over his shoulders.

"I'm sorry, Judge," he said sheepishly. "I didn't know he was still here."

"You'll have to step outside until you're called, Dr. Levin," Foxman said.

The psychologist looked embarrassed and left the courtroom. Niles apologized again and started his argument once more while Damore shook his head in disbelief. The interruption didn't seem to fluster Niles. He picked up where he had left off, his booming voice again resuming its evangelical quality.

Niles noted that Carol Ann Hunt, Deidre's mother, and three of her aunts had been treated for mental problems. He told the court that Deidre had suffered "horrendous" beatings, rapes, and attempted rapes all of her young life. Niles said abuse breeds abuse and that Deidre consistently got involved with men who brutalized her. Nevertheless, she clung to them, he said, because of past rejection and because she was easily manipulated.

Deidre's attorney said the court could not image "the most horrendous circumstances this young girl grew up in." He noted that she had followed a boyfriend, John Beauvier, to Daytona Beach and that he had beaten her, then left.

". . . Deidre was a lost waif in Daytona Beach when she fell into the hands of someone who used her," Niles said. "I'm not saying she's without fault . . . but she has been the victim of abuse and domination."

Niles categorized the people who were involved in the murder scheme as "emotionally crippled kids who were running around the Boardwalk playing video games" until they met Kosta Fotopoulos. It was Kosta's influence and domination, Niles argued, that turned these kids, including Deidre, toward violence.

"These kids were no match for him," Niles said. "This is the power. This is the killer. This is the money. This is the god. The things they did were wrong, but how did these waifs come together at the same time to become involved in murder?

"Bryan Chase had never done anything wrong," Niles said, pacing. "He was just a big, dumb kid. He was a teddy bear. But Kosta manipulated him and the others. He was a manipulative, conniving, and extremely scary person, an arch criminal."

Both Niles and Damore often drove their points home by repetition, a technique that is generally considered necessary to impress a jury. Foxman occasionally nudged them by telling them to "ask the question" or "to move on. I think you've made your point."

During a break, Damore, who was determined not to try the case in the press, noted this failing. He said it was easier to make legal points with a judge than a jury.

"There's a man sitting up there who knows the law," he said. "You don't have to keep hammering away. It's easy to forget."

Niles spent part of the break telling a small group that there was no such thing as a "minor" wound from an AK-47. He displayed considerable knowledge of armaments. He noted that military bullets had to be encased in a steel jacket so that they wouldn't flatten out like a lead projectile. This supposedly minimized the severity of injuries to soldiers who were shot in action. This was part of the agreement at the Geneva Convention, Niles said.

He explained that military munitions experts circumvented the intent of the agreement by altering the way a bullet moves through the air. Some bullets, Niles said, "worm" their way through a body, causing severe injury. A bullet from an AK-47, he said, is designed to tumble end over end when it hits something.

"The bullet has such impact that if it hits your arm, it might kill you," he said. "You won't lose your arm, you'll lose your life. The impact has a shattering effect all through the body."

When court reconvened, Niles called Dr. Levin to the stand in the hope of buttressing his contention that Deidre was easily dominated and was manipulated against her own free will when she shot Ramsey and participated in the plans to kill Lisa and Bryan Chase. This was precisely what Dr. Levin concluded when he tested Deidre on May 13, 1989.

321

There was, however, a severe glitch.

Dr. Levin discovered that Deidre had been involved in the attempted murder of Veronica Rudzinski in New Hampshire. Deidre was under no one's domination then, and this prompted Dr. Levin to write a letter to Damore saying that the new evidence made him "uncomfortable" with his previous conclusion.

Dr. Levin interviewed Deidre again on August 13, 1990, in the Volusia County Jail and decided to stand by his original finding. The psychologist took the stand with reporters expecting that Damore would use him like a punching bag on cross-examination by showing him to be indecisive.

Dr. Levin testified that Deidre had a life of abuse. He said she had been abused by her mother, sexually abused by a series of men, and that she sought abusive relationships. He noted that Deidre began using drugs and alcohol before she reached her teens. Deidre's mother, Dr. Levin testified, dominated her daughter as a child, but did a complete turnabout when Deidre reached her teens. Then, he said, her mother allowed Deidre to drink at home and have live-in boyfriends.

"There was no security in the home," Dr. Levin said. "Deidre wanted a father figure and would do anything to get the approval of a man."

Dr. Levin said Deidre thought she controlled Kosta, when the opposite was true. "He intimidated her," he testified. "He would aim a gun at her and cock it. He burned her breast with a cigarette and cut her. She thought that she better not cross him because she was afraid of what would happen to her . . . There was a lot of fear of him but also a strong attachment, which is common in people with abused backgrounds."

The psychologist put Deidre's dirty laundry in the open: she was emotionally damaged, suspicious, hostile, overly sensitive, worried, tense, indecisive, had disrupted judgment and thinking, and was unable to be logical in times of stress.

"This is a person who has poor ego development, a lack of sexual or any other kind of identity," he testified. "She has a borderline personality disorder, which is somewhere between being psychotic and normal. She can move between one or the other."

Because of her chronic loneliness, low self-esteem, and lack of sexual or any other kind of identity, Dr. Levin said "she would be susceptible to manipulation because that would give her a complete picture of herself."

Kosta, he said, was just the type of man who would attract Deidre. He was older and had money and power. She was reaching out for a father figure, Dr. Levin said, and added that "she wanted to believe his lies [about being a terrorist and CIA assassin] and never questioned them."

He added that people with borderline personality disorders impulsively seek relationships with people who can fill the gaps in their lives rather than striving for natural growth and development. "Deidre has a very complete profile," Dr. Levin testified. "She is in the highest range of being paranoid, hostile, suspicious, and having poor judgment. But not all of the time. She can have mood swings which make her appear absolutely normal."

Damore began cross-examination and, true to expectations, started to hammer Dr. Levin. First, Damore elicited testimony from the psychologist that Deidre knew right from wrong. That met the guidelines for sanity in Florida. Dr. Levin added that, although Deidre knew the difference, she simply ignored social standards.

The psychologist admitted that it would be "impossible" for Kosta to dominate Deidre completely but that his influence would be strong. "She would love him and fear him at the same time," he said.

Damore attacked Dr. Levin's contradictory thoughts concerning Deidre's psychological profile. "Would you change your mind again if you learned new facts?" Damore asked sharply.

"That could alter my opinion, yes. But the facts that I stated are still valid."

Damore shook his head and asked if Dr. Levin changed his mind about Deidre being subject to domination after he learned that she had been involved in an attempted murder when no one was dominating her. Dr. Levin admitted that was true, but said his second interview with Deidre caused him to return to his original position that Deidre participated in the murder schemes only because Kosta dominated her.

"What about Deidre emptying a full magazine of bullets into Veronica Rudzinski?" Damore snapped. "Deidre wasn't dominated then, was she?"

Dr. Levin replied that he had read the police reports of the shooting and that there were too many contradictions to convince him that Deidre did the shooting.

Damore forced the psychologist to admit that he had seen no scars to back up his claims that Deidre had been physically abused by Kosta. Dr. Levin was quick to note that the abuse had been mental.

Damore said there was a contradiction concerning how easily Deidre was to manipulate. He noted that Deidre's mother allowed her to do whatever she wanted when Deidre reached her teens. In fact,

Damore noted, Deidre's relatives had no control over her.

"Deidre did pretty much as she pleased, didn't she?" Damore asked. "Deidre had total control to decide whether to kill or not."

The psychologist doggedly maintained that Deidre only killed and schemed to kill to please Kosta.

Damore asked Dr. Levin if he would change his mind again if new facts were presented to him, then queried him on another issue before the psychologist could answer.

"Doctor, are you opposed to the death penalty?" Damore asked.

"Yes, I am."

"Doctor, was Deidre Hunt insane when she killed Kevin Ramsey? Was she insane when she plotted to kill Bryan Chase? Did she know right from wrong?"

Dr. Levin answered that people with borderline personality disorders, such as Deidre had, did what they pleased regardless of whether it was right or wrong.

Niles looked grim when Foxman called a short recess. Deidre kept her head on the table most of the time, sometimes dozing, sometimes weeping, always clutching the prayer beads. The reporters and spectators weren't sympathetic even when Deidre wept.

"They think it's a game show," said Pat LaMee, a reporter for the *Orlando Sentinel*, disdaining the gallery.

Dan Spiess, television photographer for WESH-TV in Daytona Beach, commented about Deidre's tears. "She's not shedding them for Kevin Ramsey, Bryan Chase, or Lisa," he said. "She hasn't shown one bit of remorse. She's not crying for her victims, she's crying for herself because she got caught."

Niles used the remainder of the afternoon to call several aunts and uncles to testify for Deidre. Each testified that Deidre's mother, Carol Ann Hunt, had treated her like a slave.

Carol Ann's sisters and half sisters admitted to treatment for emotional disorders that ranged from depression to overeating. They said Carol Ann had it tougher than they did. They said she was referred to by her mother as "that Irish bastard" and that she had severe emotional problems, in addition to being an alcoholic. They said Carol Ann used Deidre as a "pawn" and described Deidre's bitter, deprived childhood.

Deidre's aunts and uncles told how Carol Ann would dump Deidre and her brother in their yards, drive off, then telephone them later. Sometimes, they said, Carol Ann left Deidre in the house with nothing to eat. At other times, they said, Deidre was forced to cook meals before she was thirteen years old. Otherwise, they said, Deidre, her brother, and Carol Ann would have nothing to eat.

Niles had them answer questions that showed how Deidre had been born out of wedlock by a father who refused to recognize her existence. Deidre, desperate to be acknowledged, if not accepted by him, wrote letters that were returned unopened. She telephoned her father, and he hung up. Once, they said, Deidre followed him inside a bar where he threw a glass of beer in her face.

Niles elicited testimony from Deidre's relatives to support his "dominance" defense. Because she was so utterly rejected by her father, the witnesses said, Deidre sought relationships with older men who abused her. Deidre's aunts and uncles agreed that

Deidre thought she was dominating the men while the reverse was true.

Carolyn Louise Johnson, Deidre's oldest aunt, testified that Deidre "had abusive relationships again and again. She gravitated toward them whether they were young or old."

Carolyn's husband Howard said that Carol Ann frequently "had fits of rage" in front of Deidre. Putting Deidre and her mother together, he testified, was "like putting gasoline and a match together."

The witnesses had been flown in from New England and Foxman held the court late for their convenience. They turned out to be of little help to Deidre in spite of the direction Niles steered them.

Damore blew holes in the domination theory presented by Deidre's aunts and uncles. Deidre's Uncle Howard, a retired military noncom, had only seen Deidre occasionally, once a year at most. Although the Johnsons took Deidre into their house when Howard retired from the military, they testified that Deidre didn't obey the rules they set down for their own children. The rules, they testified, were simple: tell us where you're going, who you're going with, and be home by eleven p.m. Deidre, they said, disregarded the rules.

"Deidre knew she had to obey the rules or she would have to leave," Howard said. "She knew that she had a warm, loving home to return to if she would obey the rules. . . . She was very intelligent, but she wouldn't apply it. She had a lot of problems in school because of that.

Under Damore's cross-examination, the aunts and uncles admitted that Deidre wouldn't obey household rules, that she chose to go out with men they considered "lowlifes," all of whom were older than she.

Deidre's Uncle Howard summed up the experiences the aunts and uncles testified to: "We had no control over Deidre. She would go to a point, then gravitate back to the same people, doing the things we wouldn't condone. We could not manipulate her. She either had to follow the rules or get out."

With each relative, Deidre had been given the same choice. And each time she had chosen not to obey the rules. Damore's cross-examination had severely damaged Niles's argument that Deidre was easily dominated and controlled.

Foxman continued the hearing until well after five o'clock in the evening. Weary spectators left, as did television crews, leaving only two reporters in the courtroom when the last two witnesses of the day testified in Deidre's behalf.

The witnesses were remarkably alike—each was from the Combat Zone, where Deidre had achieved notoriety. They were both slim and had long hair bleached almost platinum. They were both prostitutes, wore heavy makeup and figure-hugging dresses. As each took the witness stand in turn, they smiled at Deidre and silently mouthed "I love you" to her. She returned the greeting.

Carie Ameda had known Deidre for five years in Manchester, New Hampshire, and said Deidre was only "slightly impressionable" even though she conceded that Deidre's childhood was terrible.

"I wouldn't have wanted to go through the same thing [as she did]," Carie said.

Carie noted that Deidre always went out with abusive men. "I was extremely shocked that she put up with that," she said. "Guys would introduce themselves and say, 'Come with me,' and I said, 'Dee, don't do it,' but it went in one ear and out the other. She didn't pay attention. She needed that [attention]."

"In other words, you couldn't control her?" Damore asked. "You couldn't manipulate her? She went anyway?"

"Yes."

Carie testified that Deidre had trouble and that "men were her problem." Carie insisted that she didn't believe Deidre was violent. Damore asked her if she knew Deidre had shot a woman six times in Manchester.

"I knew about it," Carie replied, "but I didn't think she had anything to do with it."

"Even though she pleaded guilty?" Damore asked incredulously.

Carie hedged when Damore asked how she made a living. The witness said she did "little things." Damore asked her to be more specific.

"Prostitution," Carie said. "It's a victimless crime."

Carie said that Deidre had been a prostitute but, "she got no pleasure from it [sex]. She just got money."

Carie had told about a fight Deidre had with her mother when Niles conducted the direct examination. The fight Carie described occurred at Carol Ann's house, ending with Carol Ann slapping Deidre.

Damore pressed for details on cross-examination. Carie said that she, John Beauvier, Deidre, and a girl named Jill were visiting Carol Ann. Deidre's mother didn't like for Deidre to see Beauvier. Carie, Deidre, Beauvier, and Jill were in Carol Ann's bedroom when Carol Ann unexpectedly opened the door.

"She found John and Dee in bed," Carie said.

"What were they doing?" Damore asked.

329

"Having sex."

"Where were you and the other girl?"

"Jill and I were in the room. There wasn't any hanky-panky. We were just lying around.

"So Carol Ann Hunt opened the door, found her daughter making love in her bed, with two other girls there, and she got mad and slapped her?"

Carie said that was true.

Damore wanted to know what Deidre's reputation was in the Combat Zone. Did they call her a liar? Carie replied in the negative. Well, what *did* they call her? Damore asked.

"I don't want to say it," Carie said.

Carie, who didn't look more than twenty, stumbled awkwardly out of the courtroom, head down, weeping silently. At one point she had to stop, support herself on a courtroom bench, before she could continue. Before she left the witness stand, Carie exchanged silent words of affection with Deidre.

Susan Hortoff wore a form-fitting yellow sheath dress. She gave Deidre a sympathetic smile and seemed on the verge of tears. Deidre gave her a warm smile.

Niles, who had seen Damore destroy Carie's testimony, only kept Susan on the stand long enough for her to say that John Beauvier dominated her. "She would do just about anything for him," Susan said. "There were times when I think she'd like it when he hit her. She would make him mad to see if he would hit her, then when he did, things would be okay."

Susan told Damore that she didn't know Deidre was a prostitute and said that Deidre and Beauvier fought over "stupid things." But she told the court that Deidre often asserted her independence when

330

Beauvier ordered her to do something.

"Dee would say, 'The hell with you, I'll do what I want to do!'" Susan said. "She'd push him as far she could without losing him."

The defense and the state were finished for the day. Foxman called recess and Niles hurried out, shaking his head. He looked flustered and frustrated. "It's rough," he told a reporter.

"You don't have anything to work with," the reporter answered.

"That's the problem." Niles hurried to his car.

The day had gone well from Damore's point of view, but Dr. Levin, who clung to the domination theory like a pit bull, didn't set well with him.

"I'm going to bring in a psychiatrist during rebuttal who will absolutely destroy his testimony," he said.

But the day had not gone at all well for Deidre Hunt. Niles had little material that he could use to establish mitigating factors. Each time he had tried, it had blown up in his face. Veteran court reporters agreed that he was doing a good job under the circumstances. They wondered what surprises lay in store the next day when Deidre's mother, Carol Ann Hunt, was expected to testify.

36

The courtroom was crowded the morning of September 10, 1990, with people who were anxious to hear Deidre's mother testify. There was also a rumor buzzing around that Deidre would take the stand herself. The excited gallery stopped whispering when Deidre entered with her armed guard and sat down.

Carol Ann Hunt would testify but not before Niles brought three more of Deidre's relatives to the stand. The gallery grunted its disapproval, prompting reporters to complain that the spectators were merely seeking entertainment and had no idea of how serious the proceedings were.

Niles followed his game plan by trying to convince Judge Foxman that Deidre's terrible upbringing, history of emotional disorders in the family, and her frantic search for a father figure led her to abusive men, such as Kosta, who dominated her. In view of the evidence against Deidre, the chances for his success seemed remote.

Shirley Miller was one of Deidre's aunts who had lived in Maitland, Florida, for ten years. She stressed the dysfunctional childhood of Deidre's mother, which later manifested itself by Carol Ann Hunt mistreating Deidre and her brother. Carol

Ann and Shirley had the same mother but different fathers. Both fathers, Shirley said, were alcoholics. All of the sisters were abused, Shirley said, but iterated that Carol Ann had it roughest by being considered "the bastard" of the family.

Carol Ann's emotional trauma, Shirley said, led her to get pregnant and have Deidre as an illegitimate daughter.

"She didn't love this child," Shirley said. "She didn't want it."

Shirley corroborated previous testimony that Carol Ann used Deidre as a pawn. She began to weep as she testified how she had tried to take Deidre away from her abusive mother.

"We tried to get custody but couldn't," Shirley said. "We stood up to Carol Ann and said, 'You can't have these kids.' Carol Ann said, 'You'll have to go to court.'"

Shirley said she went to court to get custody of Carol Ann's children but lost. Then, after winning custody, Shirley said Carol Ann wanted to turn her children over to the welfare department. Deidre was ten years old.

Shirley said she was worn down with worry and didn't have the energy to battle Carol Ann any further. She said she went to a priest for guidance. "He said, 'The only way these kids will develop is to be taken away from their mother,'" Shirley said. "'They all need counseling, but if there is no counseling you can no longer help this girl. You're not helping her by bailing her out every time she gets in trouble.'"

Shirley reinforced testimony concerning the abuse Deidre had suffered. It was almost impossible for even the most hardened person not to feel sorry about Deidre's upbringing. The main problem with all of this was that Shirley, like others before her, testified that Deidre rebelled. Shirley said that, as Deidre grew older, both she and Carol Ann had live-in boyfriends in the same house.

Deidre and Carol Ann lived with Shirley for a short time in 1980, but it didn't work out. Deidre, who was eleven, wouldn't follow the household rules and got kicked out, as did her mother.

"I believe that she [Deidre] was emotionally disturbed," Shirley said, "but nobody could make her do anything. The biggest thing with Deidre is that you can talk to her, but the girl has no self-worth. You can't make her do anything. She always chose her own path."

Niles succeeded in gaining sympathy for Deidre as an abused child, but testimony from Deidre's aunts and uncles portrayed her as being too strong to be dominated by anyone. Instead of clawing her way out of the dark pit she was in, Deidre seemed intent on sinking to even lower depths.

The aunts, uncles, and cousin gave similar testimony about Deidre. All had, in their own way, tried to help Deidre but had ended up making her leave their homes. Susan E. Carlin, Deidre's aunt from Nashua, New Hampshire, noted, "When Deidre left for Florida she knew we weren't going to bail her out anymore."

Susan complained that Damore was asking her trick questions. "You're twisting everything I say," she accused. "I don't blame Deidre for what she's done. Deidre never had a chance. Never."

In the afternoon, there was standing room only in the courtroom. Both Carol Ann Hunt and Deidre were expected to testify. Deidre clutched her prayer beads and looked terribly frightened.

The courtroom buzzed when Carol Ann Hunt

made her appearance. She entered wearing a pale blue suit. She was forty-three, petite like Deidre, and her bleached blond hair was shoulder length. The hostility that radiated from the gallery was thick enough to cut with a knife, but Carol Ann kept her shoulders straight and looked defiant. Mother and daughter mouthed "I love you" as Carol Ann was sworn in.

Niles quickly established that Carol Ann graduated from high school in 1965, went to work at a New Hampshire bank, got pregnant while only eighteen years old, and went to Florida where she tried to commit suicide by taking an overdose of drugs. But Carol Ann failed in her suicide attempt and was back in New Hampshire, on welfare, when she became pregnant by Dennis Drisco, a tall man that Carol Ann said had a bad temper.

Carol Ann said that Drisco was Deidre's father. She never lived with Drisco, but Carol Ann said he still dominated her. "He was very controlling," she said in a strong New England accent. "He told me what books to read, when to read. He told me to stay in my room. I thought I would go crazy."

Nevertheless, Carol Ann continued the rocky relationship with Drisco. Once she tried to jump out of a moving car after he slapped her, she said. She testified that Drisco knocked pots and pans off the stove in fits of rage while Carol Ann hid in her bedroom until she thought it was safe to come out.

Carol Ann described being beaten by her mother as a child, and when she refused to cry, her mother beat harder. She said she treated Deidre the same way but said her abuse was more emotional than physical. She described picking Deidre out of her crib, shaking her, then throwing her back. All the time she was in such a fit of rage that it seemed

335

she was watching someone else do it.

Carol Ann said that Deidre was totally under her control when she was a child. Carol Ann testified that she slapped her for no reason. Deidre was so afraid of being slapped, Carol Ann said, that she wouldn't come within an arm's length of her. If this wasn't enough, Carol Ann said, she herself suffered severe bouts of depression and alcoholism that kept her from functioning normally.

"Deidre was about seven but if she didn't cook, we didn't eat," Carol Ann said. "Deidre had to do everything. Once she made a birthday cake for me when she was nine. She used food coloring to decorate it because we had no frosting. I said, 'This isn't a birthday cake. Why did you bother?'" Carol Ann said she slapped the birthday cake away.

Carol Ann said that a neighbor named Richie, who was thirty, raped Deidre when she was just eleven. "I just ignored it because I couldn't handle it," she said. "Everything she did was insignificant."

Carol Ann said she hated Deidre. "I couldn't understand why I resented her, and it drove me crazy." She said she abandoned Deidre on numerous occasions before Deidre reached her teens.

Two significant events occurred when Deidre became a teenager, Carol Ann testified. Deidre became sexually active with "countless" older men. Carol Ann allowed Deidre to have affairs and even have older men live with Deidre at home. Deidre, she said, cut a wide swath through the ranks of older boyfriends because she needed approval.

"She would meet a guy," Carol Ann said, "then push him away and get another because she needed constant attention."

Deidre also gravitated toward "street kids." Deidre wanted to "rescue them," she said, by bringing them home, giving them a meal and a place to sleep. She said that Deidre was "terrified of being alone" and that the people she rescued were often "lowlifes" who robbed her.

Carol Ann said Deidre became obsessed with contacting her father. She telephoned him and he hung up; she wrote letters and they were returned unopened. Once, she said, Deidre followed him into a bar and he threw a drink in her face. Instead of being sympathetic toward Deidre, the memory seemed to aggravate Carol Ann.

"She just kept talking and talking after the altercation with her father," she said. "You wanted to throw a glass of water in her face to bring her out of it because she just wouldn't stop."

Carol Ann said there were no moral values at home when Deidre was growing up. "There weren't any rules," she said. "The kids could drink [alcohol]."

Lori Henderson was the person who told Carol Ann that Deidre had been arrested for first-degree murder.

"I said, 'No, no, no,' and Lori said, 'Don't worry. Kosta Fotopoulos set her up in the woods. It's all right.'"

Carol Ann said a reporter contacted her after Deidre's arrest and asked for her reaction. "I told the reporter that I didn't care, but it was a lie," Carol Ann said. "I lay a great deal of blame on myself. I feel immense guilt and blame."

She testified, "One of the reasons that Deidre got in trouble was that she tried to help others too much. She's worth saving."

Deidre's mother became combative when Damore began his cross-examination. Damore established that Deidre had been arrested for grand theft when she was twelve while Carol Ann and Deidre were living in Florida with Shirley. Carol Ann admitted that she had slapped Deidre when she picked her daughter up at the police station, but she made light of Deidre's crime.

"The counselors said it was just normal teenage rebellion," Carol Ann said.

Damore pointed out that there was no record to substantiate that Deidre had been raped when she was eleven. Carol Ann said she didn't report the rape.

"You didn't call the police?" he asked.

Carol Ann angrily shot back, "I didn't call the cops. I would *never* call the cops. *To this day I wouldn't call the cops!*"

Carol Ann insisted that Deidre was never violent even though she had been arrested and charged with attempted murder and armed robbery. Another time, Deidre had attacked someone with a knife. Damore said that Deidre wasn't passive or easily led and that, in fact, she was the "leader of the pack."

Carol Ann had no comment and downplayed the fact that Deidre had been a prostitute: "She didn't do that very long."

Damore recalled that Carol Ann said Deidre had gotten in trouble because she wanted to rescue people from the streets. "Was Deidre rescuing Mark Kevin Ramsey by blowing his brains out?" he asked.

Carol Ann paused a long moment. "No, I guess not. I don't know."

"Isn't it true that you'd say anything to keep your daughter from receiving the death penalty?" he asked.

"I don't want her to go to the electric chair,"

Carol Ann shrugged, "but if it happens, it happens."

The courtroom gasped in shock and anger. Several people shouted, "You should be the one going to the electric chair, not her!"

Judge Foxman called a short recess at Niles's request so that Deidre and her mother could talk privately in another room. There was still standing room only when court reconvened. Judges and attorneys helped make up the crowd that was waiting to hear Deidre testify.

Niles stood up. "The defense rests," he said. "My client says that she is not emotionally able to testify, and I agree with her."

Damore was surprised by this development. "She has been following and assisting counsel in her defense," he said. "The state does not think she's emotionally unstable."

Judge Foxman asked if she was sure she didn't want to take the stand in her own behalf. Deidre shook her head and spoke in a meek voice: "No. My decision was carefully thought out."

Judge Foxman adjourned court for the day. Following the highly charged atmosphere created by Carol Ann's testimony, the fact that Deidre wouldn't testify deflated the courtroom. Even Damore was affected.

"Well, that was certainly anticlimactic, wasn't it?" he said, before his usual habit of ducking reporters.

Peter Niles had already disappeared. Deidre, in handcuffs and leg manacles, accompanied by three armed deputies, was seen getting into a police van that would take her back to a high-security jail cell.

37

When court reconvened the morning of September 11, Damore called the rebuttal witness he had promised who would "destroy" the psychological profile of Deidre that had been presented by Dr. Levin.

Damore noted that unlike Dr. Levin, who had no medical training, Dr. Robert Davis was an M.D. in addition to having advanced schooling in psychiatry. Dr. Davis was older than Dr. Levin and had practiced psychiatry since 1964.

The prosecutor questioned Dr. Davis about the conclusions he had reached when he had examined Deidre. They were far different from those that had been presented by Dr. Levin. Dr. Davis noted that Deidre was sane at the time she shot Ramsey, when she participated in planning the murder of Brian Chase, and during the attempted murder of Lisa.

"Deidre has a great deal of will power," he said. "She had no disease of the mind and was under no emotional stress at the time of the Ramsey killing. Deidre was self-contained and not unduly coerced into anything. She is well-founded in her concepts and is very self-assured."

Dr. Davis said that Deidre didn't have a borderline personality but was a sociopath, which he described as being a genetic disorder. Sociopaths are not psychotic, because they haven't lost touch with reality, he said. Sociopaths know exactly what they're doing. As Dr. Levin had done, Dr. Davis had his own list of Deidre's psychological problems, which he described: "She is a sociopathic, antisocial personality. This is an accepted diagnostic, genetic disorder. Sociopaths have no conscience, no guilt; they're selfish, impulsive, blame others, never learn by punishment or experience. They are callous and don't feel guilt to any degree."

Dr. Davis had seen the videotape recording of Deidre shooting Ramsey and said there was nothing to indicate that Deidre had been coerced. Instead, he said she seemed self-assured and that she even enjoyed it.

"When she turned the man's head up, [when she shot Ramsey in the temple] it was done with relish. Deidre had no hesitation. She thought it out ahead of time and did it with purpose and with no revulsion. She knew exactly what she was doing, and she knew it was wrong."

The psychiatrist noted that Deidre was determined to kill Lisa in spite of several failures. Instead of discouraging her, they cemented her resolve to have Lisa and Chase killed. "She was driven by a desire for money and power," he said.

Niles, who had tried throughout the hearing to show that Deidre's actions were inevitable because of a history of mental illness in her family, wondered if the genetic order the psychiatrist described had been inherited. Niles noted that, in spite of the circumstances, Deidre still looked at Kosta with awe and administration. Dr. Davis admitted that was true.

When Niles asked if Deidre's history of abuse and rejection by her father could have contributed to her problems, the psychiatrist gave a weak reply: "I wouldn't know."

Niles wanted to know if Dr. Davis was familiar with the Helsinki Syndrome, where hostages were brainwashed into thinking of their captives as friends. The doctor was. He also knew about Patty Hearst, who had been kidnaped, brainwashed, and then participated in an armed robbery with her captors.

Niles maintained that this was what happened to Deidre and the others who were involved in plotting Lisa's death. They had no self-esteem to begin with, he said, and were dominated by Kosta the way Patty Hearst was won over by her captors. Deidre, who had no self-esteem, was easy prey for Kosta to brainwash into committing murder.

"She would do it if there was enough gain for her," Dr. Davis said. "I'm not sure how much Mr. Fotopoulos controlled or dominated her. He didn't control her to the degree that she would kill [for him]."

Niles tried to establish other mitigating factors in Deidre's favor but was unable to do so. Dr. Davis's cross-examination ended after he claimed that Deidre's ability to conform to social standards was impaired and that she would withstand dominance "better than most people."

Damore's redirect was brief, but he had Dr. Davis reinforce points that were critical to the state. First, Deidre could have refused to shoot Ramsey. Secondly, there was nothing in her psychological makeup to contribute to her being a pawn who would commit murder. "She was motivated by power, money, and position," Dr. Davis said. "She could have taken off any time she wanted to."

Damore called another psychiatrist to buttress the state's contention that the murders were particularly heinous because Deidre knew exactly what she was doing. Dr. Umesh Mhatre, a psychologist with extensive experience in dealing with children and adolescents, had interviewed Deidre April 2, 1990, and had seen the videotape of Ramsey's murder.

Dr. Mhatre said that Deidre was under no mental or emotional distress when she killed Ramsey. Neither was she being dominated. Instead, the psychiatrist said, Deidre had been "extremely arrogant and defiant" at the time of the shooting.

"The video speaks for itself, Dr. Mhatre said. "It started with Deidre ordering, 'Don't shine that shit in my eyes!' Deidre was assertive and confident, and her body language was aggressive. She showed no anxiety or panic. I was impressed at the calmness in which she carried out this execution."

Instead of being forced to kill Ramsey, Dr. Mhatre said that Deidre was "very much a participant." He said he found no mitigating factors during his interview with Deidre or by watching the videotape.

Niles said that Deidre's bisexuality proved that she had no identity, making it easy for men to dominate her. The psychiatrist said that Deidre's sexual habits were "the result of immoral character, not domination." Dr. Mhatre totally dismissed Dr. Levin's diagnosis that Deidre had a borderline personality disorder and agreed with Dr. Davis. "She is a sociopath who is motivated by greed," he said.

Niles maintained that Deidre had mixed feelings about Kosta. Initially, she thought he was a "nice man" who took her jet skiing and showed her a good time. Miles said Deidre was so afraid of Kosta that she stayed with him even after he abused her physically and emotionally.

Dr. Mhatre said Deidre's motives weren't that complicated. From his perspective, Dr. Mhatre said Deidre saw Kosta as someone who had the means to improve the quality of her life. "She was going to

343

hitch a ride and stay with him as long as it was good for her," he said.

Throughout the hearing, Niles tried to portray Kosta as an "arch criminal" who spun a web of murder and intrigue that captured young, petty criminals. He claimed that it was surprising for such people to become involved in murderous schemes unless Kosta was an "arch criminal" who dominated them.

Dr. Mhatre, however, wasn't impressed with Niles's defense. "It doesn't surprise me at all," he said. "Birds of a feather flock together. There's always a gang leader in every gang. Kosta's position gave him dominance."

"If you take a bunch of little lost kids on the Boardwalk with no money, no food, no jobs, no power, and no family, couldn't Kosta dominate them?"

"In a general sense, yes."

The psychiatrist testified again that Deidre was under no emotional distress resulting from her association with Kosta. "She knows right from wrong," he said, "and is able to dictate her actions. Deidre had no empathy and no remorse."

"Would you be terrified if someone had an AK-47 and threatened to shoot you unless you killed Ramsey?" Niles asked.

"Yes, but I would shoot him instead," Dr. Mhatre said. "It was not a terrifying situation for Deidre Hunt."

On redirect, Damore said it would take a meek person to be dominated and that Deidre was anything but that.

"Deidre is streetwise," Dr. Mhatre said. "A very smart street kid. She can't be easily dominated. She's a very strong person and Kosta Fotopoulos couldn't dominate her. There was absolutely no fear in her at all [on the videotape]. She wasn't trembling. I would have been trembling so much that I wouldn't have been able to hold a gun. The first thing she said was 'Don't shine that shit in my eyes!' I would not say that to a man holding an AK-47 on me unless I was suicidal."

Dr. Mhatre was the final witness. Now the attorneys would present arguments as to whether Deidre should die or spend the rest of her life in prison. To the most seasoned observers, it appeared that Niles had an uphill battle.

Niles strenuously objected to the state's contention that Ramsey's death was heinous and cruel. Nor was Chase's death. He said that neither man knew that he was going to be killed and that each died quickly. Niles admitted that the deaths where "horrible executions" but claimed that death was immediate. Therefore, the deaths were not cruel.

Sean Daly, an assistant from the Attorney General's Office, noted that, "It is clear from the videotape that [Ramsey] did in fact suffer greatly from those shots."

Foxman said, "You could see the suffering on that tape."

Damore's closing argument was intended to persuade the court that Deidre's crimes merited the death penalty. Damore was conservative in his words and body language, but he was persuasive. He reminded the court of Deidre's previous convictions, that she had killed for financial gain, that she was cold and calculating, and that Ramsey's murder was especially heinous, atrocious, and cruel.

He reviewed the evidence in a voice that snapped like a whip. He said that Deidre had a "cold, cruel heart . . . and if this is a case for which the death

345

penalty is not appropriate, then I can think of no case that it is appropriate."

Deidre put her head on the table and wept, clutching her prayer beads, as Damore conducting a crisp ten-minute assault. He called particular attention to the videotape of Ramsey's murder: "When the court goes out to deliberate its decision, it should not forget the sound of that boy's voice as he cries out in agony," he said. "Consider Deidre Hunt taking him by the hair and blowing his brains out."

Niles tried to save Deidre from the electric chair. He called attention to how young she was, her domination by Kosta, her emotional instability because of an abused childhood, and that she would not have become involved if Kosta had not been able to manipulate her.

Niles said Deidre was an emotional cripple that Kosta had her in his "evil grip," along with other Boardwalk waifs. Deidre, he said was a "poor child" who believed the fairy tale that she and Kosta would live happily together when Kosta collected on Lisa's seven hundred thousand dollar insurance policy. Niles said that Kosta controlled Deidre and "the waifs, vagabonds, scum of the earth" that he enlisted from the Boardwalk to kill Lisa.

"Kosta Fotopoulos is one of the most diabolical, manipulative, dangerous defendants that I have ever had the unseemly pleasure of being involved with in a case," Niles said. "This person [Deidre] is to be pitied. She's to be punished and a sufficient punishment would be life in prison. When you take somebody like that who is a cripple, do you kill them? A mental, physical, and emotional cripple, do you kill them? I say no!"

Foxman adjourned to deliberate the points of law and to weigh the aggravating and mitigating factors.

Most people, except Deidre, believed the judge could do nothing less than sentence her to death.

Two days later, Foxman called the court into session to deliver his verdict. Deidre wore a navy blue cardigan over her orange jumpsuit, and the circles under her eyes were darker. She was nervous and near tears as she had an animated conversation with Niles.

The courtroom was packed with tense spectators and six television cameras were strategically placed to capture Deidre's reaction to Foxman's sentence. The judge formally asked Niles if there were any reasons why the sentencing should not be imposed. Niles said, "No."

"The defendant will rise," the judge said.

Deidre stood, wiped tears from her eyes with a fist, and spoke in a trembling voice.

"In New Hampshire there is solid proof that Mr. Niles—"

"Don't start that," the judge said, referring to Deidre's on-again, off-again relationship with her attorney. "Mr. Niles did a darn good job," Foxman said. "He argued it very well for you, frankly."

Deidre nodded meekly, and Foxman asked if she wanted to make a statement before the sentence was imposed. She said yes, and began reading from several pages of notebook paper.

"What we have here is a videotape in combination with a murder. This is the first in the nation's history," Deidre said. "The video was a horrible, unthinkable thing to hold over one's head. I take total responsibility but not for first-degree murder. I think I was an unwilling participant in this horrendous crime."

347

Deidre's voice broke, and she trembled with sobs, tears streaming from her eyes as she looked back toward Ramsey's mother in the gallery. "I was confronted with a decision that Kosta Fotopoulos had absolutely already made," she sobbed. "It was my decision of living by shooting Mark Kevin Ramsey or dying with Mark Kevin Ramsey. My decision was a choice to survive, and I chose to live. If I had not chosen to live, I wouldn't be standing here facing what I'm facing."

Deidre's whole body shook, but she continued without missing a beat. Her voice quavered, "No one will ever know the horror of what I was forced to do and forced to view; the most disgusting and hideous, horrible scene I have ever viewed in my life. I was forced to commit this nightmare by my participation in this unspeakable act.

"I personally feel so repulsed by this nightmare ordeal. I wonder if any of you could have taken my place, would you have run? The only way to survive was to do exactly what you were told to do, when you were told to do it, and how you were told to do it. I chose to survive. I chose my own life, even with the horrible, disgusting fear and horrible torture at this man's hands and know it was the only reason I was alive."

Deidre stopped for a moment, sobbing almost hysterically, before she could speak again. "I realize my life by itself was not a normal upbringing," she wept. "However, this should not imply that I do not value the precious gift of life any less than you, who might have come from a decent upbringing. I feel tremendous guilt even though it was not done of my own volition. I cannot help but feel I should have died out there with Mark Kevin Ramsey.

"I still feel guilt, remorse, and responsibility for

348

my participation."

Deidre shuffled through her notes with trembling hands, weeping uncontrollably. Except for her sobs, the courtroom was deathly quiet. Deidre looked back at the gallery toward Ramsey's mother. "To the families of both these full-of-life young children I want to express great sympathy and total compassion to what you have been exposed to," she wept. "No one, I believe, should have to face this kind of horror in the death of a loved one. My heart aches to stand here knowing I had to participate in the unspeakable, most painful, most unfair nightmare ever. No nightmare like this should ever touch a family."

Although most of the people who watched the proceedings had little or no sympathy for Deidre, her anguish and fear were pitiful to see.

"Regardless of the judgment put upon me today, I will live with the memory of this horrible nightmare forever," she said. "The pain I feel inside I am never without.

"I couldn't have done anything differently, and I'm ashamed that I did not have the power to withstand the power of Kosta Fotopoulos. He is evil, vicious, and a professional assassin who eliminates other human beings for profit and power. He not only kills bodies, he kills minds. He makes Ted Bundy and (Gerald) Stano (serial killers) look like teddy bears. This is someone who has mastered the secret of manipulation of the human mind."

Deidre concluded, "It could have happened to anyone, anywhere, at any time," and sat down.

Damore rose and spoke to the judge. He was unmoved by Deidre's impassioned speech. "The only appropriate sentence is death," he said. "Justice is all that is sought by the state for the people who died at the cold hands of Deidre Hunt."

He mocked Deidre's attempt to show regret for what she had done, and making the apology that she had been coerced. "Her remorse is newly found," Damore noted. "It is not remorse for her victims but remorse for what she is facing."

The judge asked Deidre to stand for sentencing. She stood, her shoulders slumped, looking small and fragile, much like the "waif" Niles had described in defending her.

Foxman apparently wanted his unpleasant duty done quickly. He spoke in a strong, steady voice but wasted no time. In each case the aggravating factors were overwhelming. The first sentence was for the murder of Mark Kevin Ramsey.

"It is the sentence of the law and such is the judgment of the court that you, Deidre Michelle Hunt, be taken to a facility of the Department of Corrections . . . where you will be electrocuted until you are dead," Foxman said. "May God have mercy on your soul."

Deidre winced and put her hands to her face and wept silently. The courtroom erupted in a collective gasp. A woman screamed, "Oh, my God!" and there were other comments of shock and satisfaction. Carol Ann Hunt broke into tears.

Foxman continued sentencing even as the spectators were in turmoil. He imposed a second death sentence for the murder of Bryan Chase and six sentences of life in prison on each of the other charges. Foxman banged his gavel. "This court is adjourned," he said, and quickly went to his chambers.

Deidre seemed to have recovered some of her composure as she gathered her few belongings before being taken away by the armed deputies. Niles disappeared with her and the deputies through a side door. Damore looked shaken as he stood with two armed deputies waiting for an elevator.

"It's a prosecutor's syndrome," Nolin, the *News-Journal* reporter said. "They argue for the death sentence, then, when they get it, they're stunned." Nolin noted that the same was true of judges who sentenced defendants to death. "I've found some of them in their chambers crying," he said.

Damore had a different opinion in this particular case. "I value and cherish human life," he said. "I'd like to undo everything that happened. If I could I wouldn't have Kevin Ramsey killed in the woods or Bryan Chase murdered. I wouldn't have had Lisa Fotopoulos shot. But there comes a time when you have to answer for yourself on this earth, when you go too far over the line. If, by some chance, Deidre Hunt is granted a new sentence hearing or a trial and I prosecute, I will prosecute vociferously for the death penalty."

Judge Foxman was struck at how vicious the killings were. He wrote about the videotape of Ramsey's murder in his sentencing order: "Never before has this court seen a victim's suffering so graphically or visually established."

Almost immediately after the sentencing, Nolin entered the judge's chambers, expecting to find him in emotional turmoil. Instead, Foxman leaned against a bookcase, his robe unfastened, looking relaxed.

"There was nothing else I could do," Foxman said. "The law was very clear."

Carol Ann Hunt was corralled by reporters in the parking lot. She looked bitter as she dragged deeply on a cigarette and delivered her own verdict. "They're not looking for justice," she said. "They're looking for a conviction. She's going to get the maximum, and she's the scapegoat, and Kosta Fotopoulos

351

is going to get off. Her crime, in fact, was pleading guilty when, in fact, that wasn't the case."

"She was shown killing Ramsey on the videotape," a reporter said.

"She was coerced by Fotopoulos and the evil that lives in your city."

"Are you worried about her?" another reporter asked.

"She'll get an automatic appeal," Carol Ann said. "She has faith in God and believes that God will somehow turn the situation around."

38

Extensive investigative work had been done for almost a full year before Kosta's trial was scheduled to begin. There had also been complicated legal work to determine the best way to present the evidence.

On the basis of the evidence, the state had determined that Kosta's initial intent was to kill all of his in-laws, starting with Augustine and systematically murdering Mary and Dino so that Lisa would be the lone heir of the Paspalakis fortune when he killed her.

When Augustine Paspalakis died in 1986, no autopsy had been performed because he was under a doctor's care for coronary disease. Augustine's death was attributed to natural causes. Kosta told Bill and Barbara Markantonakis that he had arranged Augustine's death.

"I think that Kosta probably killed Augustine," said Wheeler, the chief investigator for the state attorney. "He had been complaining about pains in his stomach for several days before he died. I think Kosta probably poisoned him. He learned all about that stuff from those junky magazines he read."

The scenario wasn't one that Carmen Corrente,

Kosta's court-appointed lawyer, wanted brought to light in court. Damore and Corrente presented their arguments to Judge Foxman in late September.

Damore outlined the systematic murder scheme that Kosta had planned, which began with Augustine's death. Since then, Damore argued, Kosta had tried to have Mary and Dino killed, and then, out of desperation, rushed into several attempts to murder his wife to collect on her life insurance policies.

"What this case centers on is money," Damore argued. "Money and greed on the part of Kosta Fotopoulos."

Corrente countered that this evidence was "irrelevant and prejudicial" to Kosta. "It's not an essential element," he said. "We're going to have a parade of people coming in here, and there's no way it's not going to become a feature of the trial."

Foxman agreed with Damore's argument that there were a series of "well-connected similar facts" that culminated in the murders of Ramsey and Chase. The judge set a tentative trial date of October 1.

During the early phases of the investigation, some of the chemicals that Kosta used were stored in Gallagher's small office. The Daytona Beach headquarters for the state attorney was in a small, cramped building, where people almost had to walk sideways down the aisles. Their new offices were in a modern Criminal Justice Building were not ready at the time.

Gallagher thought nothing about the chemicals until they were removed. A forensic expert was cleaning some of the chemical containers when a spark ignited a small fire, which was quickly extinguished.

"It turned out that the chemicals were highly flammable," Gallagher said.

Had the chemicals been accidentally ignited in his office, Gallagher might not have been around to help conduct the investigation.

Lisa Fotopoulos told Gallagher that she believed Kosta had rented a metal detector from a company called D&B, or something similar to that. The investigator searched the Yellow Pages of the telephone directory to find advertisements for businesses that rented metal detectors. Gallagher telephoned D&F Enterprises and talked to Diana Godowa and found out that Kosta had rented a metal detector from her.

Gallagher met with Diana and her husband, Fred. Diana, the investigator thought, seemed like a nervous wreck.

"She was scared to death," he said. "She thought Kosta was with the Mafia, and she didn't want to get involved."

Gallagher managed to learn that Kosta had rented a metal detector on two separate occasions. The first time was about two weeks before he was arrested. Diana remembered that Kosta was driving a black BMW and told them that he was looking for a box with metal inside it.

Kosta returned later and said he had found what he was looking for, but said he would be back again. About a week later, Diana said Kosta returned and asked for a metal detector that would "go deeper." Diana rented him the same one.

"Do you have the rental receipts?" Gallagher asked.

"I tore them up when I saw that he was arrested on TV."

"Why did you do that?"

"I didn't want to get involved," Diana said.

Fred said his wife had been so upset and nervous that her ulcers were acting up.

Judge Foxman decided to hold Kosta's trial in Palatka, a town some thirty-five miles north of Daytona Beach, in Putnam County. He thought it was far enough removed so that the jury pool would not be completely contaminated and prejudicial toward Kosta.

Palatka isn't one of the glamorous beach cities in Florida; it's part of what some people refer to as "the other Florida." It has a small-town, Southern flavor, without all of the glitz and shimmer of sea and sand. Until recently, the largest business in the county was Weyerhauser, which operated a paper mill.

The residents in the county have mid-American values. When Damore and Corrente began voir dire to select a jury, enough men said their hobby was hunting to prompt a reporter to note, "It's a wonder that there's a deer or a rabbit left in the county."

The state and the defense were satisfied with a jury of twelve and two alternates, and opening arguments began. Damore's argument contained much of the same information that he had used in his argument at Deidre's sentencing. He warned the jurors that they would be hearing testimony from people who were convicted or who had pleaded guilty to serious crimes. The assistant state attorney asked the jury to weigh the testimony with the facts and other evidence.

Damore said that Kosta was afraid he would be broke because his wife intended to leave him. To avoid that, Damore said Kosta tried to have his wife killed by having Deidre Hunt hire people who were to do the job, only to be killed afterward. The motive, Damore said, was to collect on Lisa's insurance policies, and it led to the murders of Bryan Chase and Mark Kevin Ramsey.

These murders, this plot, was done in an attempt to gain money," Damore said. "It was done for greed."

Corrente's argument quickly revealed his trial strategy: that Deidre Hunt was behind the attempts on Lisa's life and that Kosta had killed Chase to protect his wife. A wiry man, Corrente paced and spoke with animation. He claimed that Kosta knew nothing of Deidre's plans to kill Lisa and that he had been the victim of a "mass uprising" against him in Daytona Beach. He noted that Kosta's trial was being held in Palatka because an impartial jury could not be empaneled in Daytona Beach.

The jury also heard forensic details about Ramsey's death before Foxman adjourned for the day.

An odd thing occurred in this trial when compared with Deidre's sentence hearing. At the sentence hearing, the state maintained that Deidre was too strong for Kosta to manipulate her; at Kosta's trial the state claimed that Deidre was dominated and manipulated by Kosta.

"Isn't that a fairly unusual twist?" Damore was asked.

"Yes, it is," he said. "I argued against it, but the state attorney thought it was the best way to go, and he's my boss. And he's such a good lawyer that, next to him, I feel like a journeyman."

For the next few days, the jury heard testimony from Lori, Teja, J.R., and Chumbley, who said they had been hired by Deidre to kill Lisa. Their testimony didn't vary from what it had been at Deidre's sentencing: Kosta was behind the plan to kill Lisa, and they knew that he intended to kill his

357

hired murderer to eliminate a witness against him.

The jury also saw the videotape of Ramsey being killed by Deidre Hunt. They were shocked, as was the rest of the courtroom. Foxman had it played again in slow motion, and it was as eerie and horrifying as it had been at Deidre's hearing.

Kosta, wearing a pale gray suit that looked expensive and well-tailored, sat stone-faced as he did throughout the rest of the trial, showing no emotion.

"See how nice he looks?" a woman in the gallery whispered. "Why, he looks like he could be a Presidential assistant. Instead, look what he's done!"

Clearly, the chips were falling the state's way, at least in the gallery.

Deidre, having already pleaded guilty to all charges, had changed her mind once again about testifying for the state. The gallery was anxiously awaiting her testimony and that of Lisa. The courtroom, always filled to capacity, was jammed when Deidre took the witness stand. She had not testified at her own sentence hearing, and this would be the first time she had spoken publicly about the murders. Deidre wore a baggy orange jumpsuit, and her hair was pulled back into a ponytail fastened with a rubber band.

State Attorney John Tanner had assumed the direct and cross-examination of the defense witnesses. Tanner, fifty-three, was just over six feet tall, with brown hair and an easy manner. He wore a conservative suit and rarely raised his voice, but he was an aggressive prosecutor. Tanner had been more in the news lately for battling pornography in the Seventh District than for his association with the Fotopoulos-Hunt case.

He looked relaxed when Deidre took the stand, greeted her politely, and got down to business. Tanner's questions were intended to show that Deidre had been an abused child, was subject to domination, and that she had been brutalized. The court was stunned when she testified that she had become pregnant by a former boyfriend, John Beauvier. Tanner asked if she had an abortion.

"He killed the baby himself," Deidre said.

"How?"

"He punched me and he kicked me in the stomach, and he said that he wanted to kill the baby. So he came after me and he did. It was in my mother's house in the bathroom."

There was a collective gasp of shock in the courtroom.

Deidre said she was afraid of Kosta almost from the beginning. She testified that she had tried to leave him when she lived in the house on Schulte Avenue. The door was always unlocked, she said, and Kosta entered.

"And Kosta came into the room . . . and he said, 'Where are you—what are you doing?'

"And I said, 'I'm leaving.'

"And he said, 'No you're not. Unpack.'

"And I tried my best to explain the situation to him, how I felt that it wasn't going to work. So I . . . he pulled out a gun and he pointed it at me, the gun that he always carried on him. And I said, 'You know, you're not going to shoot me with that. This is ridiculous. You know, this is crazy.'

"And he came over to me, and he put the gun up to my ear, and he pulled the trigger, or I thought he did, and I was scared. He backed up and said, 'Unpack.'

"And I was unpacking. I came across my ex-boyfriend's pictures. John. And he grabbed them

359

from me and he said, 'Rip these up.' And I said 'No. Why would . . . no.'

"And he backhanded me and stuck a gun to my cheek and said, 'Do it.'

"So I did it. And I was ripping them up. I had to rip them up and do the best I could. He wanted me to burn them. So, I—I tried. I tried. And while I was doing this he was in the closet—"

Corrente interrupted. "Excuse me for a moment," and asked if they could approach the bench. Judge Foxman allowed it. Tanner, Corrente and Judge Foxman talked quietly so the jury couldn't hear them.

"Your Honor, I would object to this testimony going into evidence of other crimes," Corrente said. "And that being that Mr. Fotopoulos pointed a gun at Deidre Hunt as she has testified." He said that the state was going to portray another incident that he considered "especially prejudicial" and "I would not want it to come out of this witness."

Tanner used Corrente's premise of Deidre being the driving force in the murder schemes against him. "Your Honor, the testimony will reveal a significant beginning of a pattern of intimidation and terror inflicted upon the witness to terrorize her and break down her will ultimately and obtain complete control of her, ultimately resulting in her carrying out the various crimes to which she has pled guilty."

Tanner continued, "Even though it does mention other criminal conduct of the defendant, it is not offered for that purpose. It is offered for the purpose to show a clear pattern of physical assault, abuse, intimidation, and coercion and . . . and the very direct and primary cause of Deidre Hunt's criminal activity."

Corrente said he didn't think the state could

360

prove the evidence it was about to present even existed unless Deidre exposed her breast to the jury.

Judge Foxman told Corrente, "To the point that you made in your opening statement that you contend that she's the principal cause behind these crimes, I feel testimony regarding their relationship and her state of mind would be relevant. So I think the relationship is one of the central issues in this case, and I will allow the question."

Tanner resumed his questioning, reminding Deidre that they had left off with Kosta being in her closet after she had tried to burn the pictures of her former boyfriend.

"What happened next?" he asked.

"I was on the floor and I was looking at the door," Deidre said. "So I started to crawl to the door because I was going to leave. And he grabbed me by the back of the hair and he pulled me back towards the bed, and I saw a coat hanger in his hand.

"It was a wire coat hanger. And he put me on the waterbed and he . . . while he was unraveling this coat hanger, he took off my shirt, my pink shirt, and he bound my hands above my head with this coat hanger. And he took my hands and he put them behind my head underneath my neck so he could cover my mouth with his hand.

"He was sitting on me . . . And he placed his hand over my mouth, and he—he said that this would never happen again if I just did what I was supposed to do. I wasn't understanding what was going on. And he grabbed one of my cigarettes and he put it in his mouth, and he lit it with my lighter, my pink lighter, and he burned me. He burned me on my right breast. And he just kept saying that this would never have to happen again if you just do what I tell you. 'You go to work and you come back' and you're supposed to do this and this, and that's it.

"And I was trying to scream, but nothing came out. And he . . . I tried to get up, and he lifted the cigarette up, and he told me to stop moving, and I did. And he did this again. And I could smell it."

"Smell what?" Tanner asked.

"Flesh. . . . He left. He just left. He told me all kinds of things before he left, though. He told me that, 'Don't tell anybody. I'll kill you. Don't do anything.'

"At one point he said, 'I ought to make you watch this videotape of me torturing somebody. And he was always threatening my life, you know, 'You don't leave.'

"And . . . I was told that someone was following me, and I was looking for someone to be following me. And I—there was nobody following me. So, I was just getting paranoid, but I didn't know what was going on.

"Then Kosta Fotopoulos came up to me and said, 'I didn't know you were bisexual.'

"And I said, 'What are you talking about?' "

"He went back into my past. So the next thing he did was he handed me all my mother's addresses and all my family's addresses. And he had my mother's address, my aunt's address. I had two aunts living up there in New Hampshire. My brother's work, my grandmother's work, and mother's work.

"And he told me that if I . . . if I left, something was going to happen to my mother."

Deidre said she believed Kosta was a trained terrorist and an assassin for the CIA. She testified that he talked about his training and killings a lot.

"The things that he told me were mean and vicious, and the training was cold," she said. "So that's how I got the impression of a terrorist."

"How did that make you feel about being able to stop him or get away from him?" Tanner asked.

"You couldn't stop the CIA."

Deidre described a time when Kosta took her into the woods to demonstrate the firepower of an AK-47.

"He shot up a tree with it . . . with this Russian rifle, AK-47, and mutilated the whole thing," she said. "There was no tree left. And he just did all kinds of things. When he did that . . . he came to me and he said, 'Here. Just look and see if I killed anybody without anybody trying.' "

Deidre said that Kosta had a throwing knife that he tossed at her. "He used to throw it at me all of the time, you know," she said. "I mean, no matter what I was doing, you know, he would just throw it at me."

"Did he hit you?" Tanner asked.

"No. He just wanted to see how close he could get without hitting me. He threw it into the floor at my feet."

Deidre said Kosta had a walking stick with a concealed knife at one end and a red button on the other. If the button was twisted just right and pushed, the knife would fly through the air. "He made me stand across the room and he shot it at me, and it hit a board that was right next to me," she said.

"Did you feel like he was trying to kill you with it or shoot it near you?" Tanner asked.

"Just for threatening purpose I believe now," Deidre said. "But I didn't know at the time what was going on. I didn't know . . . what he was going to do.

Tanner showed a photograph of a woman's partially exposed breast with "what appears to be a discolored dot. Is that where the cigarette burned you?"

"That was the burn."

Tanner asked if Kosta made bizarre threats or comments to her.

"He said that he ought to make me shoot some-one and videotape it," Deidre said. "He ought to make me watch this torture tape that he had. Things of that nature. He was bizarre."

". . . [A]nything outlandish with regard to what he would do to your body if he killed you?"

"I ought to kill you and keep your body and stuff it."

Tanner asked Deidre what she thought of Kevin Ramsey.

"He was a kid like the rest of them, and he didn't have a place to stay and not really much money," Deidre said. "So, I gave him money when he needed it. And he used to drink a lot. And I felt sorry for him like I did, you know, everybody else."

Deidre told an entirely different story about Ramsey's murder than she had before, when Tanner questioned her about it. She said Kosta had told her that Kevin and the two of them might go shooting.

"I didn't know what was going to happen," Deidre testified. "We arrived at . . . near the Strickland Rifle Range. Kosta brought me to the back of the car, and he opened up the trunk and he shut off the light, but I first saw the AK-47, which is the gun that you showed me there. . . . And he shut off the light. And he grabbed this gun, and he pointed it at me and said that I was going to . . . I was going to have to shoot Kevin or I was going to die.

"And I was going to have to shoot him twice in

the chest, twice in the back of the head, and Kevin wasn't coming back; and I was the only one with the choice to live. He told me . . . he did . . . also told me that he was going to videotape this and that I was going to use this . . . this gun, this .22. . . . He said there was four rounds . . . and he told me that if the last bullet didn't get shot he was going to shoot me."

"How did you feel about yourself as you thought about that choice?" Tanner asked.

"I was going to die," Deidre said. "I would have died if I didn't do this."

"What happened next?"

"Kosta told me that I was going to walk ahead of them, and he was going to have this gun, and he had this other gun, and there was not going to be anything I could do," Deidre testified. "He made sure I knew this. And he picked up . . . it was a video camera, a rope, the AK-47 Russian rifle, and he had his gun already. And he had a flashlight . . ."

"When you say he had his gun already, what . . . what other—"

"The gun he always carried," Deidre said. She told the court that Kosta had the AK-47 slung over his shoulder with the muzzle pointing down.

"What would have stopped you from merely leveling the gun and killing him or perhaps disarming him?" Tanner asked. "I'm talking about Kosta."

"There was no possible way," Deidre said. "He . . . he didn't feel pain anyway. So, even if there was anything that I would have thought of like that he wouldn't do . . . one shot and I would have been dead because that gun would have mutilated me."

"The AK-47?"

"Yes."

Deidre said that Ramsey had been looking around to see if there was anyone nearby and that he thought it was all a joke. This was consistent with what she had told Kathy Kelly, the reporter on the *News-Journal*. That was the only similarity.

"What was going through your mind at this time?" Tanner asked. "What were you going to do?"

"I just wanted to get it over with," Deidre said. "I was . . . I wanted it . . . I wanted it over with. I didn't want to be there. I didn't want to be there. I didn't . . . I was mad at myself because I was . . . I couldn't do anything."

Tanner asked, "Well, you had several choices, didn't you?"

"No, I did not."

"You couldn't run?"

"No, I could not," Deidre said. "The brush was really thick, and there's no way you could have run through this. And even if I tried he would have shot me."

"Well, certainly while he was busy tying up Kevin Ramsey you could have shot Kosta or at least threatened to shoot him and disarmed him, might you not?"

"No. Because he would . . . he was . . . the guns were easy access to him. And this is an automatic weapon, and if you touched the trigger it would have sprayed like four or five bullets even at one press."

"Do you remember those specific acts of your own recollection without reference to the film?"

"No. I remember picking the gun up and that was it. And that I remember walking over there . . . and reaching out my hand to stop him [Ramsey] from moving or something. I don't know."

"And what did you do with his head now that you've seen the film and you can now remember?"

"I grabbed his hair . . . and I shot him . . . in his temple. . . . Kosta put down the video camera and he went over to Kevin and he touched him. And Kevin moved because he was alive. And Kosta got mad. He was mad. I never saw him like this before. He . . . he said that . . . that I . . . that I screwed it up."

"Is that the word he used, or did he use the other word?"

"No. He said that I fucked it up," Deidre testified. " 'I knew you would fuck it up.' And he was really mad. So he said, 'Come here.' And I didn't . . . I didn't want to go over there. I didn't want to go near Kevin. And I just said, 'Please, let's go.' And he said, 'No,' because he [Ramsey] was still alive. And Kevin was trying to get up, and he was trying to talk. And he told me to catch the shell because he was going to shoot him.

"He aimed and he aimed. It was taking so long. And he aimed really carefully and he shot him. He shot him in the left temple, the same area."

Tanner asked Deidre what happened when they left.

"I was hysterical, and I was calling him all kinds of names, and I was flipping out because I didn't know why he would do this," Deidre said. "And I didn't know what was going on. So, I was just angry, and I was flipping out. And he let me carry on for a while, but then he told me to shut up, and I did."

Deidre testified that Kosta stopped at a gas station, dialed a number on a pay phone, gave the phone to her, and told her to ask for him. She said a voice she didn't recognize said, "He's indisposed."

Kosta hung up, she said, and told her, "I have an alibi in case you ever think of going to the police."

Deidre said that Kosta wanted to take her home,

367

but she didn't want to go.

"I couldn't be alone," Deidre said. "I wanted to look for Lori. And I just wanted to look for her so I could tell her because I trusted her. And he asked me where I wanted to go because . . . so I said, we should go down to Top Shots.

"And he had an erection. And he said . . . 'I'd fuck you now, but I don't have the time.'

"He told me that I would have to kill his wife. And I just listened to him at first, and he told me of a plan that he devised about his wife picking me up and that I was going to go wherever he told me to go and then shoot her in the car and then go to another place. And I was just listening to this, and he was not going into his plan. And it just dawned on me that this person could not make me hurt another person . . . without him present.

"He told me that if I didn't do it [kill Lisa], he would turn the video over to the police," Deidre said.

Deidre told the court that she acted under extreme duress to make plans to kill Lisa. Even after Chase shot Lisa in the head but didn't kill her, Deidre said Kosta wanted Lisa killed.

"He wanted her dead even in the hospital," Deidre said.

"Did you tell Teja?" Tanner asked.

"Yes. Kosta had a plan about a bomb in the hospital, and he didn't care how it got up there," Deidre said. "He was changing plans. He was going to send it up in flowers, under the beds, sneak up there, and he didn't care, you know. He didn't care. He wouldn't listen. He was mad, and Teja could make a bomb, he said."

Deidre said that Teja could make a bomb from Tide and gasoline, but he didn't. They were all arrested, she said, before Teja could.

368

"Did Kosta . . . say what was going to happen to the people that knew [about plans to kill Lisa]?" Tanner asked.

"Oh, oh, everybody is going to die," Deidre said. "He had a list of everyone that was going to die. It was a verbal list that he spoke to me about in person."

"Who was going to be killed now?" Tanner asked.

"Everyone that ever even had known any suspicions that he had. It was Teja, Lori, J.R., Michael Cox [Matt Chumbley], Tony Calderone, everyone."

"Who was going to do the killing?"

"He was going to."

"Were you on that list?"

"I believe I was," Deidre said, adding that Kosta didn't mention her name.

". . . I [thought] I was definitely going to die," Deidre said.

"What did you do?"

"There was no place that I could go, so I just stayed scared, and I was thinking of leaving," Deidre said. "As soon as he mentioned Lori and Teja, I knew I was on the list and I was gone to — I was thinking of a way to get away and just thinking. . . . I never attempted anything.

"He said that he flew somebody down from Chicago that was going to assist him in killing everyone.

"I wanted the police to take me into custody," Deidre said. "Because I believed that if the public knew where I was that he isn't going to try to kill me then."

On cross-examination Corrente struck at the domination theory Tanner had tried to construct. The wiry, energetic lawyer with thinning dark hair noted that Deidre had accompanied Kosta on at least a few outings. He asked if she was afraid of him then, or did she enjoy herself.

Deidre admitted that she enjoyed going to fancy restaurants with Kosta. She had gone with him to the Bubble Room Restaurant, to a theme park called Wet and Wild, and accompanied him on jet ski excursions, riding behind Kosta on the same powered jet ski.

Corrente noted that Deidre had often gone shooting with Kosta and went to a gun show in Orlando, where she asked Kosta to buy her a knife and a hat. She admitted that when she stayed at the Casa Del Mar she paid no rent, had a jacuzzi, and an unlimited bar tab.

Corrente asked her if she had gone to parties with Peter Kouracos and with people who were running for office such as "county commissioners, a little bit of the elite society of Daytona Beach."

Deidre said she had gone.

"You enjoyed yourself, didn't you?"

"Yes."

"So you were having a taste of the good life, and you were having a good time with Kosta and with the friends that you were associating with," Corrente said.

"I was there for a reason. I was at the parties for a reason."

"To influence votes?"

"So Kosta could keep his eye on me. He always wanted to know where I was."

Deidre admitted that she knew the gun she gave Bryan Chase to shoot Lisa would jam after the first bullet was fired. She testified that Kosta and Lori knew it, too.

Corrente noted discrepancies in Deidre's memory, her testimony, and depositions. The lawyer wondered why Deidre suddenly remembered things, such as Kosta pushing her face into Ramsey's face after he had been killed, and Kosta burning her with a cigarette. Corrente said she had never mentioned these things in a deposition that took nine hours to complete and that she had not mentioned them during her two-hour videotaped interview just before she was arrested.

Kosta's lawyer said Deidre told him that Kosta had burned her left breast.

"Oh, I was mistaken," Deidre said.

"Don't you remember that frightening moment when your hands were handcuffed, and you had the coat hanger around your wrists, and he put the cigarette into you? Don't you remember that?"

"Yes, I do."

"But you are not sure exactly which breast it happened on, is that what you are saying?"

"No, I think that I meant to say right."

Corrente cross-examined Deidre at length and succeeded in putting some holes in the state's domination theory. He painted Deidre as a vicious social climber who lusted after money and would kill to get it. But the evidence was stacking up against Kosta, who sat dispassionately with no change of expression.

39

Damore and Gallagher had prophesied that too much evidence and testimony would bore the jury. Even though they had withheld more than half of the evidence and witnesses, the trial became tedious as expert witnesses tried to convince the jurors that Kosta was behind Ramsey's murder and that he was at the scene.

Bob Ratliff, of the U.S. Secret Service Laboratory, was called to verify that the palm print found on the videotape cassette of Ramsey's murder was Kosta's. He compared it with a print of Kosta's palm and said, "They belong to one and the same person, that is, Mr. Fotopoulos. In my opinion it's a positive identification."

Corrente had tried to have the video cassette of the murder, and all of the evidence gathered from the house on Halifax Avenue, including the weapons used to murder Ramsey barred from being introduced. Corrente argued that Kosta had not signed the consent order and the evidence wasn't valid. Damore countered with an argument, which was upheld by Foxman, that Dino had already kicked Kosta out of the house before the evidence was recovered.

As the day wore on, two tables were piled high with evidence, including some of the military gear and weaponry that had been taken into custody. To bring it to the courtroom and to lock it up when court recessed became a major problem in logistics. Two baggage carts, like those used at airports, had to be piled high with evidence to move it back and forth, two men to each cart.

Tanner continued to present expert testimony to support testimony that Kosta was guilty of murdering Ramsey. Dr. Anthony Holbrook, from the University of Florida, was called to the stand to testify. Holbrook testified to the voice exemplars that Gallagher had given to him months ago, and explained how he had used a spectrograph to make voice prints.

Holbrook said there were few words to work with, but there were enough to produce an almost perfect match. He displayed the spectrographic voice charts to the jury. ". . . [T]he weight of this evidence causes me to conclude that the voice of Mr. Fotopoulos and that the voice of the Unknown [the voice on the videotape] are one and the same."

There was a brief appearance by Sheila Lorch regarding the ruckus in the holding cell with Kosta in early December. Lorch told how Kosta wanted a bobby pin to pick the lock on his handcuffs and on the holding cell door and that he had told Lorch to relay his death threat to Deidre.

Earlier in the trial, Allen Johnson, who was in the Branch Jail on his eighth count of burglary, told the jury that Kosta had talked about Ramsey's murder with him. According to Johnson, Kosta told him that "he had souped up his old lady to go ahead and shoot some guy while he videotaped it. He held the video camera and the flashlight and taped it."

Johnson had been implicated in what might have been an escape plan from the Branch Jail. Guards found Kosta with a detailed diagram of the facility in his pocket, which they thought was a guideline to escape. Kosta said Johnson was involved.

Under cross-examination by Corrente, Johnson said being caught in a planned escape was the only reason he testified.

"They came to me, they locked me up and investigated me, and I started talking," Johnson said. "I covered my butt is what I did."

Dino was called as a witness to talk about his suspicions and the evidence that he had heard concerning Kosta wanting to kill the Paspalakis family. Adamy testified that he, Wheeler, Gallagher, Crowell, Lilly, and Damore had conducted a search to find evidence, all with consent forms or search warrants.

Lisa caused a sympathetic stir when she marched into the courtroom, wearing a peach-colored dress. She was nervous, and she sometimes giggled at inappropriate times.

She testified to remembering the morning she was shot and what transpired. She recounted it to the jury and recalled that Kosta had said, "I'm going to kill him, I'm going to kill him." Only this time, she said that Kosta had said it *before* he shot the intruder.

Lisa asked Kosta, "Is that Teja?" and that Kosta had answered, "No, that's his friend from Ohio."

The state maintained that this conversation proved that Kosta had known that Teja's so-called attempted robbery was actually an attempted murder and that he had known that Chase was on a mission to kill Lisa.

Lisa also verified that the state had permission to remove evidence from the house and grounds on Halifax Avenue that investigators had found near the barbecue pit area. That particular bag contained the gun used to kill Ramsey, a bayonet, an AK-47, and a silencer and a magazine for assault guns.

This was important evidence that Corrente had objected to having entered as evidence, claiming that it had been taken illegally.

Damore then asked Lisa, "Had there been any talk of divorce between you and Kosta before October 29 during the whole time that you had been married?"

"I always had trouble with Kosta, and I guess I wasn't very happy with him," Lisa answered.

"Had you ever discussed with him or had there been discussions of what you would or would not do if you caught him cheating?"

"Yes."

"What was that?"

"I told him point-blank that if he ever cheated on me, I would leave him."

"Did you also tell him you would leave him flat? In other words without any assets or money?"

"Yes."

"Did you have occasion to confront Deidre Hunt about your suspicion that he was cheating with her, and, if so, how did that come about?"

Lisa discussed her search for Kosta, seeing his car at Deidre's apartment, and the high-speed chase in the rain that almost ended in her having a wreck. Lisa said she accused Kosta of having an affair with Deidre, and he said he would prove that she was wrong.

Lisa said Kosta called Deidre, then gave the phone to her. Kosta listened in, she said, as Deidre denied having an affair. Lisa said she was almost certain that Kosta had had an affair. Later, Lisa had gone to the Halloween party at Razzles, unaware that her life was in danger.

Tanner asked, "Did you know you were being stalked by Teja James?"

"No, I didn't."

"That he was supposed to stab you to death that night?"

"No, I didn't know that."

Lisa recounted how Teja had attempted to "rob" her the next day after Kosta had earlier insisted that he would be gone all day. Furthermore, Lisa discovered, Kosta had taken the pistol that was kept at Joyland for protection.

Lisa told about the drive to Edgewater with her husband and how he had toyed with a pistol, then told her, "I wouldn't shoot you here, it would dirty my car." Lisa said she begged Kosta that, if he was trying to kill her, "please don't do it."

Tanner asked Lisa what her feelings were toward Kosta.

"I feel sorry for him."

"Do you harbor any hatred?"

"No."

It was a day of high drama in the courtroom after the dull presentation of evidence and expert witnesses. The same day Tony Calderone, looking distinctly uncomfortable, told how he had found Kosta in his house the day that Lisa was shot. He described his fear of being killed, how Kosta had patted him down looking for a wire, and how he had told Kosta, "You did it, didn't you, you son of a bitch?" And that Kosta had given him a smile "like a cat eating a canary" and said, "I told you Greek men don't divorce their wives."

40

As the trial wore on, the state built an increasing body of evidence that depicted Kosta as a cold-blooded killer who had planned the deaths of Chase and Ramsey, as well as his wife. If the trial had been dull at times while the state presented evidence, that changed dramatically when Kosta decided to testify.

Kosta showed no remorse, denying that he had anything to do with anyone's death, and engaged in a duel of words with State Attorney John Tanner. One-minute TV segments of the two days of testimony showed Kosta as being cool and intelligent. But an entirely different picture emerged for those who sat through it in the courtroom. The accused murderer came across as cold, calculating, and arrogant.

Given the damage he did to himself, Damore asked if he was surprised that Kosta took the stand.

"We expected him to," Damore said. "Given his personality, we would have been very surprised if he had not."

During direct examination Corrente asked Kosta how he met Deidre.

"It's kind of embarrassing," Kosta said. "Basically, Miss Deidre Hunt was—I should use the word *hired* by Mr. Tony Calderone and at that point, myself, I guess—let's say exchanged sexual favors for room and board and clothes and all living expenses basically."

"Did you have any problems with Deidre?"

377

"No, not at all. We were not that—well, I felt that we were not that close to really have any problems with her."

"You didn't want her living with any of her friends from down on the Boardwalk, did you?"

"No, not at all. We both felt, me and Tony, that since we were paying for the house for her, it was just for her and not for everybody else who felt like staying with her. And she agreed that she would stay there alone and nobody else would stay there."

"Did there come a point when you gave Deidre Hunt a gun?" Corrente asked.

"Yes, that was after she moved to the second house, the one on Schulte Avenue. That was basically the third residence she stayed in. The first one was the motel and the second was the house we spoke about and the third one was the one on Schulte Avenue. . . . At the time, she did not have too many people over the first few days, and she was complaining she was alone at the house and she was afraid, so I supplied her with a stainless steel .380."

Corrente asked if it was true that Deidre was interested in guns.

"That was one of the things that really intrigued me about Deidre," Kosta said, "the fact that she was a female—and I am not being prejudiced about it—she really liked weapons and had a real interest in it and me, I have a hobby of weapons. I was very happy that she liked that, and all the time I will bring her different weapons and she asked to know anything about it and I will bring them all. And basically every gun that you see in here today, she can operate quite good."

"Did you talk to Dee about problems regarding Lisa?"

"Well, you are getting into embarrassing areas again," Kosta said, "and many state secrets have been compromised in a situation like this. When a man is in bed with a woman, he has a tendency to talk, and I hit myself on the head now for falling in the same — I don't want to use the word *trap,* but I did not think it was at the time. It was a discussion basically of everything."

Kosta said he lied to Deidre about what he owned because he didn't think it was any of her business. He said he told her that he and his wife owned everything together.

Kosta said that Deidre once asked him if he had life insurance. He also admitted that he took her to Lisa's house once. "It was a Saturday morning and I had arranged to take off from work and, of course, since I owned Top Shots, I arranged for Deidre to take off at the same time," Kosta said. "We were supposed to go shooting in the morning, so the weapons were still in my house. We drove to my house and I told her to wait in the car, I bring the weapons. She didn't want to wait in the car. She wanted to come in and see the house.

"We went in the house. I did not really take her upstairs because the bedroom was a big mess. I am not a very neat person and my wife works all day and my brother-in-law, you can't go in his room because of the stuff that is everywhere, but, you know, she took a full tour of the house, which I did show her. After the tour of the house, we moved into the area next to the swimming pool on the south side of the house where the barbecue pit is, where I had the particular weapons hidden at the time. We removed the weapons and we went to my car and left."

Corrente asked, "Why did you have weapons buried?"

"For two reasons," Kosta said. "For one, the weapons are very expensive and they are very — I am going to use the word *dangerous.* I did not want them in the house. You never know what happens. And the third reason, they were also illegal and that's why

I did not want them in the house."

Kosta said that all of the guns he had at the house were legal except for the ones he had hidden in the barbecue pit. He admitted that Lisa found out about his affair and told him to fire Deidre.

"I told her [Lisa] it was a lie and whoever was telling her just wanted us to get mad, and she said, 'Just fire her anyway, I want my mind at ease, so I said, 'No problem,' and I went down to my store and I told Deidre, 'You have to go, my wife knows what is going on,' and she said, 'That bitch'—and excuse me, you know, she said, 'What is going to happen to me now?'

"And I said, 'Well nothing, just find another job, and, you know, maybe we will keep seeing each other,' and she said, 'Okay,' and that was basically it."

Kosta said he didn't own a video camera but that his partner Angelo did. He said Deidre wanted to borrow it.

"I don't think so," Kosta said he told her. "Angelo won't like that. She said, 'Come on, I have something I want to surprise you with. At the time I knew that Deidre Hunt was having homosexual affairs with other women, and I thought that would be interesting to—it's not a laughing matter, but it's sort of ridiculous, you know, I thought she would do something like that to surprise me with.

"I gave her the camera the same day that she kept nagging at me," he said. "To operate a camera like this is the easiest thing in the world, and you just press the one button and that's it, and you press the same button again and it turns off. I gave her the camera and I told her I have to have it back before Angelo got back or we are in trouble."

Kosta said she returned the camera to him on a Sunday night. He then said he visited Deidre after she had been fired and that his wife caught him. He recalled he started to think like a guilty husband, whose motives for being there wouldn't be understood.

"On my way out, I saw my wife's car about a block and a half away," he said. "So I think to myself, 'Oh, oh, I am caught now,' and I tried to get away by turning a couple of turns and I think my wife followed me but eventually I got away.

"After I left . . . after I lost my wife, I should say, hoping that she would think it was somebody else's car, I called Deidre Hunt and said, 'If my wife calls you, you got to tell her we don't have an affair,' and she said, 'Oh, no problem, I would never say anything anyway.'

"After we went to the store, my wife confronted me about my car coming out of Deidre's apartment. . . . I told her, 'Yes, I went by Deidre's place just to give her last check and to tell her not to bother us anymore and if she sees us on the street, don't even talk to us because my wife gets upset about things like that. And if you want to talk to her,' I say to my wife, 'here is the phone, call her up.'

"Lisa called Deidre up and, you know, Deidre played the role of an innocent person. . . ."

Kosta said that he and Lisa had never had problems in their marriage. "We always got along. As a matter of fact, in four and a half years that we were married, the only argument that I ever remember having with her now was about Deidre."

Lisa had said that Kosta was a terrible businessman who looked for get-rich-quick schemes. Kosta argued against that. He said he was surprised at how much money Top Shots earned. He said there was no way to verify it because it was a cash business. All of the money was kept in a cabinet, and he had the key.

"There is no government control like a cash register, where you have to keep receipts for five or six years and report them," he said. "That allowed us a lot of freedom with the income that we were making, so what we were doing is we were depositing approximately half of the money and keeping the other half in the cash reserves."

Corrente asked if that explained some of the cash he had around his car.

"Yes, it does," Kosta said, "and there is also more money involved which we probably go into later."

Kosta said that he had lunch with Deidre on Halloween at Arthur Treacher's, and that she insisted on taking Lori and Teja, "which was not to my liking—again, without prejudice, but they are bums, you know. I just took them along and Mr. Prakash was sitting at our table and we were eating practically all of the time and after we finished eating, me and him left his place of business and we walk outside and we walk all around the perimeter of the area discussing various techniques and ways and amounts that would be necessary for us to go through in order to place an Arthur Treacher's on the Boardwalk."

He said he took back the gun he had given to Deidre because he received reports from her friends that she was reckless with it. ". . . [they said] she was being irresponsible with the weapon, and with the combination that she was drinking and doing some drugs, particularly LSD and some coke, which I totally disapprove and I tried to separate her from, I took it away from her to avoid any problems."

He saw Deidre almost every day after she was fired to give her money because she didn't have a new job. "I made it a point to call her at least once a day and maybe sometimes twice," he testified.

He explained that he met Teja in the men's restroom at Razzles because Deidre needed money to rent costumes. He told her that it would be too embarrassing to give her money with people watching. Teja, he said, met him in the restroom to get the money.

"I think it was around ten-thirty or somewhere around there, and he was motioning me so I followed him into the bathroom and I gave him forty dollars and he left. About twenty minutes later, I see him motion me again, and I am thinking to myself, well, he couldn't have got through the money so quick, and so I'm going to the bathroom again to see what is the problem, and he said, 'Deidre wants to meet you at twelve o'clock in the back bathroom.' I said, 'I am not going to the women's bathroom' and he said, 'No, no, she will be in the men's bathroom.' I told him how difficult and dangerous this was because I had too many relatives at this particular place and anyone could walk in and see me, and so he said that he will see what he can do. . . ."

Kosta said he drove a woman home and went to the bathroom when he returned to Razzles. He said that a man named Tim was standing in front of one of the stalls and that Deidre was hidden inside. He met her inside the stall.

"We are getting embarrassing now," Kosta said. "She wanted to make love. She was drunk. I told her that was a ridiculous idea and no way that I would do something like that in this place. We kissed a couple of times and I left."

Kosta said that he was "stunned" when Lisa picked Teja's picture out of the mug book and identified him as the man who had attempted to rob her at Joyland.

"Actually, I still . . . believe she was—I am going to use the word *brainwashed* and clouded about this event," Kosta said. "If she feels any aggravation or hard feelings against me, she was basically misled. You must also understand she is hurt about the affair. Not that I was really having an affair. It is a particular factor, a factor that the whole world and literally the whole world found out about.

"I know many instances when one member of the family has an affair with somebody else—be the male or the female of the couple—and you have an argument for a week and everybody forgets about it. In the society that we live today, it's not that unusual an event."

"Did you kill Bryan Chase?" Corrente asked.

"Yes, I did. I woke up by a very loud noise, which I immediately distinguished to be a gunshot from the proximity of the noise and also from the smell of the cordite, and, as you know, I am very familiar with weapons and I can distinguish the smell very well.

"When I opened my eyes, I looked to the left and there was a figure that I described to the detective of a silhouette, because that's what it looked like on the light coming in from the window. I immediately reached down to my right side. I grabbed the weapon which I had placed at that particular point. I always have them there, and I fire approximately five shots toward the target, which after the first shot . . . was moving, so I was kind of firing wildly."

"Which gun were you using?"

"A Sigsauer P-226. Well, the figure dropped to the ground and I immediately turned the light on to the right side of my bedstand. I got up and moved around the bed, and then I noticed the figure trying to get up, and he had a gun in his hand, so I fired another shot in the head.

"At that particular moment you must understand the pressure of the situation. Everything, you know, runs through your mind. You are in a state of basically panic, and the only thing I was thinking is the security of my wife and to eliminate any possible threat of any future action of whoever was in the room."

"Have you been trained as a terrorist?" Corrente asked.

"Of course not."

"Did you have any military training?"

"No, although it is a Greek tradition and a law

384

actually that it's—Greek males will eventually serve a couple of years of his life in the Greek Army. . . . I left too young for that."

Kosta said he didn't know how the rumors got started about his commando activities.

"Somebody told them I was a trained terrorist by the Israelis," he said. "I would like to caution the state that if Israel get ahold of that, you will have a lawsuit that you won't believe, because as I understand trained terrorists . . . as a matter of fact, they have two of the biggest terrorist groups in the world."

"You have no training whatsoever?"

"No. Every knowledge I have of my weapons is from magazines and literature that I pick up at different places."

Kosta said that he shot Chase in the head because he might have missed as he was firing wildly or that Chase might have been wearing a bulletproof vest. He said Chase was getting up and, "That's when I shot him in the head."

Previous expert testimony showed that the gun Chase had was jammed and that Kosta knew it. The shot in the head, the state argued, was just another aspect of Kosta's intention to murder the youth so he couldn't testify against him.

Kosta admitted that Deidre gave him a videotape, but he didn't know what was on it. "She said, 'This is a surprise that I have for you,' and I said, 'What is it?' and I take the tape out of the holder and I looked at it, and she said, 'Just look at it,' and I said, 'Okay, I will,' and she put it back in the holder and put it in my pocket, and when I went to the house, I just put it with the rest of my pictures that I had in the garage."

On cross-examination, Tanner quickly established that Kosta had been convicted for six previous felonies. Kosta said he wanted it known that they were all nonviolent. Tanner noted that there were six felony convictions in U.S. District Court for counterfeiting and witness tampering.

Corrente objected to the questions, but Tanner argued that Kosta had mentioned it and that he had also opened the door for questioning about illegal weapons by mentioning that he had them. That would include automatic, semiautomatic weapons, and grenades.

Kosta said that he had pleaded guilty to concealing and passing counterfeit United States currency, and Tanner reminded him, "You pled guilty to . . . harboring or concealing individuals from lawful federal arrest warrants that had been issued on federal felony charges so as to prevent their discovery and arrest and knowing that said lawful warrants had been issued for their arrest."

"I did hide my friends, yes . . . I didn't actually hide them. I just didn't tell anybody where they were."

Tanner talked about the big debts that Kosta had and pointed out that his income alone was just three hundred dollars a week. Even so, Tanner said, Kosta had offered seven hundred thousand dollars for a block of property near the beach in October, 1989.

"The property was for sale," Kosta said. "I was examining the possibility. I discussed it with my wife. We disagree on the income of the property, and we canceled the idea. I never went back and the incident was over. My wife is available, you can ask her."

"Did your wife say if you were cheating she would divorce you?"

"Any wife would say that."

"And did your wife say that to you?"

"Yes. I didn't take it seriously," Kosta said. "She was convinced there was nothing going on."

Kosta said he understood that he would have no money if Lisa left him. He said that wasn't an insurmountable obstacle. "That would be very tough for me, yes. I think I could make three hundred dollars shining shoes outside of this courtroom."

"You could make an honest living if you wanted to, couldn't you?"

"I can make an honest living anytime."

"It's not as much fun, is it?"

"Fun has nothing to do with it. . . . From time to time, I do something unthoughtful like the counterfeit deal, but I am paying hard for it. I am serving thirty-three months in federal prison. That taught me a good lesson, didn't it?"

"In fact," Tanner said, "you have done some other unthoughtful things. You were keeping photographs of naked women, and I would ask you, do you know these women?"

"I haven't seen the photographs. It's quite possible that I know them."

Tanner showed Kosta the photographs.

"In fact, you were having affairs with other women, were you not?" he asked.

"If you look at the photographs, and my wife will recognize this person that is displayed in this particular one right here, that was my last girlfriend which I lived with before I met my wife and which I left for my wife."

Tanner reminded him that there were photographs of other naked women.

"Is it not true that there are at least four different women pictured in those photographs?" he asked. "Take your time and look through them."

"There is the same woman with a different haircut," Kosta said, "and on this here is a girl that I knew up in Chicago over eight years ago."

"What about the blond lady?"

"Oh, the blond lady? I met her over twelve years ago when I was in Greece. This is actually one of the islands. I believe she was a lady from Dane—what do you say it?—Danish, and she was a dentist."

"How did these photographs get into the blue bag in which the murder tape was found?" Tanner asked.

"Well, whenever I have a girl from the past I always take some pictures of her so I can remember her in the future. I placed it there. It seemed to be a convenient place to be."

Kosta told Tanner that it cost him one hundred-fifty dollars a week to keep Deidre.

Tanner said, "You have heard a great many witnesses testify and present evidence against you, Mr. Fotopoulos, that if those witnesses testified truthfully it would convince most anyone that you tried to kill your wife, wouldn't it?"

"If they were reliable witnesses and what they say was true, they are very bad accusations, yes."

Tanner was reminded that he gave a statement to Detective Smith on November 8, 1989, after he had been advised of his rights. Tanner said Kosta's testimony conflicted with things he said in the statement.

"Yes," Kosta said, "but the whole night and the incident there was very confusing, misleading and that was the reason, sir, I said that the statements would have a certain answer. To give you an example, when they arrested me at three o'clock in the morning, three policemen came up to me and said, 'Well, you are under arrest.' They did not charge me with anything. I said, 'Well, what is this all about?'

"They said they wanted to talk to me down at the police department. I was thinking it was related . . . to Mr. Chase. I figured it would be some kind of mandatory prerequirement that you have to go through with after a shooting is involved to determine the proper action to be taken. . . . At the time, I did not know that the intention of the officers was to arrest me for my wife's alleged solicitation."

Tanner reminded Kosta that he told Smith that he denied having an affair with Deidre.

"I told that I did not have an affair with Deidre

Hunt. That was not—none of their business."

"You did not tell them you thought Bryan Chase was a friend of Teja's, did you?"

"No."

"But you told your wife?"

"No, excuse me. No, I did tell them. . . . I believe I made a statement when I talked to a few of the police officers."

"But when you talked to Greg Smith, you didn't tell him that you thought this was Teja's friend from Ohio?"

"I am not sure."

"You simply shot him in the top or the back of the head and killed him."

"I pointed in that direction and I fired the gun, yes."

"You intended to shoot him through the brain?"

"I intended to make sure that he would not interfere with myself or my wife," Kosta said.

Tanner recalled testimony that Teja had gone with him to Sun Bank in Daytona Beach Shores. The attorney wanted to elicit additional information from Kosta regarding the trip. What did Kosta say to Teja, Tanner asked, while they had lunch at Arthur Treacher's?

" 'Why don't you help me with the money, because it is kind of heavy,' " Kosta said. "And we just went in the bank and came right back. The bank is about two blocks away from there."

"That was the time you told him how he was to stab your wife with a knife above the third rib and puncture her diaphragm; correct?"

"He has testified about seventeen different times that I supposedly told him that," Kosta said. "I never told him anything about my wife or killing her or anything like that. If you read his testimony, every time he testifies, he says a different thing."

Tanner said that after Lisa was shot, that Kosta

and Peter Kouracos, both armed with pistols, went looking for Teja on the Boardwalk. "You were also carrying a tape recorder?" Tanner asked. "And you wanted to force Teja James to say that he was responsible for all of this."

"I wanted to find out what was going on and when my wife is in danger and being shot, believe me, I will find out what is going on."

Tanner asked him that hadn't he decided to kill Ramsey because Ramsey knew too much? Kosta replied that he never decided to kill Ramsey, that he knew nothing about it.

Tanner asked Kosta about his hand grenades. Kosta said that the grenades were homemade.

"For blowing things or people up?" Tanner asked.

"If you really want to know, it's for fishing."

"For fishing?"

"That's why they have a fuse, which is waterproof," Kosta explained.

"What kinds of fish do you catch with hand grenades?"

"All kinds."

Tanner offered the hand grenades into evidence. Then he turned to the recordings of various Greek men saying the same words that Gallagher had made some months ago. Several witnesses, including Lisa, had picked Kosta's voice out of voice exemplars.

"It was very interesting how all of the people who identified my voice were official witnesses," Kosta said. "I thought it was kind of amusing. If we listen to the particular tape exemplar . . . and one voice sticks out, which we do not know, but every member that is asked to identify that particular voice knew exactly what they were looking for . . . and they assumed that's what you wanted to hear."

"Are you saying that someone suggested that your voice was number six?"

"I am saying that it is very obvious that you

390

wanted that particular voice identified."

"And how was that made obvious to the people who identified your voice?"

"By having the voice sound different than every other voice in there. To this point, I don't know if it is my voice."

"Have you listened to it?" Tanner asked.

Kosta replied, "I listened to the tape, yes."

"It sounded like your voice, didn't it?"

"They all sounded like my voice."

"They were all very close, weren't they?"

"No, they all had a deep tone of voice."

Kosta claimed that Dino picked his voice out because he and Lisa "were very hurt right now."

"The whole world found out that I was having an affair," Kosta said, "courtesy of the state, and they are very, very, very embarrassed and disturbed, and I believe they want to see me dead and they will say anything for you."

"Now you blame your affair on the State of Florida?"

"No, I am blaming . . . the state of Florida [for] the incomplete investigation before I was arrested and the amount of the publicity that this case unnecessarily attracted. But I don't want to get into politics right now."

"Are you saying that all of these people were just out to get you?" Tanner asked incredulously.

"There were not really many people. They are . . . and you guys are just doing your job and get your picture in the paper. I mean, on the TV, right?" Kosta said sarcastically. "It's very convenient. I really don't want to get into it. Your presence alone, it's obvious that the publicity was intended."

Tanner ignored the personal attack and returned to the videotape of Ramsey's murder. "Allen Johnson, your cellmate, testified that you had told him that you had made such a videotape and in his words, 'souped' your old lady into doing it, persuaded her to do it, and she didn't want to. Correct? That's what he said, wasn't it?"

"You are talking about a man in jail. Like he said, everybody had heard, yes."

"In fact, you threatened to kill Deidre Hunt to Sheila Lorch, who happened to have shared a holding area while you were waiting to go to court. You said, 'Do you know Deidre Hunt?' and when she said 'Yes,' you said, 'Tell her I will kill her ass,' didn't you?"

"I would choke her right now if she comes in front of me for what she has done to my wife and me after all of this mess," Kosta said.

"So you meant it, didn't you?"

"Definitely, and I hope you do it for me."

Kosta admitted that he was in Tony Calderone's house and that he had answered "yes" when Calderone said, "You did it, didn't you, you son of a bitch."

"I thought he meant shooting the guy in the bedroom," Kosta explained.

"You said, 'I told you, Greek men don't get divorced,'" Tanner said. "How does that relate to the man killed in the bedroom?"

"I don't think I ever told that to Tony Calderone."

Kosta became even more sarcastic when Tanner noted that several people had testified that he had used Deidre Hunt to hire people to kill Lisa.

". . . [F]rom what you guys are saying, I put an ad in the paper looking for somebody to kill my wife. I wish sometimes you would explain what you are accusing me of."

"You are not accused of being real smart?"

"No."

"You are accused of murder?"

"Yes, but what I am saying, I hired fifteen or twenty people, and that is ridiculous."

"It was ridiculous, wasn't it?"

"Yes, I would never have done something like that for various reasons. One, I loved my wife and, secondly, there is no reason for . . . basically, to do somebody's job."

Tanner reminded Kosta that he had called Ramsey his son. "When Tony Calderone told you that Ramsey was stealing from you, you said, 'I will kill the little bastard,' didn't you?"

"It was not Tony Calderone who told me. It was Officer Grayson."

"In fact, Mr. Calderone said to you, 'Man, you can't go around killing people. What are you going to do, kill the whole Boardwalk?' and you said, 'If I have to,' didn't you?"

"I did not."

"Well, perhaps when you were going to take your wife to Key West, you had in mind that you might take her out on a boat and kill her and throw her overboard?"

"That statement right there makes me understand that you are totally misinformed about the case and about what is going on."

"For instance, I misunderstood your hand grenades. I thought hand grenades were meant for blowing up people or objects, and they are meant for fishing, according to you."

"That may be what you use them for."

"What kind of fish do you catch with hand grenades?"

"Everything. You throw it in the water and whatever comes up."

"When was the last time you fished with hand grenades?"

"I would say at least two years ago."

"About the time that you gave up counterfeiting."

"Probably before that."

"Well, you said that you gave up counterfeiting

because you got tired of it?"

"No, it was not fun anymore, but actually the people got caught so we stopped."

"Sure, that took the fun out of it, didn't it?"

Tanner asked if getting caught took the fun out of killing Ramsey.

"I did not kill Mark Ramsey."

Tanner asked if getting caught took the fun out of killing Bryan Chase.

"I saved my wife's life that night," Kosta said.

"Well, you told Deidre Hunt that you laid there in cold blood waiting for your wife to be shot and then murdered Bryan Chase."

"Are you making up stuff now like you did in my financial conditions yesterday in front of the cameras and in front of the people to mislead the jury?" Kosta asked.

"Isn't it a fact that you told Deidre Hunt that you made meatloaf out of Bryan Chase?"

"No, I told her that I shoot him five or six times."

"You were proud of the fact that you filled him full of holes, weren't you?"

"I was proud that I saved my wife."

"You don't have much regard for the truth, do you?" Tanner asked.

"You seem to be the one that doesn't have that."

"You have no regard for honesty, do you?"

"How do you know? You never met me before."

"What about counterfeiting? Was that honest?"

"No, it is fun. So I made a mistake, I am paying for it."

Tanner asked him if he were being honest when he told Lisa he wouldn't shoot her because he didn't want to mess up his car.

"I was joking."

"You manipulated Deidre Hunt to kill Mark Kevin Ramsey," Tanner said.

"I did not and you know that."

"You manipulated Bryan Chase to try to kill your wife."

"I did not and you know that."

"And then you shot him in cold blood and murdered him, didn't you?"

"I shot him down, because he came in my house and shot my wife, and if you come to my house and shoot my wife, I will shoot you, too," Kosta said.

41

Final arguments in Kosta's trial began on Thursday, October 25. By this time, Damore was weary but was getting his second wind.

"I kept telling myself that I had to hang on a little bit longer," he said. "The guy who reaches down deep in the closing stretch, regardless of how tired he is, is the guy who wins the race."

The police officers of Daytona Beach and Wheeler and Gallagher of the state attorney's office knew it was the case of a lifetime. They wanted to be able to look back on it and say, "Hey, I did all right on that case."

Up to that point, Damore had never lost a murder trial, either as a defender or prosecutor. State Attorney John Tanner, who had placed himself in the role as assistant to Damore for the Fotopoulos case, sat back as Damore began his closing argument before the jury.

Damore didn't appear tired. His use of words and body language was economical, but it was sharp and clear. Damore told the jurors that he was sorry that they had been exposed to the horror of seeing Ramsey killed on videotape. He told them it was necessary for them to see the crime committed and to hear the unmistakable calling card that Kosta had left on the video.

"There is one piece of evidence in this case that

Kosta Fotopoulos has been unable to explain away," Damore said. "His voice is on that tape. You hear that voice no less clearly than you hear the cries of agony from Mark Kevin Ramsey."

Damore's voice cracked like a whip as he described Kosta as a cold, ruthless egotist who enjoyed seeing his wife shot. He said that Kosta wanted to record his wife's murder on videotape but realized that this wasn't possible.

Kosta was so warped that he became sexually excited after watching Ramsey being killed. "He watched that tape over and over; that's the ego of the man," Damore said. "Kosta Fotopoulos kept his momento to remind him what he had gotten away with."

Damore ridiculed Fotopoulos, imitating his thick accent, and calling him "the answer man" who could explain anything. "Murder does not matter to him," Damore said. "To him it's fun. It's a game."

The assistant state attorney said Kosta had such a huge ego that he thought he could fool the jury into thinking that those who testified against him were liars, not worth listening to.

"This is a man of grand delusions. This is a man whose ego has gone beyond the bounds of all good sense."

In his final argument, Corrente used the title of a current movie called *sex, lies and videotape* to characterize the case against Kosta. The sex, he said, was provided by Deidre Hunt. The lies were from the criminals who testified against Kosta, and the videotape was the one that showed Ramsey being murdered.

Corrente said the state's case was based on Deidre Hunt's lies. She was the killer, he said, not Kosta. Corrente said that Deidre's story was riddled with lies and inconsistencies. She was promiscuous with both men and women, he said, and she was greedy.

397

It was that greed, Corrente maintained, that drove her to try to eliminate Lisa so she could get her money through Kosta, whose only involvement was having an affair with the wrong person.

"We got a woman who is lying through her teeth," Corrente said, then he made fun of Deidre in a mincing voice: "This poor girl, she's frail, she doesn't like guns." Voice changing, he then said, "She was *fascinated* by guns. She wanted to shoot kittens."

Corrente reminded the jury that he had produced his own expert, who said that Kosta's voice prints could not be positively matched with those on the Ramsey murder video. And he criticized the state for confusing the jurors by presenting so much evidence. But he maintained that it was all meaningless.

"We got a large amount of evidence out there," he said, "but not a bit of it actually points to Kosta Fotopoulos." Corrente continued that Kosta had the legal right to kill Chase. "This person came in and put a bullet into Lisa Fotopoulos's head, and if Mr. Fotopoulos had not shot him, she might be dead," Corrente argued. "Self-defense is allowable."

Tanner rose in rebuttal after Corrente had finished. His message was brief, but powerful.

"Do not judge Kosta Fotopoulos like you would a normal person," he told the jurors. "What sort of a man sits up here and laughs and jokes and flits about as if he's not on trial? He was not only frustrated and angry and desperate and terribly violent," Tanner said, "he was driven by lust, power, hatred, and greed."

With that, Judge Foxman gave the jury instructions, and they retired to reach a verdict. Three hours and forty-three minutes later the jury did just that. They were returned to the courtroom at approximately eight p.m. Fotopoulos stood up, looking pale but unemotional, as the verdicts were read. The jury found him guilty on all counts.

Kosta smirked and shrugged slightly. Foxman said that court would reconvene Monday to weigh mitigating and aggravating factors before the jury recommended a sentence.

The case had been bizarre from the beginning, and it was to end on the same note.

Kosta was taken to the Putnam County Jail after the jury had found him guilty. Nothing seemed unusual when James Dorris, a corrections officer, made his rounds at 12:55 a.m. Dorris looked in on Kosta and found him lying in blood.

Under heavy guard, Kosta was rushed to Putnam General Hospital, where he was treated and released. Somehow, Kosta had managed to cut his left wrist and ankles. Thirty-some stitches were required to close the wounds, but no one was able to determine how Kosta had cut himself. No sharp objects were found in his cell, and he refused to talk about it.

Officials at the jail thought that Kosta might have been planning to escape when he was taken outside the jail with no manacles on his ankles because of the wounds. Rather than trying to escape, Kosta remained docile.

Deidre Hunt, who was still at the Volusia County Branch Jail, speculated that Kosta had been planning an escape. She said he knew more effective ways to kill himself than cutting his wrist and ankles. Deidre said that, instead of trying to escape, Kosta might have faked a suicide attempt to elicit sympathy from the jury before it sentenced him.

The wounds weren't serious enough to keep Kosta from returning to court on Monday for arguments concerning mitigating and aggravating factors before sentencing. Kosta wore a flesh-colored bandage on his left wrist.

The jury that had convicted him on Thursday took only an hour and thirteen minutes to recommend that Kosta be executed in the electric chair. Judge Foxman, who had the power to overrule the jury's recommendations, set sentencing for two p.m. on the following Thursday. The attorneys held brief news conferences following the jury's recommendation.

"We thought the recommendation and the verdict were just," Damore said.

Corrente said that Kosta was distraught after being found guilty and had tried to kill himself "to cheat the state" from the satisfaction of executing him.

Kosta, still unrepentant, smiled when he entered the courtroom on Thursday morning to be sentenced. It took just a few minutes.

Kosta had some last words before sentence was imposed.

"I'm not going to stand here and plead for mercy, say I'm a good person, simply because I do not accept the verdict from the jury last week," Kosta read from a one-page statement. "I just feel that the trial was completely unfair. It was not actually a trial, but it was a political theater. Mr. Tanner was standing up like a peacock in front of the cameras."

Tanner rose to object, and the judge admonished Kosta to restrict his comments to the sentencing.

"No matter the outcome of this sentencing, I feel I have won the case in my way," Kosta said. "I feel I have done my duty in defending my wife and my family, and if I have to, I'll die for doing that."

When Kosta finished, Foxman sentenced him to die in the electric chair for the murders of Bryan Chase and Kevin Ramsey. Just like Deidre, Kosta was given two death sentences, and sentenced to life in prison on the charges of solicitation for murder and conspiracy to commit murder.

Kosta smiled as he was handcuffed and led away.

Epilogue

Deidre Hunt is on Death Row at Broward Correctional Institute in Florida. Death sentences are automatically appealed in Florida. Deidre could receive a new sentence hearing, a trial, or be executed. The legal procedure could take years.

Kosta Fotopoulos is on Death Row in Florida State Prison at Starke, Florida. Since his death sentence has been automatically appealed, too, it may be years before Kosta is executed or before the death sentence is overturned.

Lori Henderson was sentenced to four years in prison for conspiracy to commit murder and attempted murder. Judge Foxman said that Lori's crimes justified "a much harsher sentence" but that she had kept her part of the plea bargain. "A deal is a deal," Foxman said.

Teja James was sentenced to four years in prison for conspiracy to commit murder and attempted murder. Foxman said Teja was basically a good young man "who had fallen in with a bad crowd."

Teja said he intended to do his time, then change his name and move to another state.

J.R. Taylor is still a transient.

Matthew Chumbley has left Daytona Beach.

David Damore took a week off when Kosta Fotopoulos's trial ended and then resumed his activities. As this was written he was developing evidence to prosecute Aileen Wuornos, a woman who may be the first female serial killer in American history.

Joe Gallagher continues his work as an investigator for the state attorney.

Robert Wheeler, chief investigator for the state attorney in the Seventh District, said he was watching some of the unconvicted people in the Hunt-Fotopoulos case.

Corp. Greg Smith of the Daytona Beach Police Department was promoted to sergeant in charge of the Patrol Division.

Tony Calderone was investigated and no charges were filed against him. Damore said there was no basis for any legal action against Calderone.

Peter Kouracos retains his appointed political positions, was not charged in the case, and is expected to become an important politician in Florida.

Circuit Judge S. James Foxman moved from criminal cases to civil cases after the Fotopoulos-Hunt case.